The New Testament

GUIDES TO SACRED TEXTS

THE DAODE JING

Livia Kohn

THE RIGVEDA

Stephanie Jamison and Joel Brereton

THE YIJING

Joseph Adler

THE BOOK OF COMMON PRAYER

Charles Hefling

THE ANNALECTS

Erin M. Cline

THE NEW TESTAMENT: A GUIDE

Donald Senior, C.P.

Guides to Sacred Texts

What is a sacred text? *The Oxford English Dictionary* offers a definition of *sacred* as "set apart for or dedicated to some religious purpose, and hence entitled to veneration or religious respect." The definition is necessarily vague. What does it mean to be "set apart?" What constitutes a "religious purpose?" How formal is "veneration?" Does minimal "religious respect" qualify? The sphere of meanings surrounding the word *sacred* will depend on the religion involved. For that reason, "sacred texts" in this series is a term conceived broadly. All of the texts covered by this series have held special regard—they have been "set apart"—in a religion either ancient or modern. Such texts are generally accorded more serious attention than other religious documents. In some cases, the texts may be believed to be the words of a deity. In other cases, the texts may be part of an atheistic religion. This breadth of application indicates the rationale behind Guides to Sacred Texts.

This series offers brief, accessible introductions to sacred texts, written by experts on them. While allowing for the individuality of each text, the series follows a basic format of introducing the text in terms of its dates of composition, traditions of authorship and assessment of those traditions, the extent of the text, and the issues raised by the text. For scripture that continues to be utilized, those issues will likely continue to generate controversy and discussion among adherents to the text. For texts from religions no longer practiced, the issues may well continue to address concerns of the present day, despite the antiquity of the scripture. These volumes are useful for introducing sacred writings from around the world to readers wanting to learn what these sacred texts are.

The New Testament

A Guide

DONALD SENIOR, C.P.

OXFORD
UNIVERSITY PRESS

OXFORD
UNIVERSITY PRESS

Oxford University Press is a department of the University of Oxford. It furthers the University's objective of excellence in research, scholarship, and education by publishing worldwide. Oxford is a registered trade mark of Oxford University Press in the UK and certain other countries.

Published in the United States of America by Oxford University Press
198 Madison Avenue, New York, NY 10016, United States of America.

Library of Congress Cataloging-in-Publication Data
Names: Senior, Donald, author.
Title: The New Testament : a guide / Donald Senior, C.P.
Description: New York, NY, United States of America : Oxford University Press, [2022] |
Series: Guides to sacred texts series | Includes bibliographical references and index.
Identifiers: LCCN 2021033789 (print) | LCCN 2021033790 (ebook) |
ISBN 9780197530849 (pb) | ISBN 9780197530832 (hb) |
ISBN 9780197530863 (epub)
Subjects: LCSH: Bible. New Testament – Criticism, interpretation, etc.
Classification: LCC BS2361.3 .S46 2021 (print) | LCC BS2361.3 (ebook) |
DDC 225.6—dc23
LC record available at https://lccn.loc.gov/2021033789
LC ebook record available at https://lccn.loc.gov/2021033790

DOI: 10.1093/oso/9780197530832.001.0001

1 3 5 7 9 8 6 4 2

Paperback printed by LSC Communications, United States of America
Hardback printed by Bridgeport National Bindery, Inc., United States of America

Contents

Introduction

The New Testament as Sacred Text

The New Testament surely has a place among the most significant and influential literature in all of human history. In a series intended as a guide to "sacred texts," the New Testament could not be overlooked.

For Christians, the New Testament stands as a central and inspired resource for the origin, content, and spirit of Christian faith. Through the Four Gospels, the Christian believer encounters the foundational portrayal of Jesus and his mission. Through the Acts of the Apostles, the Letters of Paul, and the other writings included in the New Testament, the believing Christian discovers the formative experiences of the early Christian communities and the meaning of Christian life based on faith in the Risen Christ.

No wonder the New Testament is treated by Christians with a reverence reserved for no other sacred writing. Each Sunday, millions of Christians of multiple denominations and cultural traditions listen to readings from the New Testament. In many congregations the immediate response to such readings is to acclaim it as the "Word of God." Thousands of priests and ministers draw on the New Testament to preach to their congregations. Copies of the New Testament, usually embedded in the entire Bible, including the Old Testament, are treated with reverence, many bound in leather and decorated with art. Many devout Christians carry their Bible with them every day in pocket editions or now in apps on their cellphones and iPads. Particularly for Roman Catholic and Orthodox Christians, scenes from the Gospels and

The New Testament. Donald Senior, Oxford University Press. © Oxford University Press 2022.
DOI: 10.1093/oso/9780197530832.003.0001

portraits of great characters depicted in the New Testament have been the subject of religious art and adorn churches and homes. Phrases from the New Testament inspire the hymns sung in every church and Christian assembly throughout the world. And last but not least, the content of the New Testament has been the object of unending scrutiny and interpretation by Christian theologians of every generation, virtually from the time of its composition.

However, not everyone interested in the New Testament approaches it from the perspective of Christian faith. While recognizing that for Christians it is a sacred text, such a faith stance is not shared by all who have an interest in the history, content, and interpretation of the New Testament writings. For example, scholars interested in the history of Judaism or ancient Middle Eastern history consider the New Testament, composed in the first century of the common era, a prime source. For those exploring the history of religious thought, the New Testament writings are a major example of the religious map of the first century, as well as an incalculable influence on the subsequent development of Western culture. Others, for example, who are interested in the various literary forms of first century Greco-Roman and Jewish literature, analyze the Gospels as a type of ancient biography or scan Paul's letters as examples of early Greco-Roman rhetoric and letter writing. Cultural historians can examine the New Testament as reflective of the influence of Jewish and Greco-Roman cultures on early Christian beliefs.

For such scholars pursuing what might be called "secular" or purely historical interests in the New Testament, the term "sacred" might still be applied to the biblical texts, not reflecting a motivation of their own inquiry but as a respectful recognition that for other readers these texts have a unique religious authority. But in the pursuit of knowledge, the religious claims of the New Testament cannot be viewed as imposing any limitations on historical, scientific, or literary inquiry.

The object of this study is to be attentive to both these fundamentally different perspectives about the New Testament writings. The study that follows is not intended to be a standard introduction to the New Testament, of which there are many examples.[1] In such an "introduction" the reader is briefed on the historical context of Jesus and the early church and introduced to the purpose, literary style, content, and historical context of each of the New Testament writings. The author of such introductions may approach their subject from an explicitly confessional or faith stance or examine the New Testament writings from a purely historical and literary point of view. Different from such standard introductions to the New Testament, our exploration here will keep an eye on what about their history, literary form, and content contributes to making these biblical texts "sacred" to believing Christians. And we also need to consider why the ensemble of these individual books, namely the "New Testament" itself is a sacred "book."

The Meaning of "Sacred"

From the outset, it is important to understand what is meant by the term "sacred." The designation "sacred" can be applied in a broad sense to places, objects, or personages who are deserving of deep respect because of their human and historical impact. Thus, Arlington National Cemetery is "sacred" ground because it is the resting place of many men and women who have given their lives in service to their country. Mt. Vernon, the ancestral home of George Washington, or the Lincoln Memorial might be considered sacred because of their association with revered leaders of our country.

---

[1] Representative examples would be the works of M. Eugene Boring, *An Introduction to the New Testament. History, Literature, Theology* (Louisville, KY: Westminster John Knox Press, 2012); Raymond E. Brown, *An Introduction to the New Testament* (New York: Doubleday, 1997); Luke Timothy Johnson, *The Writings of the New Testament: An Interpretation* (Minneapolis, MN: Fortress, rev. ed., 1999).

The death camp at Auschwitz might also be considered sacred, not because of its hideous historical purpose but out of respect for the hundreds of thousands of people who lost their lives there as a result of Nazi genocide. "Sacred" in these contexts is a kind of "civic" sacredness—an aura of respect attributed to persons or places or objects that have had a significant impact on human experience and human history.

But "sacred" in a strict sense, and as it is used in this study, refers to persons, places, or artifacts which in the eyes of believers are associated with the presence of the transcendent, a presence that evokes awe and reverence—places associated with the divine presence and where worship is conducted. This would be the case with a church such as St. Peter's Basilica in Rome or Westminster Cathedral in London or the Belz Great Synagogue in Jerusalem, or the Masjid al-Haram, the central mosque enclosing the Kaba in Mecca. For a similar reason, "sacred" can be applied to certain persons and the roles they exercise within a particular religious tradition which in some fashion represent or point to the divine presence, such as a revered rabbi, a holy imam, or a respected priest or minister. And, obviously, the term "sacred" can be applied to certain key texts which play a normative role within a particular religion, such as the Hebrew Bible, the Koran, and, of course, the New Testament itself. For believers these "sacred" texts make possible an encounter with the divine.

As we will note in more detail later, Christians view the New Testament as inherently sacred and religiously normative for Christian life. The writings of the New Testament, along with the entire Bible of which it is a part, are traditionally considered as originating with God, but not in the sense that God is the literary author of any of the New Testament—put bluntly, God did not write a letter to the Corinthians! Yet traditional Christian belief would claim God to be the "author" of Sacred Scripture in the sense that God is the ultimate origin or source of the message of the New Testament and the entire Bible. Put another way, God's Spirit "inspired" the various biblical authors to compose the writings that make up the Bible, thus revealing in a privileged way the ultimate truth about God, about human nature, and the path needed to be taken to ensure one's salvation. For believing Christians, the New Testament, therefore, is both "inspired" and "inspiring"—that is, ultimately originating with God and at the same time pointing the way to ultimate union with God.[2] For many Christians, the Bible, including the New Testament, would itself have a revelatory or "sacramental" character. That is to say, reverent reflection on the Scriptures leads one to an encounter with the very "Word of God," an authentic and life-changing experience of the sacred.

Thus, the use of the term "sacred" as applied to the New Testament also involves the perspective of the readers of this religious text. Modern awareness of the dynamic nature of written texts emphasizes that the meaning of a text is generated in the relationship between the capacity of the text itself and the readers who engage this text. For the New Testament to be "sacred" in the fullest sense of the term requires readers who view the biblical text as inspired by God, its content normative for authentic Christian belief and practice, and having the religious authority to command reverence and obedience in accord with the patterns of the human life it portrays.

The Approach of This Study

To explore as fully as possible how the New Testament has been considered "sacred" requires a number of steps that form the successive chapters of this book.

First of all, it is important to survey the contents of the New Testament, including its nature as a "collection" of various

---

[2] In labeling such viewpoints "traditional" infers that not all present-day Christians agree on the meaning and instrumentality of biblical inspiration. See Chapter 8.

individual "books" or writings in diverse literary forms. What, in fact, is the New Testament?

We will also consider how the writings of the New Testament emerged from the faith experience of the early Christian community. This includes Paul's letters as the earliest writings of the New Testament as well as the Four Gospels and the other written texts included in the New Testament.

Then we will discuss the historical origin of the New Testament as distinct from the individual books that make up its contents, including the question on what basis the individual writings came to be included in what is called the New Testament "canon." This will also involve the relationship of the New Testament to the Old Testament and the formation of the Christian Bible as a whole.

Examining the contents of the New Testament in more detail helps illustrate why and how these materials portray what "sacred" means to the readers who accept them as normative for their lives. This includes the portrayal of the transcendent dimension attributed to Jesus in various ways in the Four Gospels. And also how Paul the apostle focused on the death and resurrection of Jesus as the definitive revelation of God's holiness. Other New Testament texts, too, focus on the proclamation of the Jesus as the definitive revelation of God and the privileged source for the Christian's encounter with the divine presence.

Also important for understanding the sacred character of the New Testament writings are the various ways these writing describe a life of holiness on the part of the believing community. In the Gospels, for example, this is found in Jesus's instructions to his disciples and the patterns of their responses, both good and bad. In Paul's letters and other New Testament writings, there are also guidelines about the virtues and patterns of life that reflect a sacred character.

And, finally, we need to consider the variety of ways in which the New Testament writings have been interpreted over the centuries, including the dramatic turn in the manner of interpretation in the modern era of historical inquiry. As noted earlier, the designation of the New Testament as "sacred" depends in large part on the relationship of readers to this text and the varied perspectives they bring to their interpretation of the biblical text.

Our quest remains determining how and why the New Testament became the central "sacred text" of Christianity. As we will see, both understanding the history of its composition and the varied approaches to its interpretation are essential for realizing the character of the New Testament as religiously "sacred."

I have had the privilege of studying, teaching, and interpreting the New Testament for most of my adult life. I welcome the opportunity this Oxford University series offers me to explore exactly why the writings of the New Testament are so compelling and rich in meaning that they can absorb a lifetime of study and reflection—and yet leave the interpreter with the feeling that you have only just begun.

My sincere thanks to Steve Wiggins of Oxford University Press who first invited me to be part of this series and then to the excellent and professional staff at Oxford University Press who shepherded my manuscript through to completion and publication. I am also grateful to my faculty colleagues at Catholic Theological Union, Professor Laurie Brink, O.P., and Professor Robin Ryan, C.P., for taking the time to read through every line of the manuscript and making helpful suggestions that I have incorporated into this final version. Thanks, too, to Lissa Romell for her always generous work on the index and assisting in preparation of the manuscript. I realize more than ever that biblical scholarship is not a solitary exercise but that to create anything worthwhile you must draw on the hard work of fellow inquirers who walked this path long before you. For all of them I give thanks.

1

What Is the New Testament?

A First Glance

The Term "New Testament"

A necessary first step in discovering why the New Testament is considered a "sacred" text is to be aware of exactly what constitutes the "New Testament." The term "New Testament," referring to the group of writings that now bears that name, seems to have been first used by the second-century Christian theologian Tertullian (155 to ca. 220 AD). In the Hebrew Bible, the prophet Jeremiah spoke of a "new covenant" or solemn agreement that God would make with Israel and Judah, a covenant written on the human heart which would replace the former covenant of the past written on stone.

> See, days are coming—oracle of the LORD—when I will make a new covenant with the house of Israel and the house of Judah. It will not be like the covenant I made with their ancestors the day I took them by the hand to lead them out of the land of Egypt. They broke my covenant, though I was their master—oracle of the LORD. But this is the covenant I will make with the house of Israel after those days—oracle of the LORD. I will place my law within them, and write it upon their hearts; I will be their God, and they shall be my people. (Jer 31:31–34)

The Letter to the Hebrews, one of the books included in the New Testament, quotes this same text from Jeremiah, identifying the "new covenant" referred to by the prophet as fulfilled in Jesus

The New Testament. Donald Senior, Oxford University Press. © Oxford University Press 2022. DOI: 10.1093/oso/9780197530832.003.0002

Christ who through his death and resurrection, forged a "new covenant," replacing the first or "old" covenant: "When he [the prophet Jeremiah] speaks of a 'new' covenant, he declares the first one obsolete. And what has become obsolete and has grown old is close to disappearing" (Hebrews 8:13). The Latin word for "covenant" is *testamentum*—thus the term "New Testament" referring to the Christian sacred writings that ultimately would be fused onto the sacred texts of the "Old Testament."

Although the wording in the Letter to the Hebrews seems to imply that the "new" covenant replaces and makes void the "old" covenant, Tertullian and the majority of early Christian theologians opposed the idea that the Hebrew Scriptures or the writings of the Old Testament were null and void. The move to cast off the Hebrew Scriptures or Old Testament was led by an early Christian theologian Marcion (85–180 AD). He believed that the teachings of Jesus were diametrically opposed to those of the Old Testament and that the God of the Old Testament worshipped by Israel was not the same as the God of the New Testament revealed by Jesus. Marcion proposed a set of eleven Christian sacred writings that eliminated the Old Testament and included ten of the Pauline Letters and a gospel that was most similar to that of Luke.

Marcion's views were rejected by the early church and he was declared a "heretic" by the Roman church in 144 AD. In opposing Marcion, Tertullian wrote: "All Scripture is divided into two Testaments. That which preceded the advent and passion of Christ—that is, the law and the prophets—is called the Old; but those things which were written after His resurrection are named the New Testament. The Jews make use of the Old, we of the New: but yet they are not discordant . . . (Against Marcion)." As we will discuss later, Marcion's attempt to forge an official list of Christian sacred books was an impetus in the early church that led to the formation of the Christian "canon" or list of official sacred books.[1]

In an attempt to avoid the implication that the writings of the "Old Testament" are somehow obsolete or void compared to the "New Testament," some modern scholars prefer alternate language such as referring to the books of the Old Testament as the "Hebrew Scriptures" and the New Testament as the "Christian Scriptures."[2] While well intentioned, there are problems with this terminology, too. First of all, strictly speaking not all of the "Hebrew Scriptures" were in fact written in Hebrew—a few parts were written in Aramaic.[3] Even more important, from the vantage point of Christian faith, the books of the Old Testament are not "*Hebrew* Scriptures," that is, belonging only to Judaism, but are now an integral part of the overall Christian Bible. While it is perfectly valid and self-evident that observant Jews consider these books their "Jewish Scriptures," for Christians these same writings take on a somewhat different meaning in the light of faith in Jesus as the promised Messiah or Christ. While retaining their validity in their own right as God's revealed word, the books of the Old Testament are read by Christians inevitably from the perspective of Christian faith. For Christians, then, the Old Testament is no longer the "Jewish" or "Hebrew" Scriptures; rather, these texts are now incorporated into the entirety of the Christian Bible. This is compatible with full respect for the "Jewish" or "Hebrew" Scriptures but simply acknowledges that, when read and interpreted in the light of Christian faith, these sacred writings take on a new level of meaning for Christian readers.

It is important to keep in mind that the term "old" used in reference to the "Old Testament" does not imply that it is obsolete

---

[1] See Chapter 3 of this volume.

[2] Another suggested alternate is to refer to the Old Testament as the "First Covenant" and the New Testament writings as the "Second Covenant."

[3] Parts of the Old Testament that were written in Aramaic include Ezra 4:8–6:18 and 7:12–26 and Daniel 2:4b–7:28.

or void. Rather the term "old" is to be used in the sense of "venerable"—the sacred and inspired writings of God's people Israel that, from the Christian vantage point, set the foundation and context for the mission of Jesus.

The New Testament: An Overview of Its Contents

Paging through the New Testament immediately reveals that it is not a single work by a single author, but a collection of diverse literary texts written by multiple authors in varied circumstances:

- This collection of writings begins with the Four Gospels attributed in turn to Matthew, Mark, Luke, and John. The names of these "evangelists," as the writers of these narratives are called, were not identified within their writings but have been attributed to each Gospel by early but still subsequent traditions. Each of the purported writers is either an original apostle or disciple of Jesus (Matthew, John) or a noted figure of the earliest post-Easter church (Mark, Luke).[4]
- Next follows the Acts of the Apostles, evidently composed by the evangelist Luke as a kind of second volume to his Gospel describing the establishment and rapid spread of the early Christian community in the wake of Jesus's resurrection. Luke alone provides a brief preface to his Gospel (Luke 1:1–4) and picks up the thread in his preface to the Acts of the Apostles, referring to his "first book" (Acts 1:1–3). The Acts became separated from Luke's Gospel in the current ordering of the books of the New Testament because of the priority given to the Four Gospels as key narratives of the life of Jesus.[5]

---

[4] See more on this in Chapter 2.
[5] See more on this in Chapter 3.

- The next series of texts are thirteen letters attributed to Paul the Apostle, forming a major part of the New Testament materials. These include the Letters to the Romans, First and Second Corinthians, Galatians, Ephesians, Philippians, Colossians, First and Second Thessalonians, First and Second Timothy, Titus, and Philemon. The Letters to Timothy, Titus, and Philemon, unlike the other Pauline writings, are addressed to individuals. Modern biblical scholarship has questioned whether the apostle Paul wrote all these letters or whether some were composed after Paul by a disciple writing in his name. The so-called undisputed letters are Romans, the Corinthian letters, Galatians, Philippians, First Thessalonians, and Philemon. Scholars debate the status of the remaining letters, with a firm majority concluding that the so-called Pastoral Letters to Timothy and Titus were written later than Paul, perhaps even in the early second century.[6]
- Next comes the Letter to the Hebrews, an exhortation that draws heavily on imagery inspired by the Jerusalem temple and its ritual. Although some ancient manuscripts connected Hebrews with the Letters of Paul, the identity of its author as well as its place of origin and its intended audience have been long debated, with most modern scholars concluding that it was not composed by Paul.[7]
- The next grouping of texts is the so-called catholic epistles— the term "catholic" referring to the fact that the intended audiences of these texts are not confined to an individual community or person. These include the Letter of James, First and Second Peter, the three Letters of John, and the Letter of Jude.
- The concluding book of the New Testament is the book of Revelation (also referred to as the "Apocalypse"—a literal rendering of the Greek word for "revelation"). This book is

---

[6] See Chapter 3.
[7] See Chapter 3.

written in the distinct literary style of Jewish apocalyptic literature. Revelation's reflection on the final destiny of the world and the ultimate triumph of Christ over the forces of evil make it a fitting conclusion to the New Testament.

The Historical Framework of the New Testament

The Life and Mission of Jesus

While the various New Testament writings were composed at different times within the framework of the first century and in various locations in the eastern Mediterranean region, their taproot is in first-century "Palestinian Judaism."[8] The trigger for the existence of early Christianity and its New Testament writings was the mission of Jesus of Nazareth, who lived and died in this region in the first third of the first century. His origin, his public ministry of teaching and healing, the controversies stirred by his mission, and his ultimate rejection, condemnation, and crucifixion, as well as the conviction of his resurrection from the dead, are the subject matter of the Four Gospels. The meaning of Jesus's identity as well as his teaching and example for Christian faith and practice is the focus of every other writing in the New Testament as well. As we will note later, although the Gospels were written in roughly the last quarter of the first century, their narrative settings are portrayed as taking place exclusively in the confines of early first-century Palestinian Judaism.

---

[8] A quick word about nomenclature. The term "Palestinian Judaism" has no connection to the present political entities of the State of Israel and Palestine and the chronic conflict in this region. Although its precise origin is debated, the term "Palestine" or "Palestinian" derives from the word "Philistine" and was already used in Greek literature prior to the first century to refer to the land bridge between Mesopotamia and Egypt. "Palestinian Judaism," as used here, then, refers to the Jewish inhabitants of this region in the first century of our era.

This period was a turbulent time for Jews living in Palestine. In the first century, a substantial number of Jews lived outside of Palestine, scattered throughout the Mediterranean and Middle Eastern world. Referred to as the *Diaspora* (i.e., the "dispersion"), these Jews numbered equal to or more than the number of those in Palestine itself. By some estimates, these Greek-speaking Jews constituted one-sixth of the population of major urban areas such as Rome, Ephesus, Antioch, and Alexandria. The Four Gospels themselves focus strongly on the circumstances of Jews living in Palestine. Paul's letters, the Acts of the Apostles, and other New Testament writings deal with Jews and Gentiles living mainly in the Diaspora.

Since the time of Alexander the Great (356–323 BC), the Jews living in the area of Roman Palestine had lived under the yoke of foreign powers—first the dynasty of the Ptolemies ruling from Egypt and then subsequently, under the Seleucid Dynasty centered in Damascus, Syria. The Seleucids proved to be harsh overlords, exacting burdensome taxation and intolerant of Jewish religious sensitivities. Against all odds and at a time when the Seleucids were distracted in having to deal with the emerging threat of the Roman Empire, the Jews rebelled against their oppressors under the leadership of the Hasmonean clan—known popularly by their nickname the "Maccabees," which in Hebrew means the "hammers." The Hasmonean family became the ruling Jewish dynasty in their own land—the first taste of freedom in centuries. The bravery of the Hasmoneans is tracked in the biblical books of the Maccabees.

Sadly, the Jewish Hasmonean Dynasty that had begun with great hope borne by the amazing success of the Maccabean revolt against their Greek overlords the Seleucids around 140 BC had gradually deteriorated. The Hasmonean rulers began to imitate the corruption and palace intrigues that had made Seleucid rule intolerable. The result was the outbreak of various Jewish reform groups in opposition to the Hasmoneans, and ultimately the triggering of a civil war among rival factions. This led to an invitation to the Romans, who by that time were encroaching on the Eastern Mediterranean and were controlling Egypt, to arbitrate the Jewish conflict. The Romans obliged and from roughly 60 BC on, would become the dominant power in the region—stretching to the end of the Byzantine period in the seventh century.

The Romans lent their support to the Herodian family among the warring factions and ultimately in 37 BC installed Herod the Great as the ruler of the entire region, incorporating Galilee, Samaria, and Judea. Herod was shrewd and powerful but remained in effect a vassal of his Roman sponsors. Upon the death of Herod in 40 BC, the Romans divided his kingdom divided among his sons into three "ethnarchies," with Herod Philip ruling in the higher elevations of the northern district known as "Upper" Galilee, Herod Antipas in Lower Galilee, that is, the region stretching from the Sea of Galilee west across the fertile plains of Esdrelon to the Mediterranean coast, and Archelaus ruling in the key districts of Judea and Samaria. Archelaus proved to be cruel and inept and was deposed by the Romans in 6 AD and exiled to Gaul. Thereafter, Roman procurators ruled directly over Samaria and, more significantly, over Judea with its capital, Jerusalem.

These historical events set the political and social stage for Jesus's lifetime. The gospel traditions are aware of the general context of this period. In Matthew's Gospel, for example, the infant Jesus and his family are threatened by the cruel paranoia of Herod the Great, leading to self-imposed exile in Egypt and, when returning, having to go to Nazareth of Galilee instead of Bethlehem to avoid the clutches of Archelaus (Matt 2:22–23). Later, the adult Jesus is warned during his Galilean mission that Herod Antipas is seeking to kill him and responds defiantly: "Go and tell that fox for me, 'Listen, I am casting out demons and performing cures today and tomorrow, and on the third day I finish my work. Yet today, tomorrow, and the next day I must be on my way, because it is impossible for a prophet to be killed outside of Jerusalem'" (Luke 13:32–33). At the time of Jesus's trial by the Romans, Luke's account notes the proper roles of Pilate as ruler of Judea and that of Herod Antipas in Galilee (Luke 23:6–12). Even though Jesus was imprisoned in Pilate's jurisdiction of Judea, as a courtesy he defers to Herod Antipas who ruled in Jesus's home district of Galilee. All four evangelists are aware that the Romans, ruling over Judea, had the power of capital punishment and that Jesus was condemned and executed by crucifixion under Roman law. It is likely that, except for some places such as their base in Caesarea Maritima and a garrison next to the Jerusalem temple, there was not an overwhelming presence of Roman soldiers in Palestine itself. The military who were present, especially in Galilee, were local mercenaries serving the ethnarchs Herod Antipas and Herod Philip. Roman troops, however, were not far away, with legions present east of the Sea of Galilee in the Decapolis region and able to respond quickly if needed.

Other features of the Gospels reflect this same verisimilitude about Palestinian Judaism in the first century. Priests, elders, and Sadducees are prominent leaders in Jerusalem and in some way responsible for public order under the supervision of the Romans. Little is known about the Sadducees except that they were elite and influential Jewish families, especially in Jerusalem, and strongly influenced by Greek culture. Apparently, the Sadducees were conservative about religious traditions but "progressive" in adapting to Greco-Roman culture. The Pharisees, by contrast, were a lay reform movement who, along with other reform groups of the period, were uncomfortable with the religious compromises of the Hasmoneans. The Pharisees intended to make a life of holiness accessible not just to the priestly class but to ordinary lay Jews as well. Therefore, they were concerned about Jewish identity and its expression in fidelity to the Law, Sabbath observance, circumcision, and the dietary and purity laws.

According to the gospel accounts, Jesus himself frequents synagogues in Galilee and is invited to preach from time to time during the service (see, e.g., Luke 4:16). There are references to various roles within the society of the time: landowners and field hands; judges and beggars; subsistence farmers and people who are visibly sick; and fishermen, merchants, and shepherds. The Gospels are aware of a certain degree of tension and competition between the region of Galilee in the north, with its mixed population of mainly Jews but some Gentiles, and Judea to the south, the traditional center of orthodoxy, the historic seat of the monarch, and the location of the Temple. For example, Matthew's Gospel notes Jesus entry into "Galilee of the Gentiles" (Matt 4:15), and Peter is apparently betrayed by his accent when confronted by a servant during Jesus's interrogation before the High Priest (see Mark 14:70). In John's Gospel, when learning that Jesus is from Nazareth, Nathanael asks, "Can anything good come out of Nazareth?"—a Galilean town (John 1:46).

The Gospels also reflect the topography of the region.[9] The images of Jesus's parables draw on the agrarian character of the land, particularly in lower Galilee: harvests of wheat and barley, flocks of sheep and goats at pasture with their shepherds, fruit trees and flowers, the importance of the olive tree and its oil. The Sea of Galilee, a dominant feature of lower Galilee, plays a highly significant and often symbolic role in the gospel narratives, serving as a boundary between the Gentile region of the Decapolis on the eastern shore of the sea (a league of ten cities originating with Alexander the Great's conquest of the region three centuries before) and the largely Jewish territory on the western side. The Sea of Galilee was also the source of the livelihood of Jesus's fishermen disciples, along with its dangerous threat of sudden storms and heavy waves that figure in several dramatic scenes in the Gospels.

Similarly, the Gospels are also aware of the impact of history on the various sectors of the region; for example, the historic

[9] See Donald Senior, C.P., *The Landscape of the Gospels: A Deeper Meaning* (New York: Paulist Press, 2020).

estrangement of the Samaritan region from that of Judea (a tension dating back to the postexilic period reflected, for example, in the famous encounter of Jesus with the Samaritan woman in John 4:1–42), the key defining role of Jerusalem and Judea for overall Jewish identity, the desert regions that border Judea on the south and east, the salt wastes of the Dead Sea and the lush oasis of Jericho on the floor of the Rift Valley, and the accustomed pilgrimage journey of Jews from Galilee to Jerusalem and its temple. Regarding Jerusalem and its environs, there is also accurate information embedded in the Gospels, particularly in John's Gospel: for example, the location of Bethany, a village east of Jerusalem where Jesus visited when staying in the Jerusalem area; the Mount of Olives overlooking Jerusalem and its temple; the Kidron valley and its olive groves; the temple precincts; the Sheep's pool; the pool of Bethesda; the pool of Siloam; the city gates and walls; Golgotha, the place of execution outside the walls; and the presents of tombs cut from the soft limestone nearby.

The Gospels place Jesus in this thoroughly Jewish, yet fractured and anxious setting. Some thirty years later the growing undercurrent of resentment toward Roman hegemony and the failure of local Jewish leaders to stem it would lead to a largely spontaneous explosion in the revolt of 66 AD—a revolt that the Roman military would brutally suppress over time, culminating in the destruction of Jerusalem and its temple in 70 AD. While Jesus lived in a prerevolutionary period in the first third of the century, the conditions of poverty and political and religious suppression experienced already in Jesus's own time and evident in the gospel narratives would ultimately lead to this later explosion.

It is also clear that the character of Jesus's mission reflects both the challenging conditions existing in Palestinian Judaism and the aspirations of Israel for freedom and justice proclaimed in its Scriptures. Thus, the keynote of Jesus's mission is the advent of God's reign (see Mark 1:14–15 and parallels) that would bring ultimate justice for the poor, the healing of bodies and spirits, and the gathering into one people the lost sheep of the house of Israel. All these longings stemmed from the heart of Jewish tradition but could still be provocative when proclaimed with authority, integrity, and persistence in troubled times.

The descriptions of Jesus's mission in the Gospels indicate that he concentrated his mission on his own people, the Jews (see, e.g., Jesus's statement in Matt 15:24, "I was sent only to the lost sheep of the house of Israel"; also Matt 10:5). However, Jesus did have relatively few encounters with Gentiles, such as the Centurion in Capernaum (Matt 8:5–13), the Syrophoenician woman at the Lebanese border (Mark 7:24–30), and the Gadarene demoniac in the Decapolis (Mark 5:1–20). Yet Jesus's attention to his fellow Jews who lived on the margins of society—the "lost sheep" as Jesus named them—coupled with his responsiveness to the Gentiles he did encounter anticipates the later mission of the post-Easter community to the Gentile world. This is also signaled in Matthew's infancy narrative when magi or astrologers "from the east"— evidently Gentiles—follow the guide of nature's star and come to Bethlehem to offer homage to the infant Jesus, while Herod and his court find the infant messiah a threat (see Matt 2:1–12). From the vantage point of the evangelists, the death and resurrection of Jesus marks a turning point in history when God's promised gift of salvation to Israel would now be extended as well to the "nations" (see, e.g., Matt 28:16–20; Luke 24:47). In the gospel portrayals, it is the Risen Christ who sends his disciples on mission to the world (see, e.g., John's account of the appearance of the Risen Christ to his disciples and the instruction, "As the father has sent me, so I send you ... " John 20:21; also 17:18).

From Israel to the Nations

The gospel narratives portray their understanding of Jesus's identity and mission in terms of the early first-century Palestinian world in which Jesus had lived, even though these texts themselves are being composed later in the first century and most, if not all, in the Mediterranean world outside of Palestine. Most contemporary scholars date the composition of the Gospels to the period after 70 AD. The rest of the New Testament writings directly reflect the transition from the exclusively Jewish milieu of Jesus and his first disciples, to the increasingly Gentile milieu of the early church as it moved out into the wider Mediterranean world. The evangelist Luke's second volume, the Acts of the Apostles, tracks that expansion in narrative form, beginning with the dynamic outreach of the Jerusalem Jewish-Christian community, and then, with the advent of Paul the Apostle, the increasing incorporation of Gentile communities in Asia Minor (present-day Turkey), Macedonia (present-day northern Greece), Achaia (present-day southern Greece), and ultimately Rome itself. We know that Christianity also moved further east into Arabia, but Paul's letters to churches in the eastern half of the Mediterranean world and the concentration of the Acts of the Apostles on Paul's missionary journeys put the focus on Christianity's spread to the west and ultimately to Rome, the imperial capital.

While Luke's account in Acts contains significant historical and geographical data, his narrative, like the Gospels themselves, also proclaims a *theological* message—that of the universal horizon of God's salvation. That salvation is rooted in Israel's sacred past, comes to fruition in the mission of Jesus, and in the wake of his death, resurrection, and ascension, is propelled beyond the boundaries of Israel by the Spirit. Thus, at the end of Luke's Gospel, the risen Christ instructs his disciples to be his "witnesses" to all nations, "beginning from Jerusalem" (Luke 24:47), and in the opening scenes of the Acts of the Apostles that commission is repeated: "you will be my witnesses in Jerusalem, in all Judea and Samaria, and to the ends of the earth" (Acts 1:8).

The Pauline Letters and the Opening to the Gentiles

The Pauline Letters explicitly reflect this transition to the Gentile world, although obviously not in narrative form. As we will note in detail later, his letters become an extension of his mission to the communities he either had founded (e.g., Philippi, Thessalonica), visited for an extended period (Corinth, Ephesus), or planned to visit (Rome). Often the content of the letters responds to specific questions or circumstances arising in the communities Paul addressed. In a letter such as Galatians, Paul wrestles directly with the tensions stirred by this transition from a predominately Jewish milieu to that of the Gentile world. For some Jewish Christians, it was imperative that any Gentile aspiring to be a follower of Jesus would need, in effect, to first become Jewish—accepting circumcision for males, and adhering to the requirements of the Mosaic Law such as kosher diet, Sabbath observance, and other moral standards of the law. Paul, however, championed the right of Gentile converts to directly receive the gift of the Spirit and baptism without such prior requirements—thus ensuring opposition and tension between his and other conflicting views. Paul notes in Galatians that he even had to correct Peter himself, when under pressure from strict Jewish Christians, the apostle had ceased to eat with Gentile Christians in Antioch for fear of violating the Jewish law and offending Jewish Christians (see Gal 2:11–14).

In many instances, the Gentile Christians in Paul's communities were "pioneers" when it came to discerning what was the proper way of life for followers of Jesus in the context of Greco-Roman society. The values of the Roman world could be very different from that of the teaching of Jesus and the strong Jewish ethical tradition in which Jesus and the earliest Jewish-Christians were steeped. Thus, in Corinth and elsewhere, Paul wrestles with such issues as building cohesion within and among the small communities or house churches, determining whether it was proper or not to eat meat that had been offered to idols, proper sexual mores reflecting the teaching of Jesus and Jewish traditions—often quite different from Roman society—the question of marriage and divorce, the use of public law courts for disputes within the community, proper behavior at the Lord's supper, questions about resurrection of the body, and so on. Paul was guided by the wise moral teaching of the Mosaic Law, but there were instances where the apostle and other early Christian leaders had to fashion explicitly Christian responses to some moral dilemmas without a lot of precedents to appeal to.

In his letter to the Romans, a community Paul had neither founded or yet visited, the apostle spent considerable time describing the moral plight of both Jew and Gentile and the significance of Jesus Christ for them both (see the opening chapters of the Letter, Romans 1–3). In chapters 9–11 of this letter, Paul wrestles with the question of why the majority of the Jews had not yet accepted Jesus as the Messiah—as Paul himself ardently had—and yet concludes that God's promises to his people Israel remained valid and enduring (Rom 11:29).

Other New Testament texts beyond the Pauline Letters reflect in varying degrees this monumental and evolving shift from the originating Jewish milieu of Christianity to that of a Gentile majority in the course of the first century. Some, such as the letter to the Hebrews, build an elaborate comparison between the priesthood and worship of the "former" covenant with Israel and that of the new and more perfect covenant forged by Jesus the High Priest of the heavenly sanctuary. The Letter of James seems to reaffirm the strong ethical tradition of Judaism, calling for a faith that is expressed in care for the poor and righteous behavior. The First Letter of Peter absorbs traditional titles that had been applied to Israel and its temple and adopts them without hesitation as descriptions of the Christian community. And the book of Revelation draws on vivid imagery and motifs from both Jewish apocalyptic literature and Greco-Roman mythology, but its focus is on the corrosive and oppressive threat of the Roman Empire and the ultimate triumph of the gospel.

Many scholars today believe that the definitive separation or "parting of the ways" between Judaism and Christianity lingered at least into the early second century and perhaps beyond, as both Judaism and early Christianity sought to establish their identities in the wake of the calamity of the Roman destruction of Jerusalem and its temple in 70 AD. There is no doubt that some of the hostility depicted between Jesus and the religious leaders in the Gospels such as those of Matthew and John in particular, reflects this later, post-70 context, in which both communities strove to assert their legitimacy. At the same time, it is evident there was also some "internal" tension between Jewish Christians and Gentile Christians as the Christian mission moved further out into the Mediterranean world. Sadly, beyond the New Testament period into the second and third centuries of the Christian era, Gentile Christianity would gradually lose contact with its Jewish Christian roots so strongly affirmed by Paul earlier in the first century. Anti-Semitism and anti-Judaism would become a tragic hallmark of many Christians, including prominent theologians and church leaders, well into the modern period.

The Character of the New Testament: Diversity within Unity; Unity within Diversity

Our initial survey of the contents of the New Testament illustrates its diversity. It is obviously not a single composition by a single writer located in one place and time. As we will discuss later in examining more closely the sacred character of the books of the New Testament, each has its own unique characteristics. Our purpose here is to illustrate how within such diversity there is a unifying focus on the person, mission, and destiny of Jesus and the significance of this for human existence. This focus will be key for the "sacred" character of the New Testament in the eyes of its believing readers.

Diversity within Unity: The Fourfold Gospels

The Gospel of Mark

All four Gospels focus on the life, mission, and destiny of Jesus, yet their accounts differ in a variety of ways. The sequence of the Gospels in the New Testament begins with Matthew, followed by Mark, Luke, and John. However, most modern scholars believe Mark was the first Gospel to be written. It is briefer than the other three, contains no information about the birth of Jesus, and has no resurrection appearances stories but only the account of the discovery of Jesus's empty tomb on Easter morning (Mark 16:1–8).[10] There the women who come to anoint the body of Jesus after the Sabbath discover a heavenly messenger (described as a "young man dressed in a white robe") who announces to them that the crucified Jesus they sought had been raised from the dead. In the body of his Gospel, Mark's description of the mission of Jesus is told in somewhat blunt and sparse language, with an emphasis on his exorcisms—that is, liberating those afflicted with demons who caused their victims physical and spiritual harm. Jesus's healings on the Sabbath, his association with "sinners" and those on the margin, and the crowds of sick who surge to him for healing cause the religious authorities to oppose him. Early on, Jesus's healing of a man with a withered arm in the synagogue of Capernaum prompts the religious leaders and the "Herodians" (presumably those loyal to Herod Antipas, the ruler in lower Galilee) to begin a plot to destroy him (Mark 3:6). This begins a focus on the death of Jesus that will dominate this Gospel.

Mark organizes the framework of his narrative along roughly geographical lines. After the opening scenes of Jesus's baptism and testing by Satan in the desert region near the Dead Sea (1:1–13),

---

[10] Note that other longer endings were added later from other sources to Mark's original ending at 16:8; see the so-called shorter ending and the longer ending, Mark 16:9–19. Both of these alternate endings are included in the canon of the New Testament.

most of Jesus's public ministry takes place in the northern region of Galilee (chapter 1–8). At certain moments during this Galilean ministry, Jesus crosses into Gentile territory: into the northern region of Tyre and Sidon (7:24, 31) and to the eastern shore of the Sea of Galilee into the region of the Decapolis, a league of ten Hellenistic cities originally established after Alexander's conquest of the region (5:1–20). These journeys seem to signal the later Gentile mission of the post-Easter community. At a crucial turning point, Mark describes Jesus and his disciples beginning a journey from Caesarea Philippi in the northernmost region, south down the Jordan valley, and eventually to Jerusalem (chapters 8–10). The climax of the gospel takes place in Jerusalem with a series of final conflicts with the religious leaders, and then the account of Jesus's passion, death, burial, and proclamation of his resurrection (chapters 11–16).

Matthew and Luke

It appears that both Matthew and Luke were familiar with Mark's Gospel and absorbed much of its content—but each in his own independent way. The geographical backbone of their narratives is similar to that of Mark, with Jesus's public ministry taking place in Galilee, followed by the journey of Jesus and his disciples to Jerusalem, and then the climactic account of events in Jerusalem, including the passion, death, and resurrection of Jesus. But Matthew and Luke each have their own distinctive characteristics. Unlike Mark they begin their Gospels with the account of Jesus's origin, birth, and infancy—but here, too, each in a very different way. Matthew's story is tense, with Joseph's initial concern about the unexplained and unanticipated pregnancy of Mary and then later the threat of Herod against the holy family. Luke, however, focuses on the Jerusalem temple with Zachary the temple priest and his wife Elizabeth—the parents of John the Baptist—and then with the visit of Mary, Joseph, and the infant Jesus to the temple and their encounter there with the prophets Simeon and Anna. Luke continues this focus on Jerusalem and the temple by recounting the story of the boy Jesus remaining behind, interacting with the religious teachers in the temple precincts, to the consternation of his parents who were looking for him (Luke 2:41–52).

In the body of their Gospels, too, Matthew and Luke diverge. Matthew's first of five discourses, the Sermon on the Mount (chapters 5–7), begins a strong emphasis on Jesus as teacher and emphasizes Jesus's continuity with the "law and the prophets" of Israel. Luke transforms this same body of material into a "sermon on the plain" (Luke 6:17–49) but gives greater emphasis to the prophetic role of Jesus as a champion of justice signaled in his unique opening scene of Jesus's preaching in the synagogue of Nazareth (Luke 4:16–30). There is much material in both Matthew and Luke that seems to derive from a common source that each drew upon independently of each other—a source not found in Mark's Gospel. Modern scholarship has dubbed this source as "Q," from the German word *Quelle*, which means "source." We have no independent copy of this source, which was apparently composed mainly of sayings and parables of Jesus. It is detected only in passages that Matthew and Luke share independently but which are not found in Mark's Gospel.

Both evangelists add resurrection appearances to their Markan source but, again, each in their distinctive ways. Matthew concludes his Gospel with the dramatic appearance of Jesus to the "Eleven" (Judas is tragically absent) on a mountaintop in Galilee where he commissions his disciples to bring the gospel message to the nations (28:16–20). Luke confines Jesus's resurrection appearances to Jerusalem—the constant focus of his Gospel—narrating the enticing story of the appearance of the disciples on the way to Emmaus (Luke 24:13–45), as well as an appearance to the rest of the disciples in Jerusalem (Luke 24:36–39). Luke's Gospel concludes with the ascension of Jesus to his Father and the promise to send the Spirit

(Luke 24:50–53; see also Acts 1:6–12)—the prelude to his second volume, the Acts of the Apostles.

The Gospel of John

Among the Four Gospels, that of John is the most distinctive of all. One author has branded this Gospel as the "Maverick Gospel."[11] While John's Gospel proclaims Jesus as the Messiah and the Son of God as do the Synoptics, he does so in a unique way. The Gospel of Mark begins his narrative with the preaching of John the Baptist at the Jordan river and the coming of the adult Jesus to be baptized by John. Matthew and Luke begin by reflecting on the events surrounding the infant Jesus's origin in Bethlehem and Jerusalem. In a quite different manner, John begins his gospel by extending the framework of Jesus's existence to cosmic proportions. His Gospel begins with a magnificent and poetic "prologue" (John 1:1–18) that locates the origin of Jesus, the "Word of God," in the very being of God before all time. That Word becomes flesh and takes on a human history which is narrated in the body of the Gospel. At the end of John's account, on the eve of Jesus's death, he speaks of his return to his Father, thus completing the cosmic framework of his account (John 17:1–5; see also John 13:1–2).

Within the body of the Gospel, there are also significant differences from the Synoptic Gospels. While Mark, Matthew, and Luke record one dramatic journey of Jesus from Galilee in the north to Jerusalem and the climax of his mission in Judea to the south, John has Jesus move back and forth between the two and gives greater attention to Jesus's presence in Jerusalem. The span of Jesus's public ministry in the Synoptics seems to be one year (embracing one Passover), but in John it seems to be three years. The

---

[11] See Robert Kysar, *John The Maverick Gospel* (Louisville, KY: Westminster John Knox Pres, rev. ed., 1993).

characteristic means of Jesus's ministry—parables and exorcisms—are prominent in the Synoptics, but they are absent in John. Where Peter is the representative leader of the disciples in the Synoptics, John introduces the enigmatic figure of the "Beloved disciple" who is close to Jesus, stands by him (with Mary the mother of Jesus) at the cross, and seems to be the privileged witness to the gospel events (John 13:23; 19:26–27; 21:20–23). While most of Jesus's teaching is done in relatively brief and often pithy statements in the Synoptics (Matthew's discourses are an exception), in John, Jesus speaks in long discourses, often reflecting on his own mission and his relationship to his Father. And some scenes prominent in the Synoptics, such as the Last Supper or Jesus's prayer in Gethsemane, are presented in a different fashion in John (John's equivalent of Jesus's Gethsemane prayer is found in John 12:27).

Scholars debate the reasons for this unique character of John's Gospel. Was the composer of John's Gospel aware of the Synoptic Gospels and yet decided to go in a different direction? Or was the stream of tradition that ultimately fed into John's Gospel completely independent of that of the Synoptics? Or were both streams of tradition independent but had some contact between them over time (there is some parallel material such as the walking on the water and multiplication of the loaves, and the passion narratives in all Four Gospels have a similar sequence of events)? For some scholars, the reason for John's unique portrayal of Jesus is that the Johannine community originated in a different expression of Judaism than that which stands behind the synoptic tradition. Judaism at the time of Jesus was diverse, as we are now aware because of the discovery of the Dead Sea Scrolls produced by a sectarian group of Jews who lived apart from the majority of their fellow Jews. Some of John's language and concepts echo the writings of this Jewish sectarian group. Likewise, John's Gospel gives a prominent role to the Samaritans in his story of the encounter of Jesus with the Samaritan Woman and then the whole village in chapter 4 of his Gospel. The Acts of the Apostles notes an early mission of the

Jerusalem community to Samaria (Acts 8:2–25). Did Samaritans form a significant part of the Johannine community that ultimately produced the Gospel? Samaritans had an aversion to Jerusalem and its Davidic traditions—perhaps this is why the metaphor of "the Kingdom of God" that plays such a prominent role in the Synoptics is rarely cited in John.[12]

Unity within Diversity

Having traced some of the distinctiveness of each Gospel, we return to our starting point. Even within this diversity of the gospel narratives, they share a singular focus on the person of Jesus— the claim of his unique identity, the fundamental character of his teaching and example, and the central significance of his death and resurrection for human destiny. A case can be made that the Gospels draw on historical traditions about Jesus of Nazareth in fashioning their narrative biographies of him. Substantial connection can be made between the gospel presentation of the story of Jesus and what we know to be true of the landscape, religious setting, and the political and social context of Palestinian Judaism in the first third of the first century. But the ultimate purpose of the evangelists and their communities was not to create a historical archive about Jesus of Nazareth. Their real purpose was proclamation of the gospel message about Jesus. The evangelists who composed the Gospels were similar to preachers who want to move and inspire their audiences. From the perspective of Christian faith, the Jesus who dominates the gospel narratives is in fact the "Risen Jesus"— with the gospel accounts, as it were, written "backward" from the vantage point of resurrection and the triumph over death that is at

---

[12] On this see Raymond E. Brown, *The Community of the Beloved Disciple: The Life, Loves, and Hates of an Individual Church in New Testament Times* (New York: Paulist, 1979), esp., pp. 35–40.

the heart of the Christian message. When the gospel writers portray the events of Jesus's origin, public ministry, and the events of his final days, the Jesus who teaches and heals and endures opposition is the now the triumphant Risen Jesus whose destiny with God is not in doubt.[13] As we will be asserting throughout this study, it is here—in the foundational religious claims of these narratives about the identity of Jesus—that one finds an essential rationale for their sacredness.

The Other New Testament Books

The "diversity within unity" that characterizes the Four Gospels also marks the rest of the New Testament writings. The Gospels have a fundamental point of comparison because each of them is a narrative about Jesus, even though with distinctive features. The remaining New Testament books take various literary forms, making comparison among them more challenging.

The Pauline Letters

The thirteen letters attributed to Paul share the literary form of a letter, with the possible exception of the Letter to the Ephesians. Some modern scholars question whether Ephesians was a letter to a specific community such as the church at Ephesus. That address is, in fact, missing in some early manuscripts. This text may have been something of a circular letter or synthesis, summarizing some of the major theological themes of Paul's

---

[13] On this see the helpful explanation of Sandra M. Schneider, *The Revelatory Text: Interpreting the New Testament as Sacred Scripture* (New York: HarperCollins, 1991), esp. pp. 97–110.

writings.[14] As noted earlier, some Pauline scholars also believe that not all of the thirteen letters attributed to the apostle were originally composed by Paul. There is no debate, however, about the Pauline authorship of Romans, 1 & 2 Corinthians, Galatians, Philippians, 1 Thessalonians, and Philemon. And the remaining list—2 Thessalonians, Colossians, Ephesians, and the Pastoral Letters of 1 & 2 Timothy and Titus—all take the form of letters and reflect the standard form of letter writing current in the Greco-Roman world of Paul's day.[15]

Despite sharing the common basic format of letters, the Pauline correspondence also exhibits remarkable diversity as well. Each of the letters attributed to Paul deals with specific communities, different pastoral or theological issues, and draws forth varied emphases and perspectives on the part of Paul or the author of the letters. For example, the challenge to Paul's conviction that God justifies humans, including Gentiles, not through the works of the law but through faith in God's liberating grace dominates Paul's Letter to the Galatians. The letter to Philemon—the shortest of Paul's letters and one addressed to an individual and the house church he apparently leads—is triggered by Paul's concern for the fate of an apparently runaway slave, Onesimus, who aided Paul during his imprisonment. It seems that Philemon is the former owner of this slave and Paul realizes that in the context of Roman law Philemon had the right to severely punish Onesimus. In an enticing personal way, Paul appeals to the fact that Philemon and Onesimus are also fellow Christians and that this is a far more compelling relationship than their different status in Roman society. Thus, the focus of this brief letter is not on justification by faith as in Galatians but on the fact that mutual love among Christians transcends any requirements of the social order.

---

[14] We will discuss the theology of Ephesians in Chapter 5, pp. 57–66.
[15] On Paul and his letter writing, see Luke Timothy Johnson, *Constructing Paul*, Vol. 1., in *The Canonical Paul* (Grand Rapids, MI: Eerdmans, 2020), pp. 62–92.

In Philippians, a community for which Paul seems to have had great affection, his focus is on the need to reconcile conflicting factions. Paul quotes what appears to be an early Christian hymn in urging the Christians at Philippi to transcend their differences by imitating the self-transcending love of Christ, who put aside his divine status to take on a human condition and to give his life for the world (see Phil 2:1–11). Paul's letters to the Corinthian community have quite different tones, as the apostle deals with one pastoral problem after another, including friction between Paul and his rambunctious Corinthian Christians. In another contrast, Paul's Letter to the Romans, a community he did not found and had not yet visited, takes on much more of a summation of his theology, moving from a review of the need for both Jew and Gentile for God's saving grace to the wrenching question of the destiny of Paul's beloved Israel, and ending with a strong encouragement for unity within the Roman Christian community.

This diversity in tone and purpose and style and context that marks the undisputed letters of Paul is, if anything, more accentuated in the so-called deutero-Pauline Letters.[16] Colossians and Ephesians reflect on the dominating role of Christ within the realm of the cosmic powers which popular Roman perspectives viewed as controlling human destiny. The exaltation of Christ is also reflected in his role as "head" of the body which is the church—a notion of the Body of Christ that differs from Paul's presentations in 1 Corinthians and Romans where his emphasis is on the mutual interdependence of the members of Christ's body rather than the dominant role of the "head." And, finally, the Pastoral Letters, in the view of many interpreters, reflect a later context, perhaps even into the early part of the second century, in which the concerns of the early church were on maintaining sound doctrine and the

---

[16] The ancient world was accustomed to what is called "pseudepigraphy," namely writings that claimed a famous author but were in fact written by a later disciple or admirer—in effect, claiming the tradition and authority of the named author. As a recognized rhetorical device, this was not equivalent to modern plagiarism.

qualities needed for various leadership roles. The image of Paul in these letters (especially in 2 Timothy) has a certain nostalgia to it, as the apostle gives advice to his trusted assistants, Timothy and Titus, and reflects on the sufferings and perseverance that marked his own history as an apostle.

Thus, the Pauline Letters are not the communication of a uniform and standardized theological perspective but express different facets of Paul's Christian faith and pastoral experience. At the same time, as we will note later, the undercurrents of Paul's tenacious faith in Jesus Christ and his constant reflection on his experiences and the concerns of his communities form a unifying foundation. Faith in Jesus as the Christ, the Son of God, the Redeemer of humankind, and the center of all history runs through all of Paul's diverse writings.[17] And, as in the case with the Four Gospels, it is this vivid faith confession of Paul proclaimed in his letters that will eventually lift this correspondence to the status of sacred writings acknowledged by the church at large.

The Letter to the Hebrews, the "Catholic" Epistles, the Book of Revelation

The diversity within unity found in the Gospels and in the Pauline Letters is also a characteristic of the remaining New Testament books. These include the Letter to the Hebrews, which in early Christianity was thought to be one of Paul's letters, and the "catholic" epistles—James, the First and Second Letters of Peter, the First, Second, and Third Letters of John, and the Letter of Jude. And, lastly, there is the book of Revelation, which concludes the series of books in the New Testament. Because these remaining books differ widely in their literary formats, the contexts that prompted

[17] See later discussion in Chapter 5.

their composition, and the theological or pastoral issues they deal with, their diversity is self-evident.

The Letter to the Hebrews, for example, is more of an elaborate exhortation or encouragement than it is a letter; it is clearly meant to fortify and inspire its intended audience (whose precise identity and location are not known). It is composed in rather elegant Greek. Its major theological and pastoral content is expressed through an elaborate metaphor, portraying Jesus's work of redemption in terms of an ideal and heavenly version of the Temple priesthood, exercised now in the heavenly sanctuary, producing a once-for-all and completely efficacious sacrifice for the forgiveness of sins. This "new covenant" succeeds the former covenant celebrated in the historical Jerusalem temple and its priesthood and worship which had been tragically destroyed in 70 AD.[18] Platonic philosophy, which views earthly realities as "shadows" of the true realities of the eternal realm, has some influence on Hebrew's elaborate metaphor. The letter concludes with a review of the faith maintained by great heroes of the Old Testament as encouragement to Christians to also persevere.

The Letter of James, by contrast, focuses on blunt moral exhortation, drawing heavily on the covenant tradition of Judaism which stressed the moral responsibility of Israel, particularly for its most vulnerable members. Faith must issue in good deeds; care for the poor is far more important than showing partiality to the rich; malicious speech is dangerous; undisciplined cravings and desires can lead one astray; patience in suffering and endurance in hope are salutary.

---

[18] While traditional interpreters of Hebrews tend to view the Letter's emphasis on the new covenant as asserting the replacement of Judaism by Christianity, it is also possible that by affirming a new and perfect heavenly temple the author intends rather to comfort Gentile Christians (as well as Jewish Christians) who mourned the destruction of the Jerusalem temple; see Ken Schenck, *The Letter to the Hebrews* (Franklin, TN: Seedbed Publishing, 2018).

There are two letters ascribed to Peter, and even these two are quite different in tone. Many modern scholars question whether either of them was composed by the apostle Peter. They probably come from later church leaders evoking the authority of Peter's name. The First Letter is an elegant and theologically rich text, written from Rome (referred to as "Babylon" in 1 Pet 5:13) directed to a series of churches in north central Asia Minor, probably composed in the last quarter of the first century. The goal of the letter is to encourage these communities who find themselves in mounting tension with the majority non-Christian population. The author refers to his addresses as "exiles of the diaspora" and "resident aliens"—terms which may suggest the communities were also composed of ethnic minorities, increasing their vulnerability. The letter's encouragement takes the form of recalling their source of hope in the resurrection of Christ and heaps on the community a series of images and qualities formerly associated with Israel in the Old Testament and now applied without hesitation to the Christians; for example, the author refers to the Christian community as "a chosen race, a royal priesthood, a holy nation, God's own people"—all titles applied to Israel in the Old Testament (see 1 Pet 2:9). They are also the "house of God" formed of living stones, that is, a new realization of the temple of Jerusalem now destroyed. The author encourages the various members of the household to live honorably and to give positive and respectful witness to the outside world.

The Second Letter of Peter is probably written later and, by contrast, has more "biographical" references, speaking of Peter's impending death and seeming to refer to his experience of the transfiguration (2 Pet 1:16–18). The tone of the letter is less bright than that of First Peter, warning about false prophets, including those who question why the second coming of Christ seems delayed. This letter may, in fact, be the last New Testament book to be written, perhaps in the early part of the second century. The author is familiar with the writings of Paul and notes that there are some things in Paul's letters "hard to understand," and, therefore, the writer warns against those who are "ignorant" and "unstable" and misinterpret Paul (see 2 Pet 3:16).

There are three letters attributed to the apostle John and, in fact, their content and style has affinity with the Gospel attributed to John as well. But here again there is great diversity even among the three letters themselves. The First Letter of John is barely a "letter" but rather a full-length communication that recapitulates the theology of the Fourth Gospel: Jesus as the privileged revelation of God as a God of love, the emphasis on the love command as the key criterion of Christian life, warnings about contrary teachings, and an exhortation to faith in Christ and his commands. The remaining two letters, by contrast, are brief and deal severely with what the author perceives as false teachers who threaten the very faith and destiny of the community.

The origin and circumstances of the very brief Letter of Jude are also shrouded in mystery. The "Jude" named as author is not identified as the apostle Jude and may refer to one of the brothers of Jesus at Nazareth named in Matt 13:53 and Mark 6:3. A striking feature is that it shares some material with the Second Letter of Peter (compare Jude 4–16 and 2 Pet 2:1–18), indicating that one borrowed from the other. Most scholars think that Jude was written before 2 Peter. Written in fine Greek, this letter is also concerned with fending off doctrinal errors that are a threat to the community. In this case, the errors seem to anticipate the kind of aberration in doctrine that blossomed later in second- and third-century Gnosticism, perhaps an indication that the letter was composed late in the first century or early second century.[19]

---

[19] Gnosticism is a term that applies broadly to a second-century philosophical and religious movement, strongly influenced by Platonic ideas, that emphasized the esoteric and privileged knowledge of its adherents and took a dim view of the material world. It posed a threat to orthodox Christianity.

The Book of Revelation

The last book in the Christian canon is the Apocalypse, or as it is more popularly known, the book of Revelation. The Greek verb *apokalypto* means to "unfold" or "reveal," and the title for this book is taken from its opening line which speaks of a "revelation of Jesus Christ" given to the book's author, "John" (see Rev 1:1). The identity of this "John" (sometimes traditionally referred to as "John the Divine") is debated; traditionally it was assumed to be the apostle John, also identified with the author of the Fourth Gospel and the Johannine Letters. Because of its unique style and theology, modern scholars generally hold that the author of Revelation is not the apostle John, but a Christian leader from western Asia Minor who was exiled by Roman authorities to the remote Mediterranean island of Patmos (see Rev. 1:1–2, 9–11).

It is not difficult to make a case for diversity among the New Testament writings when considering Revelation. It is distinctive in every way, particularly because of its literary genre. The author draws on what is called "apocalyptic" literature in composing his book. Various forms of ancient apocalyptic literature can be found in Judaism and in Greco-Roman literature. It is literature prompted by times of crisis and great suffering, when the known world seems to be dissolving in chaos and hope turns to the possibilities of a new world order.[20] Regarding the Bible, some interpreters see apocalyptic literature as related to prophecy. Just as the Old Testament prophets such as Jeremiah, Isaiah, and Ezekiel, for example, railed against the present corruption of Israel and longed for God's redemption, the overall message of Jewish apocalyptic literature usually has a more radical but similar perspective. Although there are varieties of apocalyptic literature, it often takes the form of

---

[20] On the Jewish background of apocalyptic literature, see John J. Collins, *The Apocalyptic Imagination: An Introduction to Jewish Apocalyptic Literature* (Grand Rapids, MI: Eerdmans, 2nd ed., 1998).

visionary revelations and employs vivid and mysterious symbols, as is the case with the book of Revelation. Some of the images used in Revelation echo those found in the Old Testament, particularly in books such as Ezekiel, Zechariah, and Daniel. It should be noted that the opening chapters of the book of Revelation also utilize the letter format we have seen in so many other New Testament books. The first three chapters contain letters sent to seven churches in the western region of Asia Minor, challenging their failings and exhorting them to faithful perseverance.

Some Christians throughout the centuries have interpreted the mysterious imagery and symbolism of Revelation as a secret code predicting the end of the world and have speculated which events and personages contemporary with later readers are being identified by John the author. However, most Christians interpret Revelation not as a magical prediction of future events but as a strong critique of the Roman Empire contemporary with the author. The author views his current history as a cosmic struggle between the diabolical injustices and persecutions of the Roman Empire and the divine redemptive power of the "Lamb," that is, the crucified and risen Christ. There is no doubt about the outcome: the "Lamb that was slain" will triumph over all evil power. And God's creation, wounded by evil, will ultimately be restored and a "new heaven and a new earth" will be realized. This is the fundamental and enduring theological message of Revelation.

The author is guided by the vision he has experienced to urge his fellow Christians not to compromise in any way with what he considers the inherently evil Roman Empire, expressed in its idolatrous emperor worship and its economic and political oppression of the poor (see, e.g., the vivid condemnation of Rome's injustice in Revelation 18). For example, Christians should not eat meat that had been used in pagan rituals and then put on the market. Eating this meat makes one complicit in idolatry (Rev 2:14, 20). Here is a clear example of the diversity existing among the New Testament books. Paul the Apostle had a very different perspective.

Since pagan rituals are futile and the gods they honor do not exist, Christians need not worry about eating such meat. However, Paul cautions that if a fellow Christian is scrupulous in this matter and has, in effect, a "weak" conscience, then their fellow Christians should avoid scandalizing them (1 Cor 8:1–13). Similarly, Paul in Romans 13, unlike Revelation, counsels Christians to respect their civic leaders, while at the same time, Paul's letters in their entirely espouse a view of human life and society that runs counter to the assumptions of Roman society.

Unity in Diversity

As we noted earlier, the diverse Four Gospels find their fundamental unity in their conviction that Jesus was the Christ, the Son of God, and the authentic revealer of God and God's will. His death and resurrection—the fundamental reality of all four narratives—brings redemption to the world and becomes the normative pattern of Christian existence. The same is true for the writings assigned to Paul, both the undisputed letters and those that may have been written later under Paul's name. Running through all of the letters and the particular circumstances of their composition and the different nuances of their literary form and language is the singular focus on Jesus Christ as Messiah and God's uniquely chosen Son, whose life, death, and resurrection reveal God's true face and the destiny of humankind.

The same is true of the remaining letters. Hebrews proclaims Jesus as the final "word" of God to the world and as the definitive "high priest" whose self-sacrifice assures the salvation of the world. The Letter of James is absorbed in moral exhortation, but the virtues it extolls are clearly derived from Jesus and the Jewish ethical tradition that Jesus exemplifies. The author presents himself as "a servant of God and of the Lord Jesus Christ" (Jas 1:1) and questions whether those who neglect the poor in order to heap favor on the rich "really believe in our glorious Lord Jesus Christ" (Jas 2:1). Both Letters of Peter, while quite different from each other, extoll faith in the Risen Christ as the center of one's existence (1 Pet 1:2; 2 Pet 1:1). The Johannine Letters, particularly 1 John, reflect the intense focus on the person of Jesus as revealer of the God of love that is the dominant conviction of the Gospel of John as well. From the teaching of Jesus, the Word made flesh, derives the central Christian ethical demand of love of God and neighbor. The very brief letter of Jude has a polemical focus as is the case with 2 and 3 John. Yet the author's concern is that deviation from sound doctrine in effect denies "our only Master and Lord, Jesus Christ" (Jude 4).

The book of Revelation concludes the New Testament canon and, despite its radical difference in literary form compared to the rest of the New Testament, also proclaims a singular focus on the triumphant victory of the Risen and Exalted Jesus over the diabolical power represented by the excesses of the Roman Empire. That Christological focus fittingly becomes the final verse of the New Testament canon as the author longs for the triumphant return of Christ at the end of time: "The one who testifies to these things says, 'Surely I am coming soon.' Amen. Come, Lord Jesus! The grace of the Lord Jesus be with all the saints. Amen" (Rev 22:20–21).

As we will take up later, this singular focus on the person of Jesus and his ultimate identity that transcends the diversity of these writings is key to the sacred character of the New Testament.

2

From Jesus to the Writings of the New Testament

As we have discussed, the New Testament is not a single, uniform book but is composed of multiple compositions, written by numerous authors, with diverse literary forms and theological perspectives, yet sharing a fundamental unity in its focus on the identity of Jesus and the implications of his life, death, and resurrection for human destiny. This ensemble of New Testament texts emerged within the framework of the first-century Jewish and Greco-Roman world and the experience and convictions of the earliest followers of Jesus of Nazareth. The way the New Testament was formed and transmitted to later generations has a lot to do with it being viewed as a "sacred" text. We now turn to a closer look at the formation and transmission of the New Testament writings.

The traditions about Jesus that circulated in the early church were not contained in a sealed envelope but were transmitted in and through the living reality of these first Christian communities. Stories about Jesus were told in preaching and in instruction about the Christian faith. How best to describe who Jesus is? What titles should be used to illustrate his unique identity? What were the key events of his life? The life of Jesus was viewed as exemplary. Therefore, questions of how best to live in the spirit of Jesus and his teaching were discussed and debated within the Christian community. What are the virtues that reflect the authentic Christian life? What are the vices and habits to be avoided? How do we as Christians handle disputes and tensions in the community? How should we relate to non-Christians and to the civil authorities of the

The New Testament. Donald Senior, Oxford University Press. © Oxford University Press 2022.
DOI: 10.1093/oso/9780197530832.003.0003

Roman Empire? What is the meaning of the Lord's Supper left to us through tradition? The lived experience of the early Christians reflected in such questions left its mark on the traditions about Jesus and the Christian life that circulated through the early community and acted as a kind of "filter" determining which traditions about Jesus were to be retained because they were viewed as most relevant for Christian life. Not everything originally known about Jesus was handed on: for example, we know nothing about his physical appearance or the sound of his voice. What was handed on was vital information about the perceived identity of Jesus and the purpose and spirit of his mission.

After Jesus: Stages in the Development of the New Testament Writings

Although the New Testament has a unifying focus on Jesus of Nazareth, not a single New Testament writing claims Jesus as its author. Our knowledge of Jesus and his mission derives not from his own direct testimony in any written form but from the transmission of such knowledge by his followers within the early Christian community. In the prologue to his Gospel, the evangelist Luke informs "Theophilus" (his prime reader or perhaps patron) of his intention to write an account of Jesus's life and cites previous examples:

> Since many have undertaken to set down an orderly account of the events that have been fulfilled among us, just as they were handed on to us by those who from the beginning were eyewitnesses and servants of the world, I too decided, after investigating everything carefully from the very first, to write an orderly account for you, most excellent Theophilus, so that you may know the truth concerning the things about which you have been instructed. (Luke 1:1–4)

While Luke's prologue offers a theological perspective on the flourishing of the Christian message from Jerusalem out into the Mediterranean world, the major stages of his theological perspective also reflect a historical reality about the formation and transmission of the New Testament. Luke's prologue sketches three stages in the transmission of traditions about Jesus:

Stage 1. "Eyewitnesses," that is, the contemporaries of Jesus who experienced the impact of his person, were recipients of his teaching and witnessed the dramatic events of his arrest, trial, and crucifixion, and later were caught up in the exhilarating experience of faith in his resurrection. These first followers were mainly Jews of Palestine, with Jesus only occasionally interacting with Gentiles and Samaritans.

Stage 2. A second stage emerged with the early "servants of the word," those followers of Jesus, some but not all of them eyewitnesses, who, fired by resurrection faith, began to proclaim the "gospel," that is, their shared conviction that Jesus was the Messiah and Son of God, proclaimed first to Jews and then to Gentiles. According to Acts, the very first Christians were Jews, some Hebrew-speaking native to Judea, and other Greek-speaking Jews from the Diaspora or wider Mediterranean and Arab world. Fairly quickly, the gospel message was carried by such Jewish Christians out to the wider world, including northern Africa (see the story of the conversion of an Ethiopian eunuch by Philip in Acts 8:26–40), Syria (Acts 9:1–25 refers to the Christians already in Damascus at the time of Paul's conversion), Arabia (see Paul's testimony in Gal 1:17), Asia Minor, Greece, and Rome (there are multiple references to these areas in Acts, Paul's letters, and other New Testament writings).

Stage 3. A final stage took place, roughly in the last third of the first century, when most of the New Testament books were composed, including the Four Gospels and the later writings of the New Testament (with the exception of Paul's letters, which were written during the second stage of transmission before the Gospels). These were all written in Greek, and most, if not all, were composed outside of Palestine.

Several events probably served as a trigger for this third stage, where the early traditions were put into writing, although the accompanying oral communication did not cease overnight. First of all, in 70 AD, in a violent response to the Jewish revolt that began in 66 AD, the Romans destroyed Jerusalem and its temple, causing major adjustments in both Judaism and early Jewish Christianity. Judaism had to survive without the unifying focus of the temple and the temple priesthood as a center of orthodoxy. Christians (and especially Jewish Christians) were also profoundly affected by the loss of Jerusalem and its temple. Jesus himself reverenced the temple and in Luke's Gospel called it the "My Father's house" (Luke 2:49). The Acts of the Apostles depicts the early Jewish Christian community in Rome as praying daily in the temple (Acts 2:46). Gradually, however, the epicenter of the Christian world would move west to Rome, a move accelerated by the calamity of Jerusalem's destruction. From this point on, the mission to the Gentiles would accelerate.

Another important impetus for the "third stage" in the formation of the New Testament books was the fact that the early apostolic generation of eyewitnesses and missionaries was passing from the scene, and there was a need to consolidate and make permanent traditions about Jesus that up to this point were transmitted mainly in oral form. And with advancing time, the early Christian community realized that it had a history in front of it, and the early enthusiasm for a rapid culmination of world history with the triumphant return of Christ was increasingly viewed as an event of the distant future.

In the first two stages, traditions about Jesus would have been transmitted mainly in oral form, which, in fact, was the main form of communication in the largely illiterate culture of the first-century Mediterranean world. There were, of course, educated people who knew how to read and write, but most of the population was not so equipped. Some historians estimate that less than 30 percent of the population was literate. When there was a need for official written documents, such as marriage contracts or public decrees, or business transactions or important letters sent to family, friends, or business and government associates, professional "scribes" who were literate could be engaged to produce such written texts. As we will note later, Paul's letters were obvious examples of written texts, possibly dictated to scribes or secretaries and then read to groups of Christians, most of whom were probably illiterate.[1] Oral transmission was not haphazard in such a cultural context but was carefully observed and controlled. Modern society depends on the written text and much less on memory. But ancient oral cultures cultivated careful memorization of key texts, and there were techniques that insured relative accuracy. Audiences or congregations who listened to the recital of respected literature or familiar religious texts would be attentive and ready to correct errors in the recitation. It is likely that, in many instances, a public speaker would use a written text as something of a prompt or script for his oral presentation.[2]

The third stage we are describing involved written composition such as the Four Gospels and the other texts of the New Testament. As we will point out, the traditions that had been handed on to this later generation of Christians had not passed through some kind of insulated pipeline but would have been influenced by or filtered through the faith and experience of the earlier generations of Christians. As we will note, the impact of Christian religious experience on the substance and expression of these early traditions will be an important factor in making it "sacred."

We cannot be entirely sure what Luke meant by informing Theophilus that he intended to write an "orderly account" (Luke 1:1). In Luke's own case, "orderly" might mean attempting to put

---

[1] See Chapter 5.
[2] See the work of Brian J. Wright, *Communal Reading in the Time of Jesus: A Window into Early Christian Reading Practices* (Minneapolis, MN: Fortress, 2017).

his narrative about the mission of Jesus and that of the early church into a wider and overarching perspective. For Luke this meant the rooting of Jesus's life in Judaism, as illustrated in the account of his birth in the Davidic city of Bethlehem and his early encounter with the Jerusalem temple (Luke 1–2), then showing the unfolding of his mission through Galilee and back to Jerusalem, and there the finale with his death, resurrection, and ascension back to his Father. Finally, in the opening chapters of the Acts of the Apostles, Luke describes the sending of the Spirit, which provides the dynamism to propel the apostles and disciples of Jesus from Jerusalem to the ends of the earth. Thus, the "order" in Luke's account is the unfolding of the plan of God to bring salvation to the world.

The Pauline Letters

Paul's letters are the first written New Testament texts, composed during what we have termed Stage 2, roughly from 50 to 70 AD. Although we cannot be precise about the date of Paul's martyrdom, it likely took place during the reign of the Emperor Nero around 64 to 68 AD. Therefore, what is termed the "undisputed" letters—Romans, 1 & 2 Corinthians, Galatians, Philippians, 1 Thessalonians, and Philemon—were written before that date. The other letters attributed to Paul's authorship—Ephesians, Colossians, 2 Thessalonians, 1 & 2 Timothy, and Titus—may have been composed later, citing Paul's name and authority, and therefore falling into Stage 3, that is, in the period after 70 AD.

We will consider Paul's theology later on in discussing why his writings were deemed "sacred" by early Christianity.[3] For now we can note that his letters illustrate the process of transmission we are considering. It may be that Paul happened by chance on using letters to extend his mission. After arriving in Macedonia on what

---

[3] See Chapter 5.

Acts considers the apostle's second missionary journey (covered in Acts 15:36–18:22), he went to the Roman colony of Philippi and then westward along the Via Egnatia, a major Roman road that stretched from present-day Albania clear across Macedonia (the northern region of present-day Greece) to the western shore of the Greek peninsula, in present-day Croatia. A major stop for Paul and his companion Silas was the city of Thessalonica, even then an important seaport and significant city. According to Paul's own testimony (1 Thessalonians 1–3) and the account in the Acts of the Apostles (Acts 17:1–10), his preaching succeeded in attracting both Jews and Gentiles to this new religious movement. As was typical of Paul's missionary strategy when arriving at a new city, as an observant Jew he would go first to the local synagogue and proclaim his message there. Frequenting many of the synagogues in the Mediterranean world were not only Jews but also some Gentiles enamored of Jewish tradition and moral codes. Called "Godfearers" or "devout" Greeks (see the description of the centurion of Capernaum in Luke 7:1–7; also in Acts 17:4, 7; 18:7), they were often responsive to Paul's message, enabling them to become part of God's people but without the ethnic markers of circumcision, kosher diet, and other religious observances required of Jews. Understandably, Paul's successful inroads among these Gentile participants could cause friction with some of the Jewish members of the synagogue (Acts 17:4–5).

According to Acts (17:1–10), this seems to have been the case in Thessaloniki, where those opposed to Paul started a riot in the city and attacked the home of Jason, apparently the manager of the synagogue who was accused of offering hospitality to Paul and his companions. Eventually some of the Christians spirited Paul and Silas out of the city and sent him on to Berea, a Greek city some 45 miles west of Thessaloniki. There, the irrepressible Paul again preaches in the synagogue with good success (see Acts 17:10–12). But when troublemakers pursue Paul from Thessaloniki to Berea, the Christians send Paul on to Athens, leaving behind Silas and

Timothy to continue the work of evangelization. Acts charts Paul's continuing (but apparently less than successful) mission in Athens (Acts 17:16–34) and then to Corinth, where he will stay for a considerable time (Acts 18:1–18). But his concern for what might be happening with the new community in Thessaloniki troubles Paul and, when he is not able to return there himself, he sends Timothy to check out the situation. When Paul learns from Timothy that the Christian community there is thriving in spite of everything, he is prompted to write a letter of relief and joy (see 1 Thess 3:1–10), praising the faith and courage of these new Christians and answering some of their questions and concerns (e.g., What happens to those members who pass away before the triumphant return of Christ? See 1 Thess 4:13–18).

Thus, the Letter to the Thessalonians, probably the very first New Testament book to be written, sets a pattern for Paul's subsequent correspondence. Through letter writing—a well-developed art in the ancient world—Paul is able to extend his pastoral presence both to communities he founded (e.g., Philippi, Thessaloniki, Corinth, Galatia) and to Rome, where he intended to go but had not yet visited. His letters are "occasional," often prompted by circumstances or questions raised by the community to which he writes. For example, in writing to Corinth, a dynamic and somewhat turbulent community, Paul deals with the problems of factions, of lawsuits taken to public courts, cases of incest, abuses at the Eucharist, the question of proper conduct of women in the assembly, and many other pastoral issues. His letters are, therefore, not systematic presentations of his theology. The near exception is the Letter to the Romans that lays out in a fairly comprehensive way Paul's views of salvation. Otherwise, his perspectives on Christ, on the nature of the church, and on issues of Christian conduct appear in clumps, most of the time in response to a specific question or problem.

In many ways, the content of Paul's letters is a perfect illustration of what we have described as Stage 2 in the formation of the New Testament. The substance of Paul's letters reflects his own faith experience of Christ and the apostle's exceptional ability to express the profound meaning of the life, death, and resurrection of Christ. This, no doubt, was also the content of his missionary preaching. Paul both advances Christian reflection but also is influenced by it. He includes in his letters verses of early Christian hymns (e.g., Phil 2:6–11), credal formulae that had been handed on to him (1 Cor 11:23–26; 15:3–11), and basic information about the life and teaching of Jesus about which he had been informed. In the latter category, Paul refers to the birth of Christ (Gal 4:4–5) and especially to his death by crucifixion. In fundamental ways, Paul's teaching coincides with the core teachings of Jesus, such as the love command and the need for love and forgiveness in community.[4] Paul no doubt had a profound influence on early Christian thought and experience but was also shaped by it—the kind of impact that proclaiming the Christian message has had on subsequent generations of thoughtful preachers and missionaries.

The so-called deutero-Pauline Letters such as Colossians and Ephesians, as well as the Pastoral Letters of Timothy and Titus, even though perhaps composed after the lifetime of Paul in Stage 3 of the transmission of the New Testament materials, nevertheless, reflect the same basic principle. They are texts profoundly shaped not only by the theology of their composers but also by the living tradition and the specific concerns of the later Christian communities to which they are addressed. In the latter case, particularly in the case of a letter like 2 Timothy, part of that tradition now includes Paul's own missionary sufferings and triumphs (see, e.g., 2 Tim 3:10–12; 4:6–8).

---

[4] On the impact of Jesus's life and teaching on Paul, see James D. G. Dunn, *Jesus According to the New Testament* (Grand Rapids, MI: Eerdmans, 2019), esp. pp. 99–139.

The Four Gospels and the Acts of the Apostles

The Gospels, too, emerge from the various stages of the early church we have been describing. As already noted in our discussion of the prologue to Luke's Gospel, the written Gospels do not appear until some decades after the death and resurrection of Jesus. In a very true sense, the Gospels are not a preexisting "blueprint" for the early church, but they themselves emerge from the life of the early church and are, in that sense, the "church's books."

There is much discussion today about what literary form or genre in the first-century world best describes the Four Gospels.[5] Most scholars today consider the Gospels closest to what is called a "historical biography," but ancient Greco-Roman culture had a different understanding of what constituted a "historical biography" than we do today. A good biography today attempts to reconstruct as accurately as possible the facts of a person's life—their family background, their education, their careers and accomplishments, and the impact of their life. Having access to the person's own letters, diaries, and personal documents becomes a valuable source for reconstructing their life and perspective. The author of a modern biography ultimately must interpret the meaning of all these facts about a person's life. But the ideal is to base such an interpretation on objective facts.

Ancient biographies shared some of these qualities but in a very different mode. In most instances, ancient biographers did not have access to the hard facts of a person's life or the personal effects of the object of their biography, but they were aware in a more general manner of the lives and accomplishments of their subjects. And a

---

[5] Regarding the literary form of the Gospels, see Richard Burridge, *What Are the Gospels? A Comparison with Graeco-Roman Biography* (Waco, TX: Baylor University Press, 3rd ed., 2018); see also Craig S. Keener, *Christobiography. Memory, History, and the Reliability of the Gospels* (Grand Rapids, MI: Eerdmans, 2019) and Helen K. Bond, *The First Biography of Jesus. Genre and Meaning in Mark's Gospel* (Grand Rapids, MI: Eerdmans, 2020).

primary goal of ancient biography was to extol the virtues and example of their subject, not, as is often the case in modern biography, to be as objective and factual as possible.

Although the Four Gospels reflect some of the style and goals of ancient historical biographies, the Gospels have unique features all their own. Their portrayals of Jesus are much more detailed than most other ancient biographies, and above all, there is a singular religious interest in the identity and mission of their subject. Also significant is the concentration of all Four Gospels on the circumstances of Jesus's death and the dramatic events that follow. Great details are given about the final days of Jesus's life, including his final meal with his disciples, his arrest and interrogations by the authorities, and the sequence of his condemnation, crucifixion, and burial. The Four Gospels conclude, although in varied ways, with the accounts of the discovery of the empty tomb and several appearances of the Risen Christ to his disciples. In some ways, the Gospels are built backward; that is, the entire life of Jesus is oriented to the finale of his death and resurrection. The example and meaning of Jesus's earthly ministry finds its full expression in the manner of his death and ultimate triumph over death. Similar to Paul's writings, but in a quite different literary mode, the Gospels focus on the significance of Jesus's ultimate destiny.

Again, similar to Paul's writings, the Gospels' contents are composed both of traditions transmitted and shaped by early Christian experience and by the unique circumstances of the communities and the evangelists from which each Gospel emerges. The stories of Jesus's healings, teachings, conflicts with authorities, interaction with his disciples, and the circumstances of his death had been handed on in the living traditions and faith experience of the early Christian community. As we noted earlier, the whole story of Jesus is told from the vantage point of his resurrection. At a certain moment—sometime after the traumatic events of 70 AD— the evangelists knit together these various accounts about the life and mission of Jesus into a narrative whole, a "biography." The circumstances of the Christian community from which a Gospel emerges and to which it is first directed have an influence on the tone and content of the gospel narrative.

The Gospel of Mark

Modern biblical scholarship has concluded that Mark's Gospel was the first to be so composed. While certitude about its historical circumstances is not possible, a strong possibility is that Mark's Gospel was written for the Christian community at Rome, somewhere around the year 70 AD. The third-century Christian historian Eusebius quotes Papias, a late first-century bishop of Hierapolis in Asia Minor, who asserted that Mark was a companion of Peter in Rome and served as a kind of secretary or interpreter for Peter's remembrances of Jesus's life. Given Nero's persecution of the Christians in Rome at this period, this might explain some of the tone of Mark's Gospel—its focus on the suffering of Christ, on Jesus's confrontation with the raw power of evil in his many exorcisms, and Mark's emphasis on the frailty of Peter and the disciples in the face of suffering.

The Gospel of Matthew

Mark's pioneering composition of the gospel narrative about Jesus served as a primary source for Matthew's Gospel. The evangelist absorbs almost the entirety of Mark's account, including its organization of Jesus's public life into his ministry in Galilee and then a fateful journey to Jerusalem, where he will suffer rejection and death. Matthew (along with Luke) apparently had access to other traditions about Jesus that had been circulating in the early community and fuses these onto the framework provided by Mark. But here, too, the circumstances of Matthew's own Christian community come into play. Matthew's Gospel is clearly the most Jewish of the Gospels, emphasizing continuity between the sacred traditions of Judaism and the mission of Jesus. At the beginning of the Sermon on the Mount, the Matthean Jesus declares that he has not come "to destroy the law and the prophets, but to fulfill them" (Matt 5:17). The "law and the prophets" is a kind of shorthand reference to the Hebrew Scriptures and the tradition of interpretation that surrounded them. Jesus also declares that his mission is only "to the lost sheep of the house of Israel" (Matt 10:5; 15:24). During his public ministry, the Jesus of Matthew's Gospel concentrates on his fellow Israelites. Only at the end of Matthew's Gospel does the Risen Christ extend the mission of his disciples beyond Israel to the "nations," that is, the Gentiles (Matt 28:17–20).

Matthew's assertion that Jesus's teaching and example "fulfills" the law may also explain some of the polemical material in this Gospel. In the chaotic period after 70 AD, when both the Jewish Christians and other Jewish groups were adjusting to the dramatic changes imposed by the destruction of the temple, there was a struggle to claim legitimacy. Matthew's Jewish Christian community believed that in following Jesus it was fully faithful to its Jewish heritage; however, the majority of "non-Christian" Jews would not agree with this assessment. Thus, Matthew's Gospel harshly criticizes the Jewish leaders, reflecting the tension between these communities in the period after 70 AD. Matthew's Gospel may have been written in Antioch of Syria, then the third largest city in the Roman Empire, where there was also a large Jewish community. The Acts of the Apostles (Acts 11:19–26) and the testimony of Paul in his letter to the Galatians (Gal 2:11–14) confirm that a strong Christian community, composed of Jewish and Gentile Christians, developed there—a likely place where the concerns of Matthew's Gospel would be in play.

The Gospel of Luke and the Acts of the Apostles

The two-volume work of the Gospel of Luke and the Acts of the Apostles is yet another example of the handing on of traditions about Jesus forged in the wider Christian community and now taking on a particular accent due to the circumstances of the evangelist and his community. Scholars are less certain about the location where Luke's work was composed, with both Ephesus and Antioch being strong candidates. What is clearer is that Luke directs his two-volume work to a mainly Gentile audience. In his prologue (Luke 1:1-4) the evangelist addresses his work to "Theophilus" as his ideal reader and wants to show him both the origin of Jesus's unique mission of salvation and its dynamic continuity as it moves, in Luke's phrase, "from Judea, Samaria, to the ends of the earth" (Luke 24:47; Acts 1:8). As does Matthew but in a quite different mode, Luke emphasizes the Jewish roots of Jesus and his mission. Jesus's birth in Bethlehem, the city of David, fulfills the hopes of Israel for redemption, and the presentation of the infant Jesus in the temple and his warm reception by the prophets Anna and Simeon connect Jesus to Jerusalem and its temple—the heart of the Jewish experience. Luke follows Mark's basic narrative framework of moving from Galilee to Jerusalem, but it underscores this journey of Jesus and his disciples—an anticipation of the "journey" of the gospel in the persons of Peter and Paul in the Acts of the Apostles. Luke concludes his Gospel and transitions to the Acts of the Apostles by having the Risen Jesus exalted to God's right hand through the Ascension and then sending the Spirit upon the assembly of Jerusalem apostles and disciples (Luke 24:50-53; Acts 1:1-11). The dynamic power of God's Spirit will propel these Jewish Christian missionaries out into the wider Mediterranean world, an outreach that culminates in the powerful missionary work of Paul.

Through this narrative of the Gospel and the Acts of the Apostles, Theophilus (and Luke's gentile readers) learns about the "events that have been fulfilled among us" and is assured of the "truth concerning the things about which you have been instructed" (Luke 1:1, 4). Some interpreters of the Acts of the Apostles believe that beyond providing perspective to his gentile readers, Luke also wants to make the case to Roman authorities that the Christians are law abiding and not to be feared. Where disturbances do take place, such as riots in Jerusalem (e.g., Acts 21:27–36), Thessaloniki (17:5), or Ephesus (19:21–41), these are due to false testimony against the Jerusalem apostles or Paul. Eventually, the Roman officials involved discover the apostles' innocence or dismiss the charges as groundless (e.g., Acts 16:35–40; 18:12–17). While Luke may emphasize that the Christians are not overt rebels against legitimate civil authorities, on another level, the portrayal of God's sovereignty over all these events and the kind of values exemplified in the Gospel and Acts are ultimately quite different and even counter to many of the values and suppositions of the Roman Empire.[6]

The Gospel of John

As we have noted previously, John's Gospel is obviously quite different in style and content compared to the Synoptic Gospels of Matthew, Mark, and Luke.[7] Yet John's Gospel, too, is a blend of traditions about Jesus that circulated in the early Christian community and then were fashioned into a complete narrative by the evangelist and the circumstances of his own community. Modern biblical scholarship has debated why John's Gospel is so different from the Synoptic Gospels. It is likely that the author of John's Gospel drew on a different stream of tradition than that available to Mark, Matthew, and Luke. Yet it is also possible that these two streams were not totally independent of each other, since there is

---

[6] See on this perspective, C. Kavin Rowe, *World Upside Down: Reading Acts in the Graeco-Roman Age* (New York: Oxford University Press, 2009).

[7] See Chapter 1.

some overlap such as the scenes of Jesus's walking on the water and the feeding of the multitudes (compare John 6:1–24 with Mark 6:30–44) and the passion narrative (compare John 18:1–19:42 with Mark 14:43–15:47).

As with the Synoptic Gospels, the circumstances of John's Christian community have also left their imprint on the gospel. Many scholars believe that John's community is rooted in Palestinian Judaism—yet a brand of Judaism somewhat different from that reflected in the Gospels of Mark, Matthew, and Luke. John's Gospel is very familiar with Jerusalem and some of its features (e.g., the Temple area; the Sheep's Gate, the pools of Bethesda; the Siloam pool; the Kidron valley; the Mount of Olives, Golgotha, etc.).[8] There is also evidence, as we noted especially in Matthew's Gospel, of post–70 AD conflict with the Jewish authorities. There is a sharp conflict between Jesus and the authorities at several places in John's Gospels (see the sharp exchange in John 8:39–59), and in the account of the healing of the man born blind, the narrator notes that the man's parents were fearful of the "Jews" (John's frequent term for the religious authorities opposed to Jesus): "His parents . . . were afraid of the Jews; for the Jews had already agreed that anyone who confessed Jesus to be the Messiah would be put out of the synagogue" (John 9:22)—a circumstance that reflects tension after the events of 70 AD.

At one point during the feast of Tabernacles, Jesus's opponents misconstrue his words about "going to a place where you cannot come" to mean that Jesus "intends to go to the Diaspora among the Greeks and teach the Greeks" (John 7:35). This suggests that at one point, perhaps in the chaos surrounding the Jewish revolt against Rome in 66–70 AD, the Johannine community moved away from Palestine to another location in the Mediterranean world, such as the major city of Ephesus. Some ancient traditions locate the death and burial of the Apostle John in that city that had

---

[8] See Senior, *The Gospel Landscape*, pp. xx.

a significant Christian community since the time of Paul. This probable movement of John's community also fits with the conviction of many scholars that the Gospel itself has gone through more than one stage in its composition—originating in Palestinian Judaism but reaching its final shape toward the end of the first century in a Greco-Roman city such as Ephesus. Thus, as in the case of the Synoptic Gospels, the experience of the Johannine community leaves its mark on the content and style of the Gospel. As we will consider later, some aspects of the theology of John's Gospel bear the imprint of both Palestinian Judaism and Greco-Roman thought.

Gospels for the Whole Church?

Modern biblical scholarship has demonstrated that each of the Gospels has a distinctive perspective and emerged from different locations. The question remains, When the evangelists composed their Gospels, did they intend them only for a local audience or, as one scholar has phrased it, were they written "for all Christians"?[9] This is difficult to answer, especially since the authors of the Gospels remain anonymous and except for Luke's prologue do not state their reasons for writing. And in Luke's case, his prologue is directed to one person, Theophilus, whether a real individual or a fictitious ideal reader, although we can assume he intended his two-volume work to be read by more than Theophilus! It is possible that a "both and" answer is most likely. Each evangelist, in harmony with his own local community or region, shaped the Gospel in view of the experiences and traditions he was engaged with. But, given the level of communication and travel already taking place among these early Christian communities, it is also likely that the evangelists

---

[9] See Richard Bauckham, *The Gospels for All Christians: Rethinking the Gospel Audiences* (Grand Rapids, MI: Eerdmans, 1997).

expected that the gospel narratives they composed would be shared with other Christians beyond their local communities. We know from Paul and from the traditions in Acts that Christians moved all around the Mediterranean world over the network of the good Roman roads that then existed and visited their fellow Christians in other places. Paul was able to organize a collection among several communities to be presented to the church in Jerusalem (1 Cor 16:1–4)—a feat that must have involved considerable communication and travel among these early Christian groups.

It is likely, then, the Gospels were composed both for a local community—which may have involved more than one community in a region—and for the wider church. The Gospel of Mark is a prime example of this. If written in Rome sometime around 70 AD, it had already reached a city such as Antioch and was read and heard by Christians there shortly after its composition, with enough reverence and respect that Matthew and Luke must take this Gospel into account in composing their own versions. We will take up this question from another angle in the next chapter concerning the formation of the New Testament canon.

Handing on The New Testament

By the end of the first century and the first few decades of the second century, most of the New Testament books were composed and in circulation in the early church. As we will note in the next chapter, there were debates about the inclusion of a few books, but the Four Gospels, the thirteen letters attributed to Paul, and most of the so-called Catholic Epistles and Revelation were considered part of the "New Testament." By this time, these texts were circulating among the extant Christian communities, read at their assemblies and worship, pondered and discussed by the leaders and members of these communities, and gaining status as sacred writings on a par with the Hebrew Scriptures. There were also a few early writings considered important and sacred but not considered canonical, such as the Didache and the Shepherd of Hermas, but for the most part, it was the writings now included in our New Testament that were gaining authority as both sacred and normative.[10]

Composed in Greek

Most early Christians were Greek speaking. *Koine* (that is, "common") Greek was used at least as a second language throughout most of the Roman Empire, much like English in many parts of the world today. Even among the Jewish Christians in Jerusalem, there were "Hellenists" or Greek speakers, as the famous dispute in Acts testifies. The "Hellenists" complained to the Hebrew-speaking Christians that their widows were being neglected in the daily distribution of rations (Acts 6:1–6), leading to the appointment of "deacons" to ensure equity. Thus, it is no surprise that all the New Testament writings were composed in Greek. It is possible that some previous portions of the New Testament texts were originally formulated in Hebrew or Aramaic. There are a few Hebrew and Aramaic words sprinkled throughout the Gospels and even in Paul's letters. Some are quotations from the Old Testament, such as the citation of the first verse of Psalm 22 in Mark 15:34, or key terms such as the affectionate Aramaic or Hebrew term *abba* for God as "father" found in Mark 14:36 and in Paul's Letter to the Romans 8:15 and Galatians 4:6, or the reference to *korban*, a Hebrew term for a type of sacrifice referred to in Mark 7:11, or the snatch of Aramaic prayer that concludes Paul's first Letter to the Corinthians—*maranatha*, "come, Lord" (1 Cor 16:22). But the assumption of all the New Testament authors is that their "audiences" would comprehend Greek. Likewise, for the most part, these early

---

[10] This is the issue of the formation of the canon, which we will consider in Chapter 3.

Christians also used the Septuagint or Greek translation of the Old Testament writings as their sacred scriptures.

Manuscripts

No original copies of Paul's letters or of the Gospels or any of the New Testament writings exist, presumably worn out by use or damaged and lost over time in various natural and humanmade calamities. However, early on, "scribes" who knew how to read and write made copies of these sacred texts and ensured their circulation and use among the various local Christian communities. These early texts were written on parchment (i.e., fashioned from animal skins) or papyrus (formed from the treated stalks of the papyrus plant) and were stitched together to form scrolls. These scrolls were bulky and expensive. A later technology would be the codex, the ancestor to the modern "book," consisting of folded leaves that were then sown together and given a cover. Texts in this form were much more portable, especially handy for the circulation of the New Testament texts among the various Christian communities. In 2 Tim 4:13, Paul refers to both formats when he requests that Timothy bring with him a cloak he left with Carpus in Troas (an ancient city in Asia Minor) and "also the books [in Greek, *biblia* or "books"], and above all, the parchments [*membranas*, Greek for parchment sheets]." Although we do not have access to precise historical information, it is probable that toward the end of the first century and into the beginning of the second, "collections" of Paul's letters and of the Four Gospels began to appear.

Virtually all of these earliest copies have disappeared, with only some early second-century fragments surviving.[11] Only later, into

---

[11] On the production and transmission of these early Christian texts, see Brent Nongbri, *God's Library. The Archaeology of the Earliest Christian Manuscripts* (New Haven, CT: Yale University Press, 2018).

the third and fourth centuries of the Common Era, do we find manuscripts containing substantial portions of the New Testament writings. The science of helping reconstruct the most reliable text is called "textual criticism," which by comparing the variants in extant manuscripts, scholars attempt to sort out scribal errors that may have crept into the transmission of the texts. For the most part, the transmission of the New Testament writings from their origin to their later more fixed format has been remarkably accurate and trustworthy, even though many variants exist.

Translation

With the spread of Christianity through most of the Roman world by the fourth century, the use of Greek was waning, being replaced by Latin. This led to another important phase in the transmission of the New Testament over time—namely, translations. As early as the third century BC, Judaism had translated biblical texts from their original Hebrew form into Greek, for the sake of the substantial number of Jews living in the Mediterranean world who spoke Greek and would know little or no Hebrew. In a similar fashion, the gradual transition from the use of *koine* Greek to Latin among ordinary people led to the translations of the New Testament. One of the most famous and long-lasting is Jerome's translation of the Bible into Latin, known as the Vulgate (that is, "popular"). Jerome (325–420 AD) was born in the region of Dalmatia on the eastern coast of the Adriatic but spent the last several years of his life in Bethlehem and Roman Palestine. He learned Hebrew and studied the topography of the Holy Land as background for his monumental translation work. Even earlier translations were made in Syriac and other eastern languages.

Translation, of course, is not a perfect art. The translator must choose which words and grammatical constructions best convey the meaning embedded in the original language, in this case

Hebrew and Greek. And over time usage and style of expression change in any living language, requiring that translations be revised and updated. Some modern translations are intentionally adapted to a specific readership, such as youth, or take into account the teachings and practices of a particular denomination. Others, to make the Bible more comprehensible to a modern audience, reduce the complexity of the biblical text by using explanatory "paraphrase" instead of a literal translation. In some instances, a "translation" is equivalent to an outright ideological editing of the biblical text, for example, screening out passages that speak of miracles or that call for moral stances deemed outmoded by the translators. In 1804 Thomas Jefferson produced a Bible that omitted any reference to Jesus's miracles or his resurrection!

While no modern translation of the biblical text can claim to be definitive, several modern English translations have a high degree of accuracy—choosing the most reliable reconstructions of the original Hebrew and Greek biblical text and striving to translate the Scriptures in the most accurate and consistent way possible. In most cases, the translators identify the particular Hebrew and Greek texts they are using and supply explanatory notes explaining their decision to translate a work or passage in a particular way. This would include such major English language translations as the New Revised Standard, the New American Bible Revised Edition, and the New International Version. Through such translations, the modern readers of the Bible can have confidence that what they are reading is in substantial harmony with the biblical writings of the first century.

Conclusion

Being aware of the process that led to the writings of the New Testament and the manner in which these writings were transmitted to the early Christian communities helps explain in part why the New Testament is considered "sacred." The Gospels were not the result of the evangelists searching through some ancient historical archives to construct the story of Jesus's life. The accounts of Jesus's healings, his parables and sayings, the conflicts he endured with his opponents, the example of his tenderness with the poor and rejected, the series of encounters that led to his arrest, condemnation, and crucifixion, along with the reports of his resurrection and his post-Easter appearances to his disciples—all of this fund of traditions about Jesus made an impact on his disciples and were embedded in the faith, worship, and lived experience of the earliest Christian communities. This accumulated portrayal of Jesus, sustained for most part orally, would ultimately be shaped into coherent narratives by the evangelists, but the story they attempted to tell was already profoundly influenced by Christian belief and practice. Thus, these traditions were not historically neutral but already were considered sacred.

The same is true of Paul's letters and the other New Testament writings. Paul's epistles were not in any way casual correspondence with his communities but extensions of his proclamation of the gospel and passionate testimonies of his own faith in the person and mission of Jesus Christ. Paul, too, drew on the traditions of the earliest Christian community in forging his own powerful portrayal of the Christian message. According to the Acts of the Apostles, Paul was prepared for his mission in the Christian community of Antioch (Acts 11:25–26; 13:1–3). Through his letters Paul extended what he considered his God-given mission of proclaiming the word of salvation to the world, a mission shared with Peter, Barnabas, Aquila, Priscilla, Phoebe, Silas, Timothy, and many others. The same case can be made for all the New Testament writings from the Gospel of Matthew to the book of Revelation. In the view of both the composers of these texts and of the audiences who received them, these texts revealed the divine presence and were inherently sacred.

Further stages in this process include the formation of the canon and the actual content of these revelatory texts. It is to these questions we now turn.

3

The Formation of the Canon and the Creation of the "New Testament"

In the previous chapter we traced the New Testament writings from their ultimate foundation in the person, life, and mission of Jesus to their formulation as diverse literary compositions. The next step is to consider the inclusion of these twenty-seven writings into the New Testament "canon," through which they became the authoritative and normative sacred text of Christianity. The word *canon* literally means "a tool used for measurement." It derives from the Greek word *kanon*, which in turn comes from the Hebrew word *qaneh*, meaning a measuring stick used by carpenters or craftsmen in their work. The term is used in several contexts to describe set measurements or lists or to mark territories. In 2 Cor 10:13, for example, Paul uses the term "canon" to refer to the parameters of the mission field God has assigned to him. In Gal 6:16 he uses the same term to refer to the standards of Christian conduct. But the most widespread use of the term now refers to the official list of books included in the Old and New Testaments.

The New Testament, we have seen, consists of various components: gospel narratives, letters, exhortations, a report of apocalyptic visions, and so on.[1] But the New Testament is not simply a collection of volumes on a shelf or even a designed series of books on a similar topic, such as this series on the sacred texts of different religions. The canon yokes together its twenty-seven components into a new reality that gives an added layer of

[1] See Chapter 1.

The New Testament. Donald Senior, Oxford University Press. © Oxford University Press 2022.
DOI: 10.1093/oso/9780197530832.003.0004

meaning to each of the components—and ultimately places the New Testament itself into a larger sacred framework, namely that of the Bible, which for Christians consists of the Old and the New Testaments. Tracing how the New Testament canon was formed over time is one of the most complex historical questions in all of biblical studies. Yet in wrestling with this history, we come to learn more about the meaning of the New Testament and why it is considered "sacred" by believing Christians.

Here, too, the "double track" we have encountered throughout this study is once again in play. One way of viewing the New Testament and its writings is from what we might call a "secular" viewpoint, which considers these biblical texts as important and interesting cultural and historical artifacts but not as normative for one's life. An alternate point of view, from the vantage point of the community of faith, considers the New Testament as ultimately the Word of God, a sacred text that reveals some of the most profound truths about God, about the identity and mission of Jesus Christ, and about human destiny and the meaning of life.

The question of how the canon was formed has been a source of much debate in modern biblical studies.[2] For those who take a secular viewpoint, the history of the canon is complex and the result of numerous factors, including arbitrary and unplanned factors of historical accident. The fusion of the various writings into the canon of the New Testament creates something analogous to a "classic" in human literature, a work of enduring significance from a historical and cultural point of view. But however historically important the New Testament may be, the religious claims of the "canon" as somehow directed by the church or by divine inspiration are not germane from this point of view. The formation of the canon is understood as a purely human and complex process. Along with such factors as widespread early usage of various books among the early

---

[2] A comprehensive view of the topic can be found in Lee Martin McDonald and James A. Sanders (eds.), *The Canon Debate* (Grand Rapids, MI: Baker Academic, 2019).

Christian communities (e.g., the Pauline Letters and the Gospels), other factors are seen at work. To support their own sense of correct doctrine, church leaders championed some works and suppressed others.[3] Even an emperor such as Constantine is claimed by some to have had an influence in endorsing certain biblical books. Some books seem to have been included more or less by chance, while others, popular at one point, did not make the final cut, such as the Didache or the Shepherd of Hermas.

Since the purpose of this study is to examine how the New Testament is considered a "sacred" book, our focus will be mainly on those who view the formation of the canon as ultimately guided by the Spirit of God, even as other human factors remained in play. For the community of faith, the formation of the canon is the culmination of a process guided by the very Spirit of God, and inclusion in the canon adds a new layer of meaning to the individual books.

Foundational Assumptions Regarding Scripture and Canon

Before examining the formation of the canon, it is important to note some fundamental assumptions about the biblical writings that underlie the notion of the "canon."

Divine Revelation

First is the conviction held by Judaism and continuing in Christianity that God reveals himself to humans. The God portrayed in the Bible is not a distant and incommunicable architect of the universe or an abstract "first cause" deduced by philosophical reasoning. The transcendent God of the universe to which

---

[3] See later discussion of noncanonical books.

the Bible gives homage is also the God of Israel who is close to his people.

The biblical story begins with the book of Genesis, which in its opening chapter poetically portrays God drawing order and beauty and life from the primitive chaos. The majestic account of creation in Genesis 1 portrays God as "speaking," and through the power of the divine word creating the various elements of the universe: the heavens and the earth, night and day, the sea and the dry land, all living creatures, with humans, male and female, as the culmination of the creation process. The human, unlike any other living creature, is made "in the image and likeness of God" (Gen 1:26–27), presumably meaning that humans, like God, are capable of communicating with God and are responsible for the earth. A second creation account in Genesis chapter 2 portrays God in the image of a "potter," breathing into a bag of clay and thus forming the human as a "living being" (Gen 2:7).

The following chapters of Genesis (Genesis 3–11) portray other dimensions of human experience and destiny, including the reality of evil and violence. The first humans, Adam and Eve, disobey God through arrogance, and their offspring, Cain and Abel, introduce enmity and violence into the world of human experience. This sad reality leads to the flood and the near destruction of creation, a fate offset by the righteousness of Noah. God "regrets" attempting to destroy the earth and makes a "covenant" or agreement with Noah never to destroy the world again but to restore and redeem it, sealing the agreement with the sign of the rainbow in the sky (Gen 9:1–17). This covenant with Noah is an antecedent of the one God forges with Moses and the people Israel during the Exodus from slavery in Egypt (see Exodus 19). Throughout these early chapters of Genesis, God is presented in a very anthropomorphic manner, reacting with seeming human qualities of disappointment, anger, and mercy. Above all, God communicates with his creatures in very intimate and proximate terms.

What the opening chapters of Genesis signal—namely God's self-revelation—continues as a fundamental assumption throughout the Bible, in both the Old and New Testaments. That revelation is manifest in the beauty, order, and vastness of creation itself but also in the events of history such as the liberation of the Israelites from Egypt and the gift of the Promised Land, or, as divine punishment for Israel's sin through the Assyrian and Babylonian exiles and other calamities of their history. Even a secular king such as Cyrus of Persia is presented in the Bible as God's unwitting instrument who enables the Israelites to return to their homeland (see Isaiah 45:1–6 where Cyrus is named God's "anointed one" or messiah, even though he does not know God). God's revelation in a particular way comes through human agents who are directly inspired by God to speak and act on God's behalf. The patriarch Abraham is directly guided by God to move to the land of Canaan. Moses will be the chosen leader to liberate God's people from the slavery of Egypt and speaks to God "face to face" on Mt. Sinai. The prophets utter oracles and challenges to Israel directly citing "the Word of God." The prophet Nathan is instructed to anoint David as the future king, and David, too, despite his flaws, is viewed as a reflection of God's providence toward Israel.

This sense of God's revelation continues in the New Testament. The prologue of John's Gospel explicitly portrays Jesus as the "Word of God" become "flesh" and thereby being the definitive "revealer" of God to the world (John 1:18). As we will describe in more detail later, the entire New Testament views Jesus as the privileged revealer of God to the world.[4]

Thus, a fundamental assumption of the entire Bible is that the transcendent God reveals himself to the world through creation, through the unique history of Israel and other world events, through inspired prophets and leaders, and, from the perspective of Christian faith, definitively through the person and mission of Jesus Christ. That the God who fashioned all things could be detected in the beauty and order of creation itself, apart from direct revelation, was a conviction of both Judaism and Christianity. In the opening

---

[4] See Chapter 4.

chapters of his Letter to the Romans, Paul cites this conviction that the "pagans" could have found God in nature:

> For what can be known about God is plain to them (the pagans), because God has shown it to them. Even since the creation of the world his eternal power and divine nature, invisible though they are, have been understood and seen through the things he has made. (Rom 2:19–20)

But, Paul notes, tragically their reading of nature was clouded through sin and they did not find God.

Divine Inspiration

The biblical conviction that God self-communicates not only through creation and the events of history but also through the instrumentality of human beings points to another important assumption leading to the formation of the canon. Inspired by God, the great Old Testament prophets such as Moses himself, Elijah and Elisha and others, are portrayed as directly guided by God in their assigned missions. Through the "writing," prophets whose utterances are contained in written accounts in the Bible such as Amos, Hosea, Isaiah, Jeremiah, Ezekiel, and Zachariah—to mention only some—directly communicate the "word of God" to their contemporaries. The authenticity of the prophets is manifested by God's own selection of them as his emissaries and in the integrity of their lives for which they are often persecuted by their opponents. Several of the prophets receive a direct "call" or commission from God, even when they themselves are reluctant to perform the prophetic role: Moses claims that he stutters (Exod 4:10–13); Amos that he is not a prophet but only a "shepherd and a dresser of sycamores" (Amos 7:14–15); Isaiah that he is a "man of unclean lips" (Isa 6:5); and Jeremiah protests he is too young for the role (Jer 1:6).

Jesus himself is portrayed in the Synoptic Gospels as inaugurating his public mission through a theophany when God praises Jesus as his "beloved son" at the moment of his baptism in the Jordan, as God's Spirit descends upon him (Mark 1:9–11). The impact of the Spirit drives Jesus out into the desert into direct confrontation with the power of evil—a prelude to his public mission that is about to begin in Galilee (Mark 1:12–13). In John's Gospel, it is the desert prophet John the Baptist who points out Jesus to his own disciples—"Behold the Lamb of God!"—setting in motion Jesus's own mission (John 1:29–34). This divine endorsement of Jesus occurs also in the event of the Transfiguration during Jesus's ministry. On a mountaintop Jesus's appearance is luminously transformed and the divine voice again declares Jesus to be God's Son and the three disciples who witness this spectacular vision are told to "Listen to him [Jesus]" (see Mark 9:2–8).

This form of what we might call "prophetic" inspiration is antecedent to the notion of inspiration for the biblical writers. This is a basic conviction that God "inspires" the biblical writers in the composition of the biblical books. A famous text from the Second Letter to Timothy is frequently cited in this regard: "All scripture is inspired by God and is useful for teaching, for reproof, for correction, and for training in righteousness, so that everyone who belongs to God may be proficient, equipped for every good work" (2 Tim 3:16–17). The Greek word used here for "inspired" is literally "God-inspired" (*theopneustos*). It is assumed that the author of the letter, probably writing toward the end of the first century AD or the beginning of the second century, is referring to the Old Testament Scriptures. However, the author of 2 Peter, when counseling his readers to remain virtuous while waiting for the end of the world, cautions his readers about erroneous interpretations of "our beloved brother Paul's" writings: "So also our beloved brother Paul wrote to you according to the wisdom given to him, speaking of this as he does in all his letters. There are some things in them hard to understand, which the ignorant and unstable twist to their own destruction, as they do the other scriptures" (2 Pet 3:15–16). With the phrase "the other scriptures" the author seems to consider Paul's writings as "scripture." The Second Letter of Peter may be among the very last New Testament books to be written, perhaps in the early part of the second century. As we will note later, by this time the collection of Paul's letters may have reached a status for the early church equivalent to the writings of the Hebrew Scriptures and thus, in the words of 2 Timothy, considered "God-inspired."

While most believing Christians agree that the writings of the New Testament are in some fashion "inspired," there is far less agreement on understanding precisely what "inspiration" means or how it happens. A key ingredient in the process is the role of the human author. For more traditional, and what could be called "fundamentalist," perspectives, God is the true and principal author of Scripture—in effect, prompting or even dictating to the human author what to write. In such a view, the human author's role is merely "mechanical"—writing down what God inspires the author to do. Several medieval paintings portray just that—with a dictating angel, a messenger of God, hovering over the shoulder of the evangelist as he writes down each inspired word.

Other more progressive views emphasize the role of the inspired writer as a fully human author. In this view, God would be the "author" of Scripture, not in the sense that God's writes a biblical book, but that God and God's Spirit are the ultimate "source" of the biblical message. Yet the human author, such as one of the evangelists writing a Gospel or Paul as the composer of his letters, exercises full human instrumentality. The biblical authors are "true authors," not simply copyists or secretaries taking dictation. This view of inspiration allows room for the human limitations of the biblical author who writes within the constraints of a particular language and his own literary skill, in a particular place, time, and culture, and with his own particular experience and concerns.

The "Truth" of the Bible

Acknowledging the role of the human author in the process of biblical inspiration also tempers the notion of the "truth" or "inerrancy" of the Bible. If, on the one hand, God is the direct author of the biblical text, as the traditional view maintained, then inaccuracies embedded in the biblical text about matters of science or medicine or the chronology of human history become difficult to reconcile with divine inspiration. On the other hand, if the fully human instrumentality of the biblical author is acknowledged, then the role for God's inspiration can be understood more properly. In this case, the "truth" of Scripture means that dimension of the entire Bible which reveals the truth about the nature of God and human destiny. In Roman Catholic tradition, for example, this understanding of the truth of the Scriptures is expressed by saying that the Bible communicates the truth God intended for the sake of human salvation.[5] This makes room for the limited knowledge of the biblical authors about matters of science or precise historical chronology. This confluence of the divine and the human in the process of biblical inspiration has traditionally been compared to the Christian doctrine of the Incarnation. Orthodox Christian faith since the time of the Council of Chalcedon (451 AD) has confessed that Jesus is both fully divine and fully human. While the doctrine of the Incarnation refers to the question of the unique identity of Jesus Christ, by way of analogy the Scriptures, too, can be viewed as fully divine and fully human. Fully divine in that the originator and ultimate source of biblical revelation is God; fully human in that biblical text is composed by human authors acting completely as human authors do.

---

[5] This notion of the truth of the Bible is expressed in *Dei Verbum* ("The Word of God"), an important doctrinal statement on Divine Revelation found in the declarations of the Second Vatican Council.

Such a fundamental assertion about the inspired nature of the Bible does not solve the question of how this comes about. How can one explain philosophically and psychologically the process of biblical inspiration? Drawing on the categories of medieval philosophy, some have portrayed God as the "principal" cause of the biblical text, with the human author as the "instrumental" cause. The comparison is often made to the writer and his pen. In this case, God would fully exercise God's divine wisdom as the ultimate source of the Bible, while the human authors—like the pen in the hand of the author—would also work to their full capacity. While offering clarity, this analysis depends on philosophical categories not familiar to most modern interpreters and appears to view once more the role of the human biblical author in limited and mechanistic terms.

A further complication is the realization of modern biblical studies that in many instances books of the Bible were not the work of a single author whether inspired or not. Many Old Testament books went through various revisions over time, involving many different human authors. While Paul may have written (or dictated) his letters, the Gospels and other New Testament texts may be the work of several hands, as traditions were handed down through the early Christian community and often in oral form prior to the final edition. At what point in this process does biblical inspiration play its role? Because of this, some scholars have spoken of "social inspiration"; that is, the Spirit guides the Christian community as a whole through its ongoing development as the biblical texts are codified and emerge over time as final editions expressive of the faith of the church.[6] The great German theologian Karl Rahner spoke of inspiration as an expression of the self-consciousness of the early church during its formative period.[7] As a whole, the New

---

[6] See, for example, Bruce Vawter, *Biblical Inspiration* (Theological Resources; Philadelphia: Westminster, 1972) and Gerard O'Collins, *Inspiration: Towards a Christian Interpretation of Biblical Inspiration* (New York: Oxford University Press, 2018).

[7] Karl Rahner, *Inspiration in the Bible* (Quaestiones Disputatae 1; New York: Herder and Herder, 2nd ed., 1966).

Testament writings, through the guidance of God's Spirit, reveal the constitutive nature of the church.

We should note that there is a difference between a biblical book being "inspired" and also being "inspiring."[8] In fact, most of the New Testament writings are both inspired and inspiring. The moral eloquence of the Sermon on the Mount, the enticing beauty of Jesus's parables such as the Prodigal Son or the Good Samaritan, the many eloquent passages in Paul's letters, and many more writings from both the Old and the New Testament have been a source of inspiration for believers who have read and prayed over the Bible through the centuries and found there the motivation for a life of holiness and moral integrity. The inspiring character of the Bible continues through the ages in the engagement of the believing reader with the biblical text. The narratives and teachings of the Bible have moved people to lives of heroism and generosity. Preachers of all times and places have been "inspired" to proclaim the message of the Scriptures. The vivid stories and majestic images and characters of the Bible have "inspired" artists, musicians, and architects to proclaim the message of the biblical text in various mediums and to savor its impact on human life. But it is also true that some biblical texts fail to stir the human spirit, such as the sharp admonitions of the Third Letter of John or the angry denunciations in the Letter of Jude. However, as we shall consider later, some early Christian texts not considered "inspired" and not included in the canon were viewed as "sacred" by early Christianity and seem to have a greater capacity for "inspiring" their readers than some biblical texts.[9] Here, on what might be considered the "outer banks" of the New Testament canon, the impact of divine inspiration on a particular book is less clear. In fact, as we will note, some such texts were "disputed" before making their entry into the canon and

---

[8] On this see Gerard O'Collins, *Inspiration: Towards a Christian Interpretation of Biblical Inspiration* (New York: Oxford University Press, 2018), pp. 19–42.

[9] See later discussion.

others included in the canon seem to be more favored by a majority of readers, in effect, forming a "canon within the canon.[10]

The Formation of the Canon

We turn now to the historical process through which the canon of the New Testament was formed. At the outset it is important to realize that the decision to include the twenty-seven books into the canon was not a formal or clearly defined official action of the early church made at a particular and identifiable time. Rather, the choice of which books were considered inspired and to be placed in the canon of the New Testament derived from an instinctive and collective process that took place over a long stretch of time in the early history of the church. While some parts of the New Testament were considered sacred and inspired early in the process, such as the Four Gospels and the major writings of Paul, others were more gradually, and for some even hesitantly, accepted as part of the canon.

Historical Factors

Some historical factors prompted the early church to consider which of the writings used by the early Christians should be collected and venerated as "sacred" and "inspired" texts. One significant factor was the unfolding of history. Jewish tradition anticipated that the resurrection of the just would take place at the end of the world. So the earliest post-Easter followers of Jesus assumed that with Jesus's resurrection the end of the world was near its climax. In his first letter to the Christian community at Thessalonica—probably the earliest text of the New Testament to

[10] See later discussion.

be composed—Paul reassures his newly formed Christians that indeed the end time is approaching and would take place suddenly "like a thief in the night" (1 Thess 5:2), but they need not be anxious. Some in the community were concerned about their loved ones who had already died and wondered if they would be left out when the Lord appeared at the end of time. Paul reassures them that all will be included—both the living and the dead—and gives the impression that the end would take place while those receiving the letter, including Paul himself, were still alive: "For this we declare to you by the word of the Lord, that we who are alive, who are left until the coming of the Lord, will by no means precede those who have died" (1 Thess 4:15). But as time unfolded, the Christians realized that they were facing a possibly long future until the consummation of the world. In fact, for some Christians the apparent "delay" of Christ's second coming was leading to doubts about it altogether (see, e.g., the concern of 2 Pet 3:1–13 and 2 Thess 2:1–12). Thus, in view of an indefinite future, the need for organizational structures, for competent leadership, and for maintaining sound doctrine and tradition became a focus of later New Testament writings such as the Pastoral Letters of 1 & 2 Timothy and Titus. The same realization about the need to guide the church into the future no doubt prompted the need to determine which sacred books were normative for the community of believers.

Another factor was the simple fact that the earliest disciples and eyewitnesses who knew Jesus were passing from the scene around the midpoint of the first century. Luke seems to acknowledge this in his introduction to his Gospel, where he tells "Theophilus" about the "eyewitnesses and servants of the word" who were at the "beginning," and now, later in time, Luke and others were composing written and "orderly" accounts of the formative events that had occurred (Luke 1:1–4).

Likewise the catastrophic destruction of the Jewish temple and the city of Jerusalem in the Roman suppression of the revolt in 70 AD led to the decreasing influence of the founding church of

Jerusalem and the increasing role of the Gentile world, signaling the start of a historic shift from a mainly Jewish-Christian membership to one increasingly Gentile. The geographic scope of the church was also expanding, as the work of missionaries such as Paul and others established Christian communities in the mainly Gentile regions of Asia Minor, Greece, Italy, Northern Africa, and eastward into Syria and the Arabian Peninsula. The waning influence of the Jerusalem Christian community in the wake of 70 AD accelerated this expansion into the Gentile world. A harbinger of this is found in the Acts of the Apostles, where Luke observes that the persecution that broke out in the Jerusalem church in the wake of Steven's martyrdom led some Christians to flee to Antioch in Asia Minor and to begin a Christian community there, including Gentile converts (see Acts 11:19–30). It was here, Acts notes, that the followers of Jesus were first called "Christians" (Acts 11:26). Circulation of important and defining texts to be used in worship and the instruction of these far-flung communities would require written texts, and, over time, the quality of these writings and their favored use among the communities would be an important factor leading to a formal list or "canon" of sacred books.

Also important for triggering the formation of the New Testament canon was a parallel process in Judaism itself. Here, too, the process of determining precise criteria for selection and the process of deciding which books were inspired and to be part of the official canon of the Hebrew Bible were instinctive and communal, rather than a single decisive action.[11] The Jewish Scriptures, especially in their Greek translation known as the Septuagint, were already the "Bible" of the early Christians, cited frequently in virtually

---

[11] Although some Jewish traditions believe the canon was closed at the end of the Babylonian exile, it appears that the process was still underway into the second century AD. See John J. Collins, Craig A. Evans, and Lee Martin McDonald, *Ancient Jewish and Christian Scriptures: New Developments in Canon Controversy* (Louisville, KY: Westminster John Knox Press, 2020), esp. pp. 49–97.

all of the New Testament writings.[12] Similar to the New Testament canon in its formative period, the major books of the Old Testament were known and used widely by Jews and Christians alike. This would include the five books of the Pentateuch and most of the prophetic writings, all of which are cited in the New Testament. In Matthew's Gospel, Jesus speaks of fulfilling the "Law and the prophets" (Matt 5:17)—a typical Jewish way of referring to the entirety of Scripture.[13] Judaism viewed its Scriptures as divided into three major divisions: the "Law," which included the books of the Pentateuch; the "prophets," which included the "major" prophets such as Isaiah, Jeremiah and the other writing prophets but also the so-called minor prophetic books such as the books of Joshua, Judges, Samuel, Kings, and Chronicles; and the last and least defined segment was the "writings," which included the psalms, the wisdom literature, and other biblical books. In fact, there would be much debate later in both Judaism and in early Christianity about which of the "writings" were inspired and to be included in the Hebrew canon, a dispute that would linger in the church's history through the time of the Reformation in the sixteenth century.[14]

In the process of defining their respective identities, particularly in the wake of the loss of the Temple, both Rabbinic Judaism and early Christianity determined to give more formal recognition to their sacred books—thus defining the "canon" of what in Christian terminology would become respectively the Old and the New Testaments.

---

[12] "Septuagint" is the Greek term for seventy, based on the legend that seventy Jewish scribes had been commissioned to translate the Hebrew text into Greek. When each had finished their work independently of each other, their translations were miraculously identical. Most Christians in the first century were Greek speaking and used the Septuagint as their version of the Bible.

[13] Jews traditional refer to the Scriptures as "Tanak," an abbreviation of the first letter of the Hebrew terms: *Torah* (Law), *Nevi'im* (Prophets), and *Kituvim* (Writings).

[14] See later discussion.

Criteria for Inclusion

What criteria did the Early Church use to determine which sacred books were inspired and should be included in the canon? Here again there was no official set of criteria available beforehand to guide such decisions. What in fact were the operative criteria must be deduced from an analysis of the overall process and its results. The criteria determining the inclusion of some books seem self-evident. In other cases, the choice may be more difficult to discover. At least three major and interlocking criteria seem to have been at work.

1. **Apostolic authorship.** One of the most important qualities that determined the inclusion of a sacred writing in the canon was its association with the early apostles. Because the person and mission of Jesus remain the central focus of all the New Testament, proximity to this monumental reality was a deciding factor. Such is the case, for example, with the Four Gospels. Although originally these texts did not bear the name of their authors, early traditions assigned them to either apostles or those closely associated with apostles. Thus, the Gospels of Matthew and John bear the names of those belonging to the Twelve chosen by Jesus (see Matt 10:1–4). Luke and Mark were not on the list of the Twelve, but both are associated with apostles. Luke was viewed as a companion of Paul on his missionary journeys. The name Luke is mentioned by Paul in his letter to Philemon 24, as well as in Col 4:10–11 and 2 Tim 4:11.[15] Likewise, the author of the Acts of the Apostles, traditionally assumed to be Luke, may have been including himself as a companion for part of Paul's journeys signaled by the "we passages" where he uses the first-person plural, "we," including Paul's final journey to Rome on a prison ship (see Acts 27:1–28:30; also 16:10–18; 20:4–21:19). Early traditions may have identified the author of Mark's Gospel as the "John Mark" of the Acts of the Apostles who

---

[15] The latter two letters may have been written by a later author in Paul's name. In any case, the early tradition identifies a "Luke" as a trusted coworker with Paul.

accompanied Paul and Barnabas on their first missionary journey (Acts 12:12, 25; 13:5, 13–14; 15:37–40; also mentioned by Paul in Philemon 24; Col 4:10; 2 Tim 4:11). The fourth-century historian Eusebius of Caesarea quotes Papias, a first-century bishop of Hierapolis in Asia Minor, who refers to Mark as a companion of Peter and as the one who composed the Gospel of Mark based on Peter's testimony. Modern scholarship may question the historical reliability of these early traditions, but the connection of these writings with "apostolic" authorship was certainly an important factor for the early church for their inclusion in the canon.

The same apostolic connection holds for the Letters of Paul. From Paul's own testimony he is to be included in the list of the apostles through his encounter with the Risen Christ, albeit as Paul himself notes, as the "last" of the apostles, which seems to be almost a badge of honor for Paul (see 1 Cor 15:8–11). Early on, the thirteen letters assigned to Paul's authorship gained inclusion in the lists of canonical books. Hebrews, too, was considered by many in the early church to be composed by Paul, but there were some church leaders who doubted this, so it took a while for Hebrews to be included. There is little doubt that Paul's letters were circulated not just to the communities addressed but soon to other communities. Paul himself is presented as suggesting precisely that at the conclusion of the Letter to the Colossians. The apostle asks that his letter be sent on to the community at Laodicea, a city near Colossae, and that a previous letter Paul had sent to the Laodiceans be read in Colossae (see Col 4:16). There is no extant Pauline Letter to the Laodiceans, and it may have been lost to history.[16]

Connection with apostolic authorship probably proved decisive for the inclusion of 1 Peter and 2 Peter, although 2 Peter was disputed by some and was included in the list of canonical books only later. Likewise, the letters of James, Jude, the three Johannine

---

[16] There may have been other letters of Paul that were not preserved; some scholars see evidence of this in 1 Cor 5:9; 2 Cor 2:4; 10:10.

letters, and the book of Revelation could all claim apostolic connection. In the case of Revelation, the author "John" mentioned in Rev 1:1 was traditionally identified with the apostle John. Modern biblical scholarship has questioned whether any of these writings were in fact composed by the apostolic figures assigned to them. Even in antiquity the apostolic authorship of 2 Peter, Jude, 2 & 3 John, and Revelation was questioned by some, leading to some dispute before these works were included in the canon.

There is no question, however, that proximity to the first apostolic generation was a major consideration for inclusion in the canon. The title of every New Testament book is either assigned to an apostle or was assumed to have a clear connection to this founding generation. The decisive importance of these biblical books having such proximity to the life, death, and resurrection of Jesus again points to the fundamental source of the "sacredness" of the New Testament writings in the eyes of the community of faith.[17]

2. **Reception by the churches.** Alongside the criterion of apostolic authorship and, in a sense confirming it, was the use of these sacred writings in local communities, particularly in their public worship. As noted in our previous discussion about the transmission and formation of the New Testament texts, there was considerable travel and communication among the early Christian communities.[18] This was facilitated by the Roman road system which had reached a significant degree of development in the first century, by some estimates covering some 63,000 miles. The roads were constructed primarily for military purposes, but ordinary people used them for travel and commerce.

A vivid example of this mobility is found in Paul's Letter to the Romans. When Paul wrote his letter to the Romans, a community he had not yet visited, he greets a list of twenty-nine friends and coworkers, including men, women, and married couples he had

[17] See, especially, Chapter 4.
[18] See earlier discussion.

apparently met in the course of his ministry, coworkers who currently were now part of the Christian community at Rome (Rom 16:1–23). Additionally, Paul is writing from Corinth and has enlisted Phoebe, a deacon leading the Christian community at Cenchreae, one of the ports of Corinth, to carry his letter to Rome. Paul praises her and asks the community in Rome to welcome her:

> I commend to you our sister Phoebe, a deacon of the church at Cenchreae, so that you may welcome her in the Lord as is fitting for the saints, and help her in whatever she may require from you, for she has been a benefactor of many of myself as well. (Rom 16:1–2)

The greetings at the beginning and end of Paul's other letters reveal the names of numerous friends and coworkers, such as Timothy, Titus, Silas (or Silvanus), Aquila and Priscilla, Onesimus, and others who traveled with Paul and no doubt carried his letters to various Christian communities. We can presume that these letters from the Apostle were read in the public assemblies of the communities, particularly during their worship. We can also presume that these coworkers were not simply carriers of the letters but, as collaborators with Paul, would also be invited to read them publicly and be able to offer explanation and reflection on Paul's message to the community.[19]

Another indicator of frequent communication among the early Christian communities is found in a major enterprise of Paul, namely his plan to take up a collection among the several communities he had evangelized as a tribute to the mother church of Jerusalem. Paul's description of the process is found in 1 Cor 16:1–4:

> Now concerning the collection for the saints: you should follow the directions I gave to the churches of Galatia. On the first day

---

[19] See Wright, *Communal Reading in the Time of Jesus*, pp. 35–38.

of every week, each of you is to put aside and save whatever extra you earn, so that collections need not be taken when I come. And when I arrive, I will send any whom you approve with letters to take your gift to Jerusalem. If it seems advisable that I should go also, they will accompany me. (Paul also refers to the collection in 2 Cor 8:1–9:15; Rom 15:14–32.)

The elaborate year-long collection demonstrates Paul's gratitude to the Jewish Christian community in Jerusalem, but it also reveals the degree of organization, communication, and travel taking place among these early Christian communities.

Other examples revealing the wide network of early Christian communities in approximately the third quarter of the first century include the opening of the First Letter of Peter that is sent, presumably from Rome, to Christian communities in north and central Asia Minor: "Pontus, Galatia, Cappadocia, Asia, and Bithynia" (I Pet 1:1). Similarly, the opening section of the book of Revelation consists of a series of challenging letters to seven Christian communities in western Asia Minor: Ephesus, Smyrna, Pergamum, Thyatira, Sardis, Philadelphia, and Laodicea—each a significant city (see Rev 2:1–22). And many modern scholars believe that the Letter to the Ephesians was in fact a tract written by a later disciple of the Apostle, synthesizing Paul's theology and circulated among various communities; in many early manuscripts the reference to Ephesus (1:1) is missing and probably was added later to conform to the other Pauline Letters. The Acts of the Apostles lists numerous early Christian communities throughout the Roman Empire, in Palestine, present-day Lebanon (i.e., region of Tyre and Sidon), Syria, Alexandria, Ethiopia, Asia Minor, Greece (Macedonia and Achaia), and in Rome itself.[20]

This interactions between Paul's letters and the communities he had either evangelized or planned to visit (i.e., Rome) set up a special relationship to these writings. Paul's letters, as we noted

[20] See Senior, *The Landscape of the Gospels*, pp. 76–96.

earlier, were extensions of his apostolic preaching and testimonials to his relationship with Christ. Through his letters Paul addressed in a profound and vivid way his understanding of the dynamics of Christian faith and the moral demands of being a follower of Jesus. The coherence of Paul's proclamation through his letters with the recipients' own experience of their Christian faith became an important motif for preserving these letters and circulating them to other Christian communities.

This use and reception of the Pauline Letters by a network of early Christian communities probably reflect a similar process in the dissemination of the Gospels. While the literary genre of the gospel narratives does not provide information on how they were circulated, we do know that there was a literary relationship among them. We know, for example, that the composers of Matthew's and Luke's Gospels were acquainted with the Gospel of Mark, absorbing a large portion of Mark's narrative into their own versions. Although an educated guess, it is likely that the Gospel of Matthew, for example, was composed in the city of Antioch—at the time, the third largest city in the Roman Empire and on a major east-west trade route. The Acts of the Apostles describes the early arrival of Christianity there and the ground-breading inclusion of Gentiles into the Jewish-Christian community there (Acts 11:19–30). Paul, too, in his Letter to the Galatians describes a dispute he had with Peter who at first had dined with Gentile Christians in Antioch but later, faced with criticism from strict Jewish Christians in Jerusalem, had withdrawn from table fellowship with Gentile Christians—earning a stiff rebuke from Paul (see Gal 2:11–14). Acts also tells us that from Antioch would be launched the first missionary journey of Paul, Barnabas, and Mark (Acts 13:1–3). All of this makes Antioch a likely place for the composition of Matthew's Gospel, concerned as it is with the relationship between Jews and Gentiles and its strong missionary character (see Matt 28:16–20).

If Matthew's Gospel was composed in Antioch somewhere around 80 AD, that means that Mark's Gospel—a major source for Matthew—was already well known in the church of Antioch. And if Mark's Gospel was composed, as seems likely, in Rome around 70 AD, then it had already made its way to Antioch, testifying again to the circulation of treasured sacred texts among the early Christian communities. We can also assume that if Luke's Gospel was possibly composed in Ephesus, there, too, the Gospel of Mark was known and respected.

As would clearly be the custom in the early centuries of the church, selections from the Gospels, Paul's letters, and other New Testament texts, as well as selections from the Old Testament, were read at the church's liturgy. Bishop, priests, and deacons would offer reflections or "homilies" drawing out the meaning. As we will see, much of the theology of the early church well into the Medieval period was based on commentary and preaching of biblical texts.[21]

It makes sense that such a custom had its roots in the earliest practices of the Christian community, which, by the way, also reflect the customary ingredients of Jewish synagogue services, such as the one described for the opening of Jesus's public mission in the Gospel of Luke. On a Sabbath in the synagogue of Nazareth, the attendant gives Jesus the scroll of the prophet Isaiah to read to the assembly, and afterward Jesus offers his challenging message of justice drawn from the reading of Isaiah 61 (see Luke 4:16–21). Thus, it is not surprising that the evidence even from the New Testament texts themselves suggests that the reading and reflection on certain sacred texts in the setting of the community's worship was a major criterion for the ultimate inclusion of these works in the New Testament canon. Being acceptable to and revered by the early Christian communities was a trusted sign of the inspired (and inspiring) character of these select writings judged suitable for use in public worship.

Adding to the importance of this local endorsement of sacred texts was also the significance of the major Christian communities located in important urban centers, such as Rome, Ephesus,

---

[21] See Chapter 6.

Corinth, Philippi, Thessalonica, and Antioch. The larger Christian communities in these centers, coupled with the prestige of such cities, gave added weight to the use of select sacred texts in the public worship of these locations. No doubt, too, from the major Christian communities in these urban centers smaller, more isolated communities would receive with confidence sacred works already acceptable to significant numbers of Christians.

3. The "rule of faith." A third criterion for including a sacred text into the canon of the New Testament is called the "rule of faith." It means that the contents of a particular writing are in fundamental harmony with the deepest instincts and convictions of Christian faith and practice. We noted earlier that there is quite a bit of diversity of perspective in the New Testament writings, but there is also a deep-seated unity revolving around fundamental belief in the person and mission of Jesus.[22] Some of these core beliefs were already embedded in credal formulas found in the New Testament writings themselves. In 1 Cor 11:23, for example, Paul states that the fundamental meaning of Christ's action at the Last Supper is something that had been handed on to him and he now shares it with the Corinthian community: "For I received from the lord what I also handed on to you, that the lord Jesus on the night when he was betrayed took a loaf of bread . . ." (1 Cor 11:23). Paul also seems to quote such a formula in affirming that the death, burial, and resurrection of Christ was "in accord with the scriptures:" "I handed on to you as of first importance what I in turn had received . . ." (1 Cor 15:3).

The essentials of Christian faith affirmed across the span of the New Testament writings would include the unique character of Jesus as both authentically human but also as an embodiment of the divine presence (later defined as a bedrock doctrine of Christian faith by the church at the fifth-century Council of Chalcedon); the continuity of Jesus and his mission with God's dealings with his

[22] See Chapter 2.

people Israel in the Old Testament; the redemptive power of Jesus's death; the reality of his resurrection from the dead; the necessity of faith in Christ; the character of God as unconditional love; the need for faith to be expressed in love of God and neighbor; the call for justice and virtue, care for the poor and vulnerable, the obligations to fellow Christians in community; the mission of the church for the salvation of the world; the expectation of the final coming of Christ at the end of time. Not all these basic convictions are expressed in every New Testament book nor would they be expressed in the same way. But the "rule of faith" would require that no canonical book could explicitly deny these basic truths or grossly distort them.[23]

In many ways, this criterion makes explicit what is implicit in the first two criteria we have discussed. A writing whose origins are rooted in the founding era of the community and one that had gained widespread acceptance by numerous Christian communities and was proclaimed in their worship would, by definition, be in harmony with the "rule of faith." In some instances, church leaders explicitly rejected books because they did not meet this criterion, proof of which was their use by heretical groups. Such would be the case with the "Gospel of Peter," which at first was used by the church of Antioch but was ultimately rejected by the second-century Bishop Serapion of Antioch because it was favored by Docetists, an early heresy that denied the humanity of Jesus (Eusebius HE 6.12.2). Similarly, Marcion around the mid-second century promoted a canonical list that excluded the Old Testament writings, preserved only ten letters of Paul, and contained only a single gospel which appears to be an adaptation of Luke's Gospel minus the first two chapters. A motivation for Marcion's truncated list was his aversion to the Hebrew Scriptures and the

---

[23] See Lee Martin McDonald, "Identifying Scripture and Canon in the Early Church: The Criteria Question," in *The Canon Debate*, ed. Lee Martin McDonald and James A. Sanders, *Debate* (Grand Rapids, MI: Baker Academic, 2019), pp. 416–439, esp. pp. 428–430.

connection of Jesus and the Christian community with its Jewish roots. Marcion considered the God of the Old Testament to be a different and inferior God to that revealed by Jesus. Because this was a radical departure from orthodox Christian faith, Marcion was considered heretical and his list of canonical books invalid. He was excommunicated by the church of Rome in 144 AD. Another prominent example was the third-century theologian Irenaeus (130–202 AD), a disciple of Polycarp of Smyrna, the famed bishop and martyr. Later Irenaeus was appointed bishop of Lyon and was an influential writer and church leader. He vigorously opposed the books claimed sacred by heretical groups and made a strong case for the Four Gospels, arguing that the number was in harmony with the four corners of the earth and the four winds.[24] Toward the end of the second century, Tatian, an Assyrian theologian, produced the "Diatessaron" (from the Greek meaning "out of four ingredients"), a single Gospel that attempted to harmonize the Four Gospel accounts. It was popular for a while in the Syrian church but was not widely accepted in the West.

Gnosticism, a general term for a variety of Christian movements developing in the second century and later, particularly in Egypt and northern Africa, produced several religious texts that were circulated among Christian communities. Most of them deviated strongly from the portrayal of Jesus and his teaching found in the Gospels and the Pauline writings and, therefore, did not make their way into the New Testament canon. In other cases, questions about the orthodoxy of such texts as Jude, 2 Peter, and Revelation led to debate and some delay before their widespread acceptance. At the same time, other texts whose content seems completely within the

---

[24] "The Gospels could not possibly be either more or less in number than they are. Since there are four zones of the world in which we live, and four principal winds, while the Church is spread over all the earth, and the pillar and foundation of the Church is the gospel, and the Spirit of life, it fittingly has four pillars, everywhere breathing out incorruption and revivifying men. From this it is clear that the Word, the artificer of all things, being manifested to men gave us the gospel, fourfold in form but held together by one Spirit" (*Adversus Haereses* 3.11.8).

bounds of the "rule of faith," such as the Didache, the Shepherd of Hermas, and the First Letter of Clement, ultimately did not gain acceptance in the canon for reasons that are not clear. Not until the fourth century would the set number of twenty-seven books be widely accepted among the churches.

As with the other two criteria we have considered, judging whether a particular writing conformed to the "rule of faith" was an instinctive action on the part of the early church and its leaders— sometimes becoming clear only when a text or teacher departed radically from the fundamental faith of the Christian community.

The Final Determination of the Canon

Although the principal books of the New Testament, such as the Four Gospels, the Letters of Paul, and key texts such as 1 Peter and 1 John, were in common use in the early church at the beginning of the second century, it was not until the fourth century that the full twenty-seven-book canon was firmly established. Prior to this it seems that acceptance of some books differed in some areas. Evidence for the gradual acceptance of the full canon is found in the lists of books cited by certain prominent early theologians and local church councils.

One of the earliest such lists is the so-called Muratorian fragment or canon. It is a "fragment" of a larger now lost Latin document, consisting of some eighty-five lines, dating from the seventh century AD but believed to be a translation from an earlier Greek text that is dated roughly around the second or third century. The fragment lists twenty-two of the twenty-seven books in the canon. Missing are Hebrews, James, and 1 & 2 Peter. It also lists two books that did not make it into the final form of the canon, the Apocalypse of Peter and the Wisdom of Solomon (which would be included in the canon of the Old Testament for the Catholic and Orthodox churches). Other theologians such as Origen (184–253 AD), a widely respected theologian from Alexandria, lists all twenty-seven books but had his doubts about 2 Peter and the 2 & 3 Letters of John. Eusebius, the fourth-century bishop of Caesarea Maritima in Palestine, was a well-known early historian; he also lists the books of the canon but states that James and Jude are "disputed," while admitting they were used in a number of churches.

Finally, in the fourth century there is widespread uniformity in the number of books to be included in the New Testament canon. Athanasius (296–373 AD), bishop of Alexandria and one of the leading Patristic theologians, was among the first to list all twenty-seven of the New Testament books as belonging to the canon. Augustine, too, perhaps the most famous of early church theologians, also listed the full canonical number of New Testament books. In 393 AD, the synod of Hippo in Northern Africa, the region in which Augustine was bishop, officially listed all twenty-seven books, a list ratified by the Third Synod of Carthage in 397 AD.

Alongside the growing consensus of theologians and church councils about the final list of books, there was also some possible pressure from political events. In 303 AD, the Emperor Diocletian, a fierce persecutor of the church who ruled from 284 to 305 AD, ordered Christians to turn in their sacred books in an attempt to impose religious uniformity on the empire. Many Christians turned in only less important books but refused to give up their most sacred texts, even at the price of martyrdom. Those who relinquished the most sacred texts were deemed to be traitors.[25] Some historians believe that this external political pressure revealed to the early Christians which books were most sacred to them, even to the point of being willing to die for them.

Another, more benign political influence, may have resulted from a decision of Constantine (306–337), the successor of Diocletian, who also became the first Christian emperor. Possibly to encourage more unity among the Christians, Constantine requested Bishop

---

[25] See McDonald, *The Canon Debate*, p. 417.

Eusebius to prepare fifty bibles in the Greek language to be used in the major cities of the Empire. Eusebius quotes the Emperor's request in his "Life of Constantine":

> I have thought it expedient to instruct your Prudence to order fifty copies of the sacred Scriptures, the provision and use of which you know to be most needful for the instruction of the Church, to be written on prepared parchment in a legible manner, and in a convenient, portable form, by professional transcribers thoroughly practiced in their art.[26]

Some historians claim that Constantine's influence at the Council of Nicea in 325 AD also played a role in fixing the number of books in the canon. While the Emperor convened the Council and was a major influence, there is no record that the biblical canon was an item on the Council's agenda.

Thus, several factors converged in the formation of the New Testament canon. For those viewing this process from a strictly historical point of view, the end result was largely a product of religious ideology, political control, and random historical forces. For many believing Christians, the guiding hand of God's Spirit was also at work, helping the church and its leaders discern which sacred books best expressed the constitutive elements of Christian faith.

The Sequence of the New Testament Books.

Like the formation of the New Testament canon itself, the rationale for the order in which the books are traditionally placed is also somewhat complex. The sequence varies in many ancient manuscripts. One author has noted that the only constant seems to be that the sequence begins with the Four Gospels (but not always

---

[26] Eusebius, Vita Constantini, IV, 36.

in the same order!) and ends with the book of Revelation—in between there are a lot of variations. One thing is clear—the order is not chronological, even though Augustine, who is given credit for firming up the traditional order we now have, thought that was the case. A strong consensus of modern biblical scholarship is that Mark's Gospel was probably the first to be written, with the final edition of John's Gospel composed late in the first century, while all of the authentic Pauline Letters were written prior to any of the Gospels during the 1950s and early 1960s.[27]

A number of scholars have detected a possible theological rationale for the current arrangement of the books. The Gospels come first because of the centrality of the figure of Christ in the totality of the New Testament. Everything began with Jesus, even though the accounts of his life and mission were composed later. Some believe Matthew is listed first among the Gospels because of his emphasis on Jesus as the fulfillment of the Old Testament Scriptures—thus sealing the relationship with the Old Testament canon and the Jewish roots of Jesus and Christianity itself.[28] Presenting the Four Gospels together meant that the Acts of the Apostles was separated from the Gospel of Luke. There are a number of links between Luke's Gospel and Acts, including the preface to the Acts where the author again addresses "Theophilus" and refers to his "first book" (Acts 1:1; see Luke 1:1–4).

The Acts of the Apostles now comes immediately after the Four Gospels and before Paul's letters. The very title, "Acts of the Apostles," which is not original to the work itself, may reveal the rationale for the order of books that follows. Acts is presented by Luke as an "orderly" narrative of the spread of the gospel from its origin in Jerusalem out to "ends of the earth" (see Acts 1:8). Within Luke's narrative, the power of the Spirit drives the early witnesses, often

---

[27] See earlier discussion.

[28] See Robert Wall, "The Significance of a Canonical Perspective of the Church's Scripture," in *The Canon Debate*, ed. Lee Martin McDonald and James A. Sanders (Grand Rapids, MI: Baker Academic, 2019). pp. 528–540.

beyond the expectations of the apostles and the early community itself. Such was the case, for example, with Peter being led through a dream to baptize the Roman centurion Cornelius at Caesarea Maritima (Acts 10–11) as well as the unexpected spread of the gospel to Antioch, where those dispersed by the persecution in the wake of Stephen's martyrdom baptize Greeks—much to the consternation of the Jerusalem apostles (see Acts 11:19–22). The title of Luke's narrative might more accurately be called the "Acts of the Spirit," but by the focus on the "Apostles" the traditional title paves the way for the remaining books of the New Testament canon, each of which is attributed to an apostle mentioned in Acts.

The thirteen letters of the "Apostle" Paul follow immediately after the Acts of the Apostles. This includes several letters that many modern scholars consider "deutero-Pauline," that is written by a later disciple writing in Paul's name, namely Ephesians, Colossians, 2 Thessalonians, and the "Pastoral Letters" of 1 & 2 Timothy and Titus. Some but not all early Christian leaders thought the Letter to the Hebrews was also written by Paul, so it is coupled with the Pauline Letters. The order in which the ensemble of Paul's letters is placed varies in many early manuscripts; some assume the present line-up is according to size, with Romans, the longest of Paul's letters coming first and Philemon the shortest, last. However, that rationale is not consistent—Galatians comes before Philippians, but it is shorter.

Other letters attributed to the "Apostles" come next: James, 1 & 2 Peter, the three Letters of John, and Jude. In later times these were called the "catholic" epistles because they were not addressed to individual churches or individuals but more widely, thus "catholic" in the sense of universal. Tradition assumed that Revelation was composed by the apostle John so it, too, falls under the rationale of Acts. Its strong apocalyptic character, with its emphasis on the end of the world, made it a fitting conclusion to the New Testament canon.

Thus, even in its structure, the New Testament canon is viewed as no accident but as an inspired sacred text that reveals the major story of Christian faith: linked to the history of God's people in the Old Testament, reaching its culmination and fulfillment in the person and mission of Jesus, whose death and resurrection mark the turning point in sacred history as the Spirit inspires the apostles to proclaim the good news of salvation to the ends of the earth, a mission that will lead to the ultimate triumph over the forces of evil, the consummation of the history, and the new heavens and new earth created by the victorious Lamb of God.

Extra-canonical Writings

The writings included in the New Testament were obviously not the only sacred books that circulated in the early church. As we noted previously, some of Paul's own letters may have been lost. And other widely circulated and seemingly worthy early texts such as the Didache, the Shepherd of Hermas, and the First Letter of Clement were, for reasons unclear, not included. And some texts judged heretical, such as the Apocalypse of Peter, were explicitly rejected. As Christianity expanded over time and territory, other religious writings began to appear, particularly from the second century on, posing the question whether they should have been included among the canonical books.

There is considerable interest today among biblical scholars and historians about these "extra-canonical" writings. In the views of some, the exclusion of certain extra-canonical books was an act of suppression on the part of church leaders, sometimes in collaboration with political authorities, in order to preserve their own authority and doctrinal convictions. The impression is sometimes given that many of the extra-canonical works represented a more charismatic and creative form of Christian tradition than that of the books selected for the canon.[29] The

---

[29] See, for example, Elaine Pagels, *The Gnostic Gospels* (Vasalia, CA: Vintage Press, 1989).

claim is made that in some instances, the words of Jesus and the spirit of his mission are more faithfully retained in some of the extra-canonical writings. Such a scenario, detecting the repressive efforts of religious and political establishment authorities over against more creative and free-spirited movements, may impose more of a modern twenty-first-century perspective on a second- and third-century context.

One of the most significant movements judged heretical by traditional Christianity in the second and third centuries was "Gnosticism," a term derived from the Greek word *gnosis*, meaning "knowledge." This label covered a variety of sectarian groups that had a particular view of the world ultimately judged heretical by mainline Christianity. Gnostics claimed the esoteric knowledge and spiritual insight necessary for ultimate salvation. They considered the material world as ultimately inferior and corrupt, created not by the God of Jesus Christ but by a demiurge. They had a sharply dualistic view of reality, pitting the material world against the spiritual world. Salvation was achieved by freeing one's soul or spiritual self from the material world through spiritual awareness in order to participate in the authentic spiritual world of God. Many devotees practiced extreme asceticism, and their religious texts often involved esoteric celestial descriptions and reflections on the dynamics of creation. Unlike the canonical New Testament texts, Gnostic writings limited their interactions with the Old Testament mainly to reflections on the early chapters of Genesis and ignored most of the prophetic and historical books. Many of the early church fathers, such as Origen, Tertullian, Irenaeus, Eusebius, and others, vigorously opposed Gnostic teachers and beliefs as dangerous heresies. In fact, many of the beliefs of Gnostics are known only through their condemnation in the writings of orthodox Christians.

One prominent extra-canonical example is the Gospel of Thomas, an ancient text written in Coptic (ancient Egyptian language) and discovered among a series of ancient manuscripts found in Nag Hammadi in Egypt in 1945. It is likely that the original version of Thomas was composed in Greek. Although dubbed a "gospel," it is quite different in form from the four canonical Gospels. It consists of a series of sayings and parables attributed to Jesus but has no account of Jesus's passion, death, or resurrection—something at the heart of the canonical Gospels. Several of the sayings found in the Gospel of Thomas are similar to sayings of Jesus found in the Four Gospels. Some scholars contend that, in fact, the version of some sayings in Thomas is more authentic in form than those found in canonical texts. However, much of the content and tone of the sayings in Thomas are similar to second- and third-century Egyptian Gnostic texts. It is more likely that the content of the Gospel of Thomas relies on the canonical gospel tradition instead of the other way around. The value of this "gospel" and other such texts is to demonstrate the variety of Christian life and thought in the early centuries of the church but not as substitutes for the canonical Gospels.

Many other extra-canonical texts exist only in fragments and often in quotations from other early writers. One such example is the so-called Gospel of Peter, a small portion of which was discovered in a manuscript dating from 800 AD, although the original text probably dates from the second century. The fragment describes the passion of Jesus from his trial. In this version it is Herod and the Jews who put Jesus to death—a version very different from the canonical Gospels. As noted earlier, it was explicitly rejected by Bishop Serapion of Antioch in the second century because of its use by heretical groups. Very few scholars contend that its account is more original than that of the canonical texts.[30]

---

[30] Although see John Dominic Crossan, *The Cross That Spoke: The Origins of the Passion Narrative* (San Francisco: HarperCollins, 1988), who contends that the canonical passion narratives derive from the Gospel of Peter.

A different kind of extra-canonical text is the "Protoevangelium of James," a Greek text that dates from the second century. It contains many vivid—and fanciful—stories about the boyhood of Jesus and his life with the Holy Family. The curiosity about this period in the life of Jesus—a period for which there is little information in the canonical Gospels (see, however, Luke 2:41–52)—no doubt sparked the imagination of the early Christians and made this a popular work cited in numerous Greek manuscripts from the third century. In this case, there does not seem to have been any attempt to include it in the canon.

Our focus here is on the books that were included in the New Testament canon, Christianity's sacred text, rather than on those who were not. The rise of numerous and varied Christian religious texts in the second century was no doubt a stimulus for the early church to discern which books were at the heart of the Christian experience and which were not. It is here that the criteria we cited earlier came into play. Each of the three is important—apostolic origin, widespread reception by the early Christian communities, and harmony with the "rule of faith."

The array of early Christian texts that developed in the second century raises another interesting question. What if modern archaeological quests were to discover an authentic but lost letter of Paul? Or a third letter of Peter? Would such a text attributed to an apostle and whose content seems orthodox then be eligible for inclusion in an expanded version of the canon? Although the scenario is unlikely, the answer would probably be "no." Missing in such a case is the criterion of the long-term reception and use of a sacred book by the early Christian community. The books included in the New Testament represent the self-consciousness of the early church in its early formative period. The canon of the New Testament, with all its diversity and complexity, serves as a unique foundational source for the ongoing self-understanding of the Christian community. Other subsequent writings continue to nourish and inspire the church, but they cannot replace or substitute for the historical foundational role of the New Testament.

Conclusion

As we noted earlier, while there is growing contemporary interest in the history of its formation, many scholars working from a "secular" point of view do not ascribe any special religious authority to the New Testament canon. From this perspective, inclusion in the canon does not give any special significance to the individual writings it contains. However, for the community of faith, inclusion in the New Testament adds another layer of meaning to each New Testament book. It is not simply the Gospel of Matthew or Paul's Letter to the Colossians that has religious authority as sacred Scripture for the Christian community but also the New Testament canon itself that has meaning.[31] That significance might be summarized as follows:

1. The New Testament canon, in a true sense, stands in continuity with the Old Testament and is something of a "commentary" on its portrayal of God, of God's people, and the history of salvation presented in the Hebrew Bible. Jesus is proclaimed through the Gospels and the reflections of Paul and the other New Testament writings as the culmination and flowering of the promises of God inherent in the Old Testament. This should not be seen as invalidating Judaism and its Scriptures as somehow now being obsolete or to be discarded. As Paul proclaims regarding his fellow Jews in his Letter to the Romans, "the gifts and the calling of God are irrevocable"—an affirmation that rules out "supersessionism," that is, a view that sees Christianity as completely replacing

---

[31] See James G. D. Dunn, "Has the Canon a Continuing Function?" in *The Canon Debate*, ed. Lee Martin McDonald and James A. Sanders (Grand Rapids, MI: Baker Academic, 2019), pp. 558–579; see also Christopher R. Seitz, *Convergences. Canon and Catholicity* (Waco, TX: Baylor University Press, 2020), pp. 93–122.

or "succeeding" Judaism.[32] In fact, the acceptance of the New Testament writings as "Sacred Scripture" comes about because of its fusion with the Old Testament that was already recognized by the earliest Christian community as God's Word and as inspired and sacred Scripture. Therefore, from a Christian point of view, each individual book of the New Testament must be understood as a part of a "whole"—a whole that includes the Old Testament itself. No individual book or a passage within a book of the New Testament (or, for that matter, the Old Testament) can be interpreted in isolation from this wider biblical context.

2. The New Testament canon, despite its diversity in varied human authors, its different literary forms, and its diverse theological perspectives, is the source of Christian unity. As we will consider in detail in our next chapter, the most compelling unifying factor of the New Testament is its proclamation of the person and mission of Jesus Christ. There is no other center point among all the books included in the canon of the New Testament.

3. At the same time, and with some degree of paradox, the canon of the New Testament also is the foundation of the church's diversity. Drawing into one entity such diverse individual books opens the way to the church's necessary embrace of cultural, theological, and structural differences—differences finding a source of unity in a common faith in Jesus Christ. As we will consider later in sketching the varied interpretation of the New Testament writings in Christian history, such diversity has not always been acknowledged or celebrated. But, in fact, the sacred foundational writings of Christianity are not found in a single book by a single author, but in multiple and varied

---

[32] A number of mainline Christian denominations expressly reject the notion of supersessionism; see, for example, the ground-breaking and influential statement of Roman Catholicism in the Second Vatican Council declaration, *Nostra Aetate*.

expressions of Christian faith and practice fused together in the canon of the New Testament.

4. The span of books included in the New Testament also paves the way for the development of Christian theology over time. Even within the New Testament itself—as is the case with the writings of the Old Testament—there is development. Matthew and Luke's Gospels build on the foundation of the Gospel of Mark, their principal source. The deutero-Pauline Letters develop some aspects of Paul's original theology. The Pastoral Letters reflect the growing concerns of the early community for doctrinal fidelity and organizational structures. The Second Letter of Peter notes concern about proper interpretation of Paul's letters regarding the imminence of the Parousia. As we will note later, later Christian traditions and denominations will appeal to different dimensions of the New Testament to articulate their theology and ecclesial structures.[33]

5. Finally, the New Testament also sets the limits of diversity and development within the church. To be faithful to its roots, contemporary Christianity must engage in an ongoing dialectic with its New Testament scriptures. Not all later portrayals of the person and mission of Jesus are legitimate. Not all Christian practices and ethical stances may cohere with the spirit of the New Testament writings. Development of church doctrine and the evolution of church structures can be signs of health, but if they drift too far from the fundamental values and spirit of the New Testament, they can be toxic. Only thoughtful and communal discernment among the varied Christian traditions can ensure fidelity to the sacred writings of the New Testament.

[33] See Chapter 8.

4

Jesus Christ and the New Testament

Our examination of the New Testament as a sacred text has so far revealed its singular focus on the person and mission of Jesus Christ. The Four Gospels, each in its own way, proclaim through narrative the unique identity, exemplary mission, and ultimate significance of Jesus for Christian faith. The Pauline Letters serve as a powerful testimony of the apostle's faith in Christ and the meaning of such faith for the lives of the communities he addresses. So, too, the rest of the diverse New Testament writings find their unity in reflection on faith in Jesus and the impact of his mission and teaching on Christian life. If the New Testament serves as a sacred text for Christianity, it is because it collectively proclaims Jesus as the ultimate embodiment of what it means to be "sacred" and "holy." Jesus both reveals and partakes of the divine.

It is time to explore more deeply this fundamental conviction of the New Testament. Who is Jesus Christ according to the New Testament? Here again the "two tracks" we have noted from the outset are in play. Working from what we are calling a "secular" perspective, the interests of modern biblical scholarship are mainly historical. The Bible itself, and the New Testament in particular, are viewed as important historical, literary, and cultural artifacts that have had an enormous impact on human history, but beyond such a "retrospective" or historical interest, these ancient biblical texts have no inherent normative claim on human life today.

The New Testament. Donald Senior, Oxford University Press. © Oxford University Press 2022.
DOI: 10.1093/oso/9780197530832.003.0005

Searching for the "Historical Jesus"

Recognizing the decidedly theological and confessional nature of the New Testament writings themselves, scholars in the modern era have spent a lot of time distinguishing between the actual historical figure of Jesus of Nazareth and the faith-suffused portrayal of Jesus developed in the New Testament. Characteristic of this distinction has been the so-called quest for the historical Jesus that has been a preoccupation of many scholars over the past century or more. Such a quest is difficult because the virtually exclusive sources for detecting the "historical" Jesus are the Gospels and other New Testament texts themselves.

For many, but not all, scholars seeking the historical Jesus of the early first century, there is a presumption of substantial discontinuity between the historical realities of the Jewish Jesus who lived and died in Roman Palestine and the exalted, sacred figure portrayed in the New Testament.[1] Scholars pursuing this "quest" have developed a set of criteria to help sort out in the gospel portrayals of Jesus which aspects might have some claim to historical authenticity and those that should be attributed solely to the theological convictions of early Christian faith.[2] As with all historical inquiry, it is very difficult to claim complete "objectivity." At times, the tastes and convictions of the inquirer will come up with a "historical" portrayal of Jesus that may reflect some of their own assumptions about Jesus rather than a completely reliable historical reconstruction. In a true sense, all writings about history involve interpretation.

---

[1] See, for example, the recent work of M. David Litwa, *How the Gospels Became History: Jesus and Mediterranean Myths* (New Haven, CT: Yale University Press, 2019), who asserts that the evangelists drew on Greco-Roman stories of heroic characters to fashion history-like accounts of Jesus, but without any real historical basis.

[2] See John P. Meier, *A Marginal Jew: Rethinking the Historical Jesus. Volume One: The Roots of the Problem and the Person* (Anchor Bible Reference Library; New Haven, CT: Yale University Press, 1991), pp. 167–195.

By contrast, what we might call a faith-based perspective has less interest in contrasting the "historical" Jesus from the Jesus portrayed in the New Testament. The "real" Jesus important for Christian faith and life is the Risen and Glorified Jesus proclaimed in and through the New Testament. This actual or present Jesus, in the view of Christian faith, is the same Jesus as Jesus of Nazareth but as he is *now*, not as he was *then*.[3] For most New Testament scholars, whether working from a perspective of faith or not, this does not exclude interest in discovering as much historical information as possible about the actual circumstances of Jesus's life. Refined historical methodologies, new information provided by modern archaeology, and access to textual evidence such as the Dead Sea Scrolls have provided scholars with rich and more accurate information about the historical context of Jesus's times and a more complete picture of the Judaism at the heart of Jesus's own experience and that of the early church. But for scholars working from a perspective of faith, there is continuity between the historical realities of Jesus and his religious and social context and the admittedly confessional portrayal of him in the New Testament writings. The theological portrayal of Jesus in the New Testament is considered not contrary to the historical reality of Jesus but views his life through the perspective of resurrection faith.

Key to this is the postresurrection vantage point of the New Testament writings. The Jesus they portray is not simply the Jesus of Nazareth who lived and died in the early decades of the first century but also the Risen Christ, uniquely suffused with God's Spirit, who truly died by crucifixion but also, by the power of God, overcame death and is now the exalted Risen Christ. The New Testament portrayal of Jesus, from this viewpoint, remains human and therefore a legitimate subject of historical inquiry but also has divine status

---

[3] See the helpful discussion of this distinction in Sandra Schneider, *The Revelatory Text: Interpreting the New Testament as Sacred Scripture* (New York: HarperCollins, 1991), pp. 100–102. Also, Luke Timothy Johnson, *The Real Jesus: The Misguided Quest for the Historical Jesus and the Truth of the Traditional Gospels* (San Francisco: Harper, 1996).

evident through the gift of faith and the testimony of the community of faith.

The inquirer who comes to the New Testament solely from a secular point of view may respect Christian reverence and esteem for the biblical writings but will not share a conviction about the religious and moral authority of these texts. For the inquirer who views the New Testament from the vantage point of faith, there can and should be an interest in the historical grounding of the life of Jesus and the New Testament. But there is also a conviction that the Jesus proclaimed through the ensemble of the biblical texts is the authentic Jesus who himself embodies the divine presence and, therefore, the portrayal of Jesus through the New Testament is sacred and normative for Christian life. Ultimately Christianity is not a "religion of the book" in the manner of Islam, which views the Koran as directly dictated by God to the prophet Mohammed and is therefore itself the source of revelation and worthy of the deepest reverence. For Christianity, the parallel to the role of the Koran is not the New Testament as such but the person of Jesus himself proclaimed through the biblical writings. It is the capacity to authentically portray or proclaim Jesus, the embodiment and source of all true holiness, that makes the New Testament a "sacred" book.

The Gospel Portrayal of Jesus

So what is the New Testament portrayal of Jesus? We turn first to the Four Gospels, the texts that stand first in the line of New Testament books. In subsequent chapters we will turn to Paul's letters and to the other writings of the New Testament.[4] As we have already discussed, the Gospels are narratives, each in a distinctive way telling the story of the life, mission, and destiny of Jesus.[5]

---

[4] For Paul, see Chapter 5; for the other New Testament writings, see Chapter 6.
[5] See earlier discussion.

As narratives, the complete dimensions of a Gospel's portrayal of Jesus coincides with the overall impact of the story each evangelist narrates. The events of Jesus's life have a sequence from his origin, through his public ministry, to his climactic crucifixion and resurrection. There is, in a sense, a "plot" to each gospel story as there is for all cogent narratives. But within the confines of each story there are shared elements or various sorts of affirmations that amplify the "sacredness" of Jesus, the dominant character of the gospel plots. If we use the metaphor of thinking of the Gospels as verbal "portraits" of Jesus, then we are examining the various colors and tones that the evangelists, as portrait artists, bring to their work. It is to these gospel affirmations of the sacred quality of Jesus that we now turn.

The Origin of Jesus

Like many biographies, the Gospels begin by considering in differing ways the origin of Jesus of Nazareth. Those origins reveal at the outset his unique character and destiny. Mark, probably the first Gospel to be written, has a very brief account of Jesus's ultimate origin.[6] Entitling his narrative as "the beginning of the good news of Jesus Christ, the Son of God," the evangelist ties the advent of Jesus to the Old Testament by a citation of the prophet Isaiah, "See I am sending my messenger ahead of you, who will prepare your way; the voice of one crying out in the wilderness: 'Prepare the way of the Lord, make his paths straight'" (Mark 1:1–3). In fact, this quotation is not simply from Isaiah but is a blend of Isaiah 40:3 along with Malachi 3:1 and Exodus 23:20, suggesting it may have been a quotation used prior to Mark to describe the advent of the Messiah. In any case, the quotation identifies Jesus as the Messiah and the Son of God, two powerful titles we will consider later, and introduces the mission of John the Baptist as a messenger of God announcing

---

[6] On the chronological order of the Gospels, see earlier.

the momentous and long-awaited moment for Israel, the coming of the Messiah who will liberate the people from their burdens.[7] As is true of the New Testament as a whole, the Old Testament is an essential context for understanding Jesus and his mission. As Mark's story unfolds, the reader/listener will learn more about the unique identity of Jesus.

Jesus's Origin in Matthew's Gospel

Matthew and Luke, each in his own distinctive way, will push the story of Jesus's origins much further back into the history of Israel and, in Luke's case, to the origin of humanity itself. Matthew's Gospel also begins with a title that signals the origin and scope of Jesus's mission: "Jesus the Messiah" is also acclaimed as "Son of David"—continuing the promise of the Old Testament about King David's enduring dynasty which reaches its climax with the coming of the Messiah—and "Son of Abraham"—the reference to Abraham, designated in Genesis as the "father of many nations" (Gen 17:4–5; cited by Paul in Rom 4:11–12) and thus anticipating the worldwide mission of the Risen Christ. A strong emphasis of Matthew's narrative is Jesus's essential continuity with Judaism and, at the same time, embodying the fulfillment of the promises of God to Israel, promises that will ultimately take the story of salvation to the "nations."

Matthew's infancy narrative (Matthew 1–2) ties Jesus to the events of Israel's history in multiple ways. The Gospel begins with a genealogy that traces the family tree of Jesus from Abraham to the reign of David, then through the tragedy of the Babylonian exile, and then ending with the birth of Jesus, the Messiah.[8] Joseph is the decisive character in Matthew's account, and Jesus's Davidic

---

[7] On the use of titles, see later discussion.

[8] Matthew signals the structure of his genealogy in 1:18; the contents of the genealogy are taken mainly from segments in the first book of Chronicles and Ruth.

heritage is traced through him. By taking Mary as his spouse, Joseph adopts her child Jesus into the messianic line.[9]

Matthew's account of Jesus's origin is filled with remarkable and significant events. Joseph is startled to learn that Mary, his betrothed, is pregnant before they have come together and determines to divorce her "quietly," but he is informed by an angel in a dream that the child she bears "is from the Holy Spirit" (Matt 1:20). The angel, acting as a messenger from God, also declares that the child's name will be "Jesus" (which means in Hebrew, "God saves" or "God's salvation") "for he will save his people from their sins" (1:21). At this point Matthew also introduces the first of several "fulfillment quotations" that will occur throughout his narrative, that is, quotations from the Old Testament introduced by a standard introduction that affirms that Jesus and his mission "fulfill" the hopes of Israel expressed in the Old Testament. The first of these is a quotation from Isaiah 7:14, affirming the virginal conception of Jesus and adding another name for Jesus, that of "Emmanuel," which Matthew translates for his Greek-speaking audience as "God is with us" (1:22–23). Thus, in the opening chapter of Matthew's Gospel, the reader has already learned the unique identity of Jesus: he is rooted deep in the history of Israel and fulfills God's promises to his people; he is the longed-for Davidic messiah; he is conceived not by normal human means but by the power of God's Spirit; he is designated as "Jesus," the one who will save his people from their sins; and he is also named "Emmanuel" who embodies the divine presence itself.

In the remainder of Matthew's infancy narrative, the evangelist once again ties Jesus to some of the paradigmatic events of Israel's

---

[9] Matthew adds several women to the genealogy—Tamar (Genesis 38), Rahab (Joshua 2), Ruth (book of Ruth), Bathsheba (2 Samuel 11,12), and Mary herself (Matt 1:16). Biblical genealogies usually trace only the male descendants. Each of the women in Matthew's account breaks into the messianic line in a unique way, perhaps signaling the unexpected turns in history that will also be exemplified in the mission of Jesus and the early community.

history and anticipates the drama of the gospel narrative itself. Although in the body of his Gospel, Matthew will focus on Jesus's mission to Israel, in the concluding scene of the narrative (28:16–20), the Risen Jesus sends his apostles "to all nations" and promises to remain with them until the end of time (fulfilling the meaning of his name "Emmanuel"—"God with us"). That emphasis on a worldwide mission is anticipated even in the events of Jesus's conception and birth. In a scene unique to Matthew, "wise men from the east" (a translation of the Greek term *magoi*, meaning magicians or astrologers who have been studying the pattern of the stars) come seeking the child "who has been born king of the Jews" (Matt 2:1–2). By contrast, Herod the Great, the then reigning king, has murderous intentions, wanting to eradicate any rival to his power, even to the extent of killing all the male children of Bethlehem under two years old (itself reminiscent of Pharaoh's cruelty at the time of the Exodus). His attempt to trick the "Magi" will be thwarted by another angelic intervention, warning them to return home by a different route. Meanwhile the Gentile visitors are "overwhelmed with joy" when they find the child and offer Jesus homage and precious gifts. A paradoxical pattern of the gospel drama is set: many of the leaders of God's own people will reject Jesus, and Gentiles will pay him homage.

A final echo of the Old Testament history is played out in Matthew's account of Jesus's origin. Like Moses's encounter with Pharaoh, Jesus is hounded by a wicked despot, Herod. Like Israel of old, Jesus is protected by another "Joseph" who is also a "dreamer," echoing the story of Joseph in Genesis 37–50, who, although at first rejected by them, ultimately saves his family in Egypt. And as with a sad chapter of Israel's own history in the Babylonian exile, Jesus and his family must flee into exile, now though in Egypt. And from there, like Israel's own liberation from slavery in Egypt and subsequent exiles, God will call them back home (Matt 2:13–15). Yet the threat to the life of the child still lingers in the person of Archelaus, Herod's despotic son who is now ruling over Judea, the region that includes Bethlehem. So the family cannot return home to Bethlehem but must displace to Nazareth (Matt 2:19–23). All of this anticipates the rejection and sufferings that Jesus, God's chosen one, will endure later in the gospel drama. At the same time, Matthew affirms at the very outset of his Gospel the fact that Jesus embodies the hopes of God's people. Through his mission, particularly through his death and resurrection, the Jesus of Matthew's Gospel will indeed "save his people from their sins."

Jesus's Origin in Luke's Gospel

Luke and Matthew share a few basic elements in their reflection on Jesus's origin: Mary and Joseph are Jesus's parents, with the virginal conception affirmed in both accounts; Bethlehem is the birthplace of Jesus (although each evangelist understands this in a different way); each offers a genealogy of Jesus (but again in different ways); and John the Baptist is presented as the precursor of Jesus. Nazareth is the Galilean hometown of Jesus, Mary, and Joseph. Other than these basic elements, their accounts are quite different in content and tone.

Luke organizes his infancy narrative by paralleling the conception and birth of John the Baptist with that of Jesus himself. While John is revered as a prophet, his identity and preparatory role are subordinate to that of Jesus. The first set of scenes tells of the unusual conception of John; his parents, Elizabeth and Zachary, are old and barren, but through God's intervention they will conceive a child, John, whose destiny will be to announce the advent of the Messiah (see Luke 1:5–25). The setting for these first events is the Jerusalem temple where Zachary performs his duties as a priest. For Luke's Gospel as a whole, the setting of Jerusalem and its temple is of paramount importance, signaling the Jewish roots of Jesus and, as narrated in the Acts of the Apostles, of the post-Easter community formed in his name. Jesus's life and mission begin in the shadow of Jerusalem and its temple and will end there, with the death, resurrection, and ascension of Jesus.

The parallel scenes narrating the annunciation to Mary and the conception and birth of Jesus proclaim the unique identity of this child. The angel Gabriel announces that Mary is God's "favored one" and assures her that "the Lord is with you" (Luke 1:26–38), and describes her son in exalted terms: "He will be great, and will be called the Son of the Most High, and the Lord God will give to him the throne of his ancestor David. He will reign over the house of Jacob forever, and of his kingdom there will be no end" (Luke 1:32–33). When Mary asks how this will come about since she is a virgin (a parallel to the barrenness of Elizabeth), the angel affirms (similar to Matthew's account) that "The Holy Spirit will come upon you, and the power of the Most High will overshadow you, therefore the child to be born will be holy; he will be called Son of God" (Luke 1:35).

A series of enticing scenes closes out Luke's infancy narrative and continues to affirm for the reader the unique identity of Jesus. Mary comes from Nazareth to visit her cousin Elizabeth in the southern region of Judea, the one scene in all the Gospels where two women, both pregnant, command the stage (Luke 1:39–56). Here, too, the unique identity of Jesus is underscored. Elizabeth, "filled with the Holy Spirit," acclaims Mary, "Blessed are you among women and blessed is the fruit of your womb. And why has this happened to me that the mother of my Lord comes to me?" Elizabeth's praise is prompted by the fact that John in her womb "leapt for joy" at the sound of Mary's greeting—a beautiful way of signaling the preparatory role of John. The scene concludes by once again acclaiming Mary's unique role as mother of the Lord: "And blessed is she who believed that there would be a fulfillment of what was spoken to her by the Lord" (Luke 1:39–45). Elizabeth's praise triggers Mary's exuberant and prophetic canticle, the Magnificat (Luke 1:46–56). Both this canticle and the earlier one of Zachariah emphasize God's fidelity to the promises made to Israel that are now fulfilled in the advent of Jesus the Messiah.

The actual birth of Jesus in Luke's account takes place in Bethlehem (Luke 2:1–21). Jesus's family is there to take part in the census decreed by the Emperor Augustus.[10] Note that Matthew and Luke diverge here. Both place the birth of Jesus in Bethlehem, but Matthew's account assumes that Joseph and Mary were natives of Bethlehem and move to Nazareth out of fear of Archelaus, who now rules in Judea (the province where Bethlehem is located); while Luke assumes that Nazareth is the hometown of Mary and Joseph, and they go to Bethlehem, the home of their ancestors, only for the census and then return to Nazareth.

After Mary gives birth to her son, the first to pay him homage is a group of shepherds. An "angel of the Lord" brings them "good news of great joy for all the people." Luke stresses the Davidic heritage of Jesus, the Messiah: "to you is born this day in the city of David a Savior, who is the Messiah, the Lord." The announcing angel is joined by a chorus "of heavenly host" who exuberantly praise God. The shepherds then go to the birthplace to pay homage to the child and then return to their fields, "glorifying and praising God for all they had heard and seen, as it had been told them." The birth account concludes with the circumcision of the child and his naming as "Jesus" (Luke 2:21).

Luke's concludes his reflections on the origin of Jesus with episodes in the Jerusalem Temple itself. When Mary and Joseph bring the child to the Temple to be "purified according to the law of Moses" (Luke 2:22–24), they encounter there two "prophets." Simeon, prompted by the Spirit (as is true of virtually every character in Luke's infancy account), takes the child in his arms and praises God for fulfilling the promise of a Messiah, one will bring "salvation . . . to all peoples" and who will be "a light for revelation to the Gentiles and for glory to your people Israel" (Luke 2:29–32).

---

[10] The census administered by Quirinius, the governor of Syria, took place in 6 AD, creating some historical dissonance with the fact that Luke places Jesus's birth under the reign of Herod the Great (Luke 1:5), who died nine years earlier in 4 BC.

At this point, Luke introduces one of the few discordant notes in his account of Jesus's origin—Simeon's prophecy that "this child is destined for the falling and the rising of many in Israel, and will be a sign that will be opposed so that the inner thoughts of many will be revealed..." (Luke 2:34–35). Anna, a prophet who "never left the temple," also praises God for the fulfillment of his promises to Israel and spoke about the child "to all who were looking for the redemption of Jerusalem" (Luke 2:38).

The finale scene of Luke's infancy narrative also takes place in the temple and represents the sole story in the gospel literature about Jesus's childhood. After the story of his conception and birth, Mary, Joseph, and the child Jesus return to "their own town of Nazareth," where "the child grew and became strong, filled with wisdom and the favor of God was upon him" (Luke 2:39–40). Later, when Jesus was twelve, he accompanies his parents to Jerusalem to celebrate the feast of Passover (Luke 2:41–51). When his parents and their other relatives begin their return to Nazareth, they discover that Jesus is missing and return anxiously to Jerusalem to find him. After three days they find him in the temple, dazzling the teachers there with his answers. When his mother confronts him with their anxiety, Jesus replies, "Why were you searching for me? Did you not know that I must be in my Father's house?" An enigmatic response that baffles his parents but signals to the reader of the Gospel the unique mission of Jesus. The account closes with their return to Nazareth and the assurance of Jesus's obedience to his parents, adding: "And Jesus increased in wisdom and in years, and in divine and human favor" (2:52).

Note that in Luke the genealogy of Jesus comes only after the account of the baptism, in contrast to Matthew's account where it comes before the description of his conception and birth. Luke also tracks Jesus's ancestry in reverse order, beginning with the notation of Joseph (his father, "as was thought," adds Luke) back through the Davidic line all the way through to Adam and to God himself (see Luke 3:23–38).

The Cosmic Perspective of John's Gospel

The exalted portrayal of Jesus's origins in the Synoptic Gospels is more than matched in the preface to John's Gospel. In so many ways, the entire Gospel of John has a distinct format compared to the Synoptic Gospels and that includes its portrayal of the origin of Jesus. John begins his Gospel not with an account of the circumstances of Jesus's conception and birth, as is the case with Matthew and Luke, but with a poetic reflection that takes the origin of Jesus back into the very being and timeless presence of God: "In the beginning was the Word, and the Word was with God, and the Word was God" (John 1:1). Many commentators believe that the evangelist adopts here an early Christian hymn that reflects on the identity and mission of Jesus from a cosmic perspective.

The dominant image used is that of Jesus as the "Word"—a Word uttered by God and so perfectly articulating what God wants to say that the "Word" *is* God. The prologue then moves in a descending structure. The Word that originates in God becomes the pattern of all created things (John 1:1–5) and then the pattern of the "world," that is, the human realm capable of either receiving or rejecting God's Word (John 1:10–13). And, finally, the "Word became flesh and lived among us, and we have seen his glory, the glory as of a father's only son, full of grace and truth" (John 1:14). Spliced into the hymn are references to the testimony of John the Baptist, whom the prologue emphatically states was not the "light" (as Jesus is) but was sent to give testimony about the true light (John 1:6–9, 15)— a role not unlike the one John the Baptist plays in the Synoptic Gospels. By stating that the Word "became flesh" the evangelist refers not simply to the moment of the conception of Jesus but to his taking on the entirety of a human existence. This is John's unique way of referring to the "Incarnation," the Divine full embrace of the human, one of the bedrock doctrines of Christianity.

John's prologue concludes with an emphatic statement of the unique mission of Jesus the Word Incarnate: "No one has ever seen God. It is God the only Son, who is close to the Father's heart, who has made him known (literally, "revealed" him, John 1:18). This unique mission of Jesus to reveal God's Word to the world is reaffirmed in John 3:16–17, one of the most quoted verses of John's Gospel: "For God so loved the world that he gave his only Son, so that everyone who believes in him may not perish but may have eternal life. Indeed, God did not send the Son into the world to condemn the world, but in order that the world might be saved through him" (John 3:16–17). Some interpreters of John's Gospel consider the prologue not simply as a "prologue" or introduction to the Gospel but as its conceptual "center"—a core vision of Jesus and his God-given mission from which all of the other features of John's Gospel radiate. In any case, John's unique description of the origin of Jesus, rooted in the very being of God and then "becoming flesh," strongly affirms the unique identity and mission of Jesus in a manner different from the Synoptic Gospels but, at the same time, complementary to their proclamation of Jesus. Jesus's origin is with God and from God. He brings that Divine Presence into creation itself and into the world of humanity. In "becoming flesh" the Word of God is manifested to humanity ("We have seen his glory"); the Jesus of John's Gospel is the unique and authentic revealer of God in and through his "flesh." The ultimate message of God's Word is not a word of condemnation but one of redeeming love (3:16–17).[11]

Conclusion

Examining the diverse ways the Four Gospels describe the origin of Jesus demonstrates that from the outset of their narratives, the evangelists affirm the unique and profound religious identity of Jesus. In the Synoptic Gospels, Jesus's person and mission are strongly fused onto the backdrop of the Old Testament. He is identified as God's promised Messiah or "anointed one"—the

---

[11] For John's Gospel the ultimate expression of Jesus's mission of love for the world paradoxically is his death, which the Gospel interprets as an act of friendship love (see John 15:13).

longed-for royal figure who would lead Israel to the fulfillment of its hopes for peace and justice, hopes anticipated but unfulfilled in the reign of Jesus's ancestor David. Particularly in the accounts of Matthew and Luke—but in different tones—Jesus's conception is described as taking place not by ordinary human means but through the power of God's Spirit. Jesus is acclaimed as the "savior" of Israel and of humanity itself; he will free the people from their sins. He is confessed as "Lord" and "Son of God." He is named "Emmanuel," the embodiment of God's presence among his people. Diverse peoples pay him homage: the shepherds, the gentile Magi, the temple prophets Simeon and Anna. The experiences of his life, even in his infancy, mirror those of God's people Israel— aided by Joseph, a dreamer like the Joseph of old; threatened as was Moses by Pharaoh; pushed into exile like his own people under the Assyrians and Babylonians; brought out from Egypt like Israel of old. His death is anticipated as revealing the hearts of many. Luke, we should note, presents the Jewish context of Jesus's conception and birth in positive tones, reflecting the deep piety and devotion of Judaism. Matthew, however, introduces discordant notes of hostility and violence on the part of Herod and his court.

John's Gospel, too, affirms in poetic fashion that the origin of Jesus is in God and that the Word of God has fashioned all of creation, including the human realm of the "world" (in Greek, *cosmos*). Jesus, in John's portrayal, is the ultimate revelation of God to the world—not simply as another in the line of Old Testament prophetic figures but definitively revealing God in his very being, as the Word made flesh.

Obviously, these are not ordinary birth stories but a proclamation of one uniquely chosen by God and one whose mission is no less than the salvation of the world; one whose being embodies the divine presence and on whose destiny the destiny of the world itself hangs. Clearly the evangelists begin their accounts of the life and mission of Jesus not as a dispassionate historical rendering but from the vantage point of the Risen Jesus's triumph over death and the belief of the Christian community in Jesus as the Son of God.

Theophanies

The assertion of Jesus's unique identity rooted in God in the opening scenes of the Four Gospels finds reaffirmation in several dramatic scenes in the body of their narratives. These are termed "theophanies," from the fusion of the Greek words *theos* ("God") and *epiphanos* ("appearance" or "manifestation"). In such scenes the veil of human circumstances shrouding the divine presence seems to be torn away, momentarily revealing to the reader the unique bond between Jesus and God.

At the Baptism
A first dramatic example takes place at the baptism of Jesus by John the Baptist in the Jordan River, which prefaces Jesus's public ministry in all Four Gospels, although here, too, each evangelist has some subtle accents of his own. Mark's account sets the pattern and is typically brief (see Mark 1:9–11). Jesus comes from Nazareth in Galilee to the southern desert region near where the Jordan River flows into the Dead Sea to be baptized by John, and as he emerges from the water, "he [Jesus] saw the heavens torn apart and the Spirit descending like a dove on him. And a voice came from heaven, 'You are my Son, the Beloved, with you I am well pleased.'" In Mark's version God speaks to Jesus alone; in Matthew, the pronouncement of God appears to be public, "*This* is my Son, the Beloved, with whom I am well pleased" (Matt 3:17). Luke does not narrate the actual moment of Jesus's baptism but concentrates on the divine voice that immediately follows (see Luke 3:21–22). In all three Synoptic Gospels, the voice of God reaffirms for the reader the unique status of Jesus as he is about to begin his public ministry. After the descent of the Spirit on Jesus and the affirmation by God of his status

as the "beloved Son," Jesus is propelled into the desert to confront the raw power of evil, an anticipation of his mission of exorcism and healing that is about to begin (Mark 1:12–13). Note that John's Gospel does not mention the baptism of Jesus by John the Baptist, but it does refer to the Spirit's "descent" upon Jesus and the Baptist's recognition that Jesus is the "Son of God" (John 1:33–34).

The Transfiguration

Another theophany described in the Synoptic Gospels takes place at the transfiguration of Jesus, at the conclusion of his Galilean mission and immediately prior to the beginning of his fateful journey to Jerusalem.[12] In a mountaintop setting reminiscent of God's encounter with Moses on Sinai (see Exodus 19), the divine voice once again declares Jesus's unique identity as the beloved Son of God: "This is my son, the Beloved, listen to him!" (Mark 9:7). The setting for this event enhances its dramatic significance. In view of his disciples Peter, James, and John, Jesus's appearance is transformed, "his clothes became dazzling white, such as no one on earth could bleach them." And appearing with Jesus are Elijah, the great prophet of Israel, and Moses, the one who led Israel out of slavery and received the Law on Mount Sinai. A dazed Peter offers to make three "tabernacles" "one for you, one for Moses, and one for Elijah," as an act of homage (Mark 9:5).

In all three Gospels, the event is tied to the first of Jesus's predictions of his passion. In Mark and Matthew, "six days" after; in Luke, "eight days." In effect, the manifest transfiguration of Jesus and the endorsement by the voice from heaven ("listen to him") affirm for the disciples (and the reader) the unique identity and authority of Jesus even as he faces the power of death that looms in Jerusalem (see Mark 8:27–33).

---

[12] See Mark 9:2–8 and the parallels in Matthew and Luke. The three versions are similar.

John's Gospel does not have the transfiguration scene, but there is a unique moment that has intriguing echoes of this event. At the conclusion of Jesus's public ministry in John's account, Jesus has a moment of anguish that may be John's equivalent of Jesus's intense prayer for deliverance from death in the garden of Gethsemane found in the Synoptic Gospels, "Now my soul is troubled. And what should I say— 'Father, save me from this hour? No, it is for this reason I have come to this hour, 'Father, glorify your name'" (John 12:27–30). At that moment in John's account there comes in response "a voice from heaven" that affirms Jesus's unique identity: "I have glorified it, and I will glorify it again." The crowd present there thought they heard thunder, while others believed "an angel has spoken to him." But Jesus himself declares, "This voice has come for your sake, not for mine"—a comment equivalent to the instruction of the voice from heaven in the Synoptic account, "listen to him."

On the Sea

Another dramatic theophany is the scene of Jesus's walking on the water, found in the Gospels of Mark, Matthew, and John (see Mark 6:45–52; Matt 14:22–33; John 6:16–21; Luke has the similar story of the calming of the sea—Luke 8:22–25). The pattern is again set by Mark's version: Jesus remains on the shore, praying alone on a mountain, while the disciples struggle in a boat in a violent storm. During the "fourth watch of the night" (according to the Roman calculation, the last "watch" between 3:00 and 6:00 a.m.), Jesus appears "walking on the water." In all three accounts, the disciples are terrified at this specter, but Jesus calms them: "Take heart, it is I; do not be afraid" (Mark 6:50). The English translation—"it is I"—masks the significance of Jesus's words. The Greek phrase is *ego eimi* (literally, "I am"), a recurring version of the divine name used in the Septuagint, or Greek translation of the Old Testament. The phrase "I am" (*ego eimi*) appears to evoke the enigmatic name of God revealed to Moses in Exodus 3:14 (see also Is 41:4, 10, 14; 43:1–3, 10, 13). The entire setting of this scene reinforces its function as a theophany; Jesus's power to walk on the raging waters recalls the description of God's own power over the forces of nature as in Psalm 77:19 ("Your way was through the sea, your path, through the mighty waters; yet your footprints were unseen") and in Job 9:8 ("[God] who alone stretched out the heavens and trampled the waves of the Sea"). Jesus who bears the divine name also exercises God's power over the chaos of the sea.

Each of the evangelists adds his own nuance to the story. In Mark this theophany is met with bewilderment on the part of the disciples (Mark 6:52), a recurring theme in Mark's Gospel. Matthew splices into the story the attempt of Peter to walk on the water and, when he begins to sink out of fear, crying out to Jesus for deliverance: "Lord, save me." The title "Lord" (*kurios*, in Greek), as we will see, also evokes the divine name.[13] When Jesus and Peter enter the boat, the other disciples acclaim Jesus, "Truly you are the Son of God"—unlike in Mark, an appropriate response to the theophany (see Matt 14:33). In John, the sea theophany comes immediately before Jesus's bread of life discourse and prepares for the portrayal of Jesus as the living bread come down from heaven (John 6:22–59).

Jesus and the Divine Name

We should note that John's Gospel brings the use of the "I am" designation to a new level. Several times in the Gospel Jesus declares this divine name in reference to himself; for example, in 8:58 Jesus asserts to his opponents that he existed before Abraham came to be: "Amen, amen, I tell you, before Abraham was, I am" (see also John 8:24, 28; 13:19). When Judas and the soldiers come to arrest Jesus in Gethsemane, Jesus twice asks them whom they are seeking and when they answer, "Jesus of Nazareth," he responds: "I am," causing them "to step back and fall to the ground!" (John 18:5–6, 7–8)—a remarkable assertion of Jesus's power even at the moment of his arrest. John also uses the "I am" designation for Jesus fused onto

---

[13] See later discussion.

other significant words that express human longing, as for example, "I am the bread of life" (6:35,51), "the light of the world" (8:12), "the resurrection and the life" (9:25), and "the way, the truth, and the life" (14:6). John's Gospel had already affirmed in the prologue that in Jesus the community recognizes his "glory, the glory as of the Father's only son" (John 1:14). The Greek term for "glory" (*doxa*) that John uses here translates the Hebrew word *kabod*, a frequent reference in the Old Testament to the presence of God (literally, the "heaviness" or "weight" of God's felt presence; see, e.g., Exod 3:19; Ezek 1:27–28). For John's Gospel, Jesus's primary mission is to reveal through his humanity God's presence in the world. Thus, it makes sense for Jesus to bear the very name of God, an extraordinary affirmation of the unique identity of Jesus himself.

These gospel scenes affirm in an explicit way the unique identity and authority of Jesus. In the baptism and transfiguration scenes, God's own voice ("the voice from heaven") endorses Jesus as the beloved "Son of God" and authenticates Jesus's mission. In the sea story, Jesus himself both exercises and reveals God's power over the chaotic forces of nature, a divine attribute. Breaking into the ongoing narration of Jesus's public mission, these scenes reveal the Gospels' conviction of Jesus's unique identity.

Jesus and His Father

Reinforcing this sense of the unique bond between God and Jesus are also those moments in the gospel narratives where on his part Jesus expresses his intimacy with the "Father." Several times in all Four Gospels, Jesus is depicted in solitary prayer (e.g., Mark 1:35; Luke 5:16; Matt 14:23), and in Matthew's Gospel there is a moment of intense piety:

> I thank you, Father, Lord of heaven and earth, because you have hidden these things from the wise and the intelligent and have revealed them to infants; yes, Father, for such was your gracious will. All things have been handed over to me by my Father, and

no one knows the Son except the Father and no one knows the Father except the Son and anyone to whom the Son chooses to reveal him. (Matt 11:25–27)

Repeatedly, in all Four Gospels Jesus affirms his commitment to "doing the will of my Father" (see Matt 7:21). This is presented in an intense way in the Synoptic Gospels' portrayal of Jesus's anguished prayer in Gethsemane on the eve of his arrest and the beginning of the passion narrative (Mark 14:36). In Mark, Jesus addresses God as *abba*, a Hebrew or Aramaic diminutive for the word "father" (*ab*), displaying a deep bond of love and affection as an adult or child has for one's father. As noted earlier, John's Gospel does not have an explicit narrative of the Gethsemane prayer, but the soliloquy of Jesus with his Father in chapter 17 of John's Gospel is a remarkable and extended prayer of intimacy with God, claiming "oneness" with the Father. Throughout John's Gospel the unique bond of Jesus with his Father is affirmed.

These multiple assertions of Jesus's sense of intimacy and unity with his Father correspond to the manifestations of the divine found in the dramatic theophanies of the gospel narratives.

Titles for Jesus

The gospel accounts of Jesus's origin and the theophanies that take place during Jesus's public ministry contain a profusion of titles ascribed to Jesus: "Son of God," "Lord," "Savior," "Christ," "Messiah," and so on. These titles were no doubt embedded in the traditions about Jesus that circulated in the early community and were available to the evangelists. Many of these titles were drawn from the Old Testament scriptures and already had a range of meaning before they were applied to Jesus himself. However, the titles were not applied to Jesus in a mechanical or rigid fashion, as if they had a singular, fixed meaning. When used of Jesus, his own unique character and actions gave new layers of meaning to these traditional titles.

Son of God

Some titles applied to Jesus are "royal" titles, used in the Old Testament to describe the singular God-given power and authority of the kings of Israel. God was the true "king" of Israel (see, e.g., Psalm 97, "The Lord is King! Let the earth rejoice; let the many coastlands be glad!"), and the earthly monarchs of Israel were designated to act in God's place and to exemplify the qualities of justice and mercy that characterized God's own rule. Such is the case with the title "Son of God" applied to the king in his role as the representative of God and protector of God's people. Psalm 2:7 speaks of the king as God's "son": "He said to me, 'You are my son; today, I have begotten you.'" Thus, the title "son of God" as traditionally understood did not convey divine status but revealed the authority and commitments required of the king. In many ways, the Old Testament viewed David, despite his flaws, as the ideal king. And thus, Jesus himself was designated "Son of David" and his birth in Bethlehem, the ancestral town of David, also affirmed his Davidic status (see, e.g., the title of Matthew's Gospel that designates Jesus as "Son of David"; Matt 1:1; also Luke 1:32).

However, when the term "Son of God" or my "beloved Son" is used of Jesus in the Gospels, it takes on another layer of meaning that goes beyond that of the traditional royal title, namely the unique bond of intimacy with God described earlier in reflecting on the origin of Jesus and the theophanies in the Gospels. Now the term "Son of God" addressed to Jesus in the Gospels moves closer to the later Christological affirmation that Jesus is the divine Son of God, the second person of the Christian trinitarian conception of God.

Lord

Similarly, the term "Lord" (in Greek *kurios*) could simply be an honorific title such as the modern usage of the term "sir," but when applied to the king it took on a deeper connotation. Adding further depth of meaning was the fact that the term "Lord" was also used as a title of respect and reverence in speaking of God. Later Jewish tradition avoided enunciating the name of God ("Yahweh") and when reading the Scriptures would substitute the term "my Lord," in Hebrew, *adonai* (i.e., in Greek, *kurios* or "Lord"). In a setting such as the story of the walking on the water in Matthew's account, Peter cries out, "Lord (*kurie*), save me!" (Matt 14:30). Here the title is being applied to Jesus with a strong connotation of his divine character, able to save Peter from the threat of the sea. Similarly, in one of the most dramatic confessions of Jesus in the New Testament, the apostle Thomas addresses the Risen Jesus as "my Lord (*kurios*) and my God (*theos*)" (John 20:28). Here, the meaning expressed obviously goes far beyond the traditional usage as a royal title.

The Christ
The same is true of another important royal title applied to Jesus in the Gospels, namely that of "Christ" or the "messiah." The Hebrew term "messiah" and its Greek translation as "Christ" both mean the "anointed one" and refer to the anointing of the king for his role. Israel's longing for ultimate peace and security incorporated the hope for an ideal leader or royal figure (i.e., the Messiah) who would be God's instrument to fulfill the hopes of Israel. Here again, the idealized figure of David the king was seen as a foretaste of this final triumph. While several times in the Gospels people refer to Jesus as the "Christ" or "messiah," he does not use it as a self-designation. In any case, the messianic role of Jesus is expressed in a manner different in many ways from some traditional expectations. For example, the Jesus of the Gospels enters his royal city Jerusalem not as a dominant warrior or hero but with humility, riding on a donkey (see Matt 21:1–41, where the crowds acclaim Jesus as "Son of David").[14] In other New Testament writings "Christ" is used almost

---

[14] At the time of Jesus, expectations of a "messiah" took a variety of forms in Judaism; in some instances, there was an expectation of a triumphant royal figure, but other expectations were less defined, anticipating a final era of peace and security.

as a "family name" for Jesus. Its use in the Gospels does not directly assert any divine status for Jesus but underscores his authority as the one designated by God to deliver Israel and restore the people.

Teacher

Other titles are used for Jesus in the Gospels. One of the most common was "teacher," applied to Jesus some forty-five times in the Gospels, both by his disciples and opponents. This title for a revered role in Jewish tradition does not carry any divine character as such. But when used of Jesus, his singular status as God's Son sent to redeem Israel and the world implies that his teaching is definitive. Matthew's Gospel, in particular, emphasizes the authoritative teaching role of Jesus, as, for example, in the Sermon on the Mount where Jesus contrasts his teaching as more intense and deeply interior than traditional teachings: "You have heard it said . . . but I say to you . . ." (see Matt 5:21–48). Another recurring phrase emphasizing Jesus's singular teaching authority is the emphatic phrase "Amen, amen, I say to you . . ." that introduces Jesus's sayings seventy-five times in the Gospels, implying that Jesus's teaching has a unique personal authority behind it. In the first act of Jesus's mission in Mark's account—the exorcism of the man in the synagogue of Capernaum (see Mark 1:21–28)—the amazed synagogue congregation asks, "What is this? A new teaching—with authority!" The Greek word used for "authority" here is *exousia*, meaning "force" or "power"—hinting at the definitive authority of Jesus as teacher.

Son of Man

Another title found in all Four Gospels is that of "Son of Man," one of the most elusive tiles for Jesus and one that often is used by Jesus as a self-reference. The phrase "son of man" derives from an Aramaic idiom which means in effect "a human being" (i.e., one who is a son of the human species). But the phrase seems to take on additional meaning from its use in the book of Daniel, where in a vision Daniel sees the future appearance of one coming at the end of the age as a "Son of Man," implying a certain role for this mysterious human-like figure in the final judgment (see Daniel 7:14). In the Gospels, the title "son of man" is applied to Jesus in his role as the one who will return to judge humanity at the end of the age (see, e.g., Mark 13:24–27), but it is also used in reference to the humiliation and rejection of Jesus as "the Son of Man," as in Jesus's predictions of his own suffering (e.g., Mark 10:33–34). Both humiliation and suffering as well as final exaltation are fundamental assertions about Jesus in the Gospels; Jesus is a "human being" subject to rejection and death, but he is also exalted by God and returns in triumph at the climax of human history. Thus, the "son of man" title, too, asserts the unique character of Jesus and his participation in the realm of the divine.

The Mission of Jesus

The Gospels also proclaim the unique character of Jesus and his God-given authority through their portrayal of Jesus's mission. In the Synoptic Gospels the keynote of Jesus's mission is his announcement of the imminent arrival of the "kingdom" or "reign" of God: "Now after John was arrested, Jesus came to Galilee, proclaiming the good news of God, and saying, 'The time is fulfilled and the kingdom of God has come near; repent and believe in the good news'" (see Mark 1:14–15 and parallels). The Greek word *basileia* can refer both to the realm of the king—thus "kingdom"— or to the rule exercised by the king, thus "reign." This term has its roots in Jewish biblical tradition. God is acclaimed as the true king or sovereign; the human kings of Israel such as David or Solomon and their successors in both Israel and Judah acted in God's stead and were expected to act justly and protect God's people, as God would. However, the Bible portrays the actual history of the monarchy as far less than successful—ultimately to be destroyed in a series of catastrophes, first by Assyria in the north and then by Babylon in the south, leading later after the return of Judah from exile in the sixth century to a sequence of domination under various regimes such as the Persians, Greeks, and Romans. The brief respite of Israelite self-rule under the Jewish Hasmonean Dynasty (c. 160–40 BC) would also end in corruption and chaos and lead to Roman rule that would remain in place until the Arab conquest in the seventh century AD.[15] In the century or two before Jesus, the moral and civil bankruptcy of the monarchy to achieve peace and security led to the motif of longing for the "reign of God" that would finally and decisively effect peace for the people.

Thus, the longing for the "kingdom" or "reign" of God was, in effect, a longing for God's own redeeming presence to be experienced in Israel. The Synoptic Gospels portray Jesus as the one who not only announces the coming kingdom of God, but through his healing and teaching inaugurates it. Jesus's healings of those desperately ill and his liberation of those under the grip of evil anticipate the full liberation associated with God's final rule. A saying found in both Matthew and Luke makes this explicit. When his opponents accuse Jesus of casting out demons by the power of Beelzebul, "the ruler of demons," Jesus replies, "But if it is by the Spirit of God that I cast out demons, then the kingdom of God has come to you" (Mt 12:28; see also Luke 11:20 who refers to the "finger of God"). Jesus's power to heal and to cast out evil—which from the vantage point of the Gospels' perspective is the same experience—plays a major role in Jesus's public ministry. Jesus's healing power "lifts away" or "liberates" those burdened by sickness and the threat of death (see, e.g., the vivid story of the woman bent double in Luke 13:10–17 whom Jesus "unties" from the power of Satan") and restores those isolated from the community such as the cleansing of the leper (see Mark 1:40–45) or the healing of the paralytic whose friends lower his pallet down into the room of the house where Jesus is preaching

---

[15] See Chapter 1.

(see Matt 9:2–8). Jesus's attention to the poor and the outcasts who experienced marginalization restores their rightful place in God's people and is a dominant motif of the Gospels. Jesus's parables such as the search for the lost sheep (Luke 15:1–7) or the opening of the banquet invitation to those in the "highways and by-ways" (Luke 14:15–24) make this point. As we will see, care for the poor and suffering becomes a major criterion for authentic discipleship.[16]

John's Gospel does not give much attention to the kingdom of God motif but includes Jesus's healings in his portrayal of Jesus's mission. John calls the healings of Jesus "signs" (the Greek word *semeion*) that reveal to the believing witnesses the God-given power of Jesus, the "Word incarnate" (see e.g., John 2:11; 4:54; 20:30–31).

Jesus's ministry of healing and care for the poor evokes memories of the great prophets Elijah and Elijah, who also were healers and feeders of the people. When Jesus asks the disciples, who do people say that I am, Peter notes that some think of Jesus as "Elijah" (Matt 16:14; see also Mark 8:28). The Gospels make clear that Jesus, who stands in the line of the great spirit-filled prophets of the Old Testament, nevertheless is greater than these.

The Gospels' portrayal of Jesus as healer and exorcist—and therefore the one who on behalf of God overcomes evil and restores God's people—complements his role as teacher whose words bring truth and vitality. Through his teaching, expressed in his parables and in the discourses of the Gospel, Jesus reveals God's mercy and calls men and women to a life of holiness and integrity. Thus, Jesus's teaching, like his healing power, redeems humanity. From the point of view of the Gospels, the entire mission of Jesus can be viewed as a restoration of God's people. His healings, his revelation of the truth about God and human destiny, his feeding of the multitudes— together represent an assault on the power of evil forecast in the temptation stories at the beginning of Jesus's mission (see Mark 1:12–13; Matt 4:1–11; Luke 4:1–13). Jesus is described more

---

[16] See Chapter 6.

than once as having "compassion" for the crowds (Matt 9:36) and declaring, as in Matt 10:5 and 14:24, "my mission is to the lost sheep of the house of Israel." In multiple ways, the Gospels affirm Jesus's teaching that the primary command of God is the love command— love of God and neighbor (see, e.g., Matt 22:34–40; John 15:12–17). Through his teaching, as John 3:16–17 affirmed, Jesus reveals a God of love.

Death and Resurrection

The death and resurrection of Jesus form the climax of all four Gospel narratives and are the ultimate claim to his unique identity and authority. As fully human, Jesus experiences death as all humans do. But Christian faith affirms that, through the power of God, Jesus overcame death and experienced the fullness of new life. This passage from death to life, first experienced in Jesus of Nazareth, is, again from the vantage point of Christian faith, the promised destiny for humanity.

As has been the case so often in our study, we encounter here the differences between a purely "historical" or "secular" point of view and the perspective of the community of faith. The vast majority of scholars, whether secular or not, affirm that the crucifixion of Jesus was a historical event. There is a vast literature on the question of the historical circumstances that led to Jesus's condemnation and crucifixion. Crucifixion was a form of Roman capital punishment, reserved in Roman practice for noncitizens, especially for violent criminals, rebellious slaves, vanquished enemies, and those who challenged Roman rule of law.[17] One of the explicit purposes of crucifixion was deterrence; death by crucifixion often was slow

---

[17] On the historical circumstances of crucifixion, see Martin Hengel, *Crucifixion in the Ancient World and the Folly of the Message of the Cross* (Philadelphia: Fortress, 1977); John Granger Cook, *Crucifixion in the Mediterranean World* (WUZNT 327; Tübingen: Mohr Siebeck, 2014).

and agonizing, exposed the condemned to public view, and consequently was considered a heinous and greatly feared form of death.

There is considerable debate about the historical circumstances that led to Jesus's condemnation and crucifixion. Most historians believe that under first-century Roman rule, Jewish authorities in Judea (the region of which Jerusalem was the capital) did not have the legal power to impose capital punishment. Therefore, the crucifixion of Jesus was a Roman decision, as, in fact, the Gospels affirm. A more challenging question is to what degree Jewish leaders collaborated in Jesus's condemnation. John's Gospel proposes a scenario that may reflect the complexities of the situation (see John 11:45–53). Alarmed by the public response to Jesus when crowds filled Jerusalem during the Passover festival and afraid of more widespread Roman intervention, the reigning high priest Caiaphas concludes that it was preferable "to have one man die for the people than to have the whole nation destroyed." Judea was under direct Roman rule, but there may have been an expectation that local rulers would help keep the peace.[18] At a time of rising tension between the Jews and their Roman overlords, the stirring of the crowds by Jesus's preaching and healings and his invocation of the coming reign of God could be perceived as a threat to public order on the part of the Romans, making them wary of Jesus as they were of other potential threats.

The Passion of Jesus

The religious viewpoints of the gospel writers were more concerned about the rejection of Jesus by the Jewish leaders than they were about the actions of the Roman authorities who were expected to be hostile. Reconciling the response of God's people Israel to the one whom Christian faith claimed as the promised Messiah was a

[18] See Raymond E. Brown, *The Death of the Messiah from Gethsemane to the Grave: A Commentary on the Passion Narratives in the Four Gospels.* Vol. 2 (New York: Doubleday, 1994), pp. 1419–1434.

much higher stakes question.[19] Thus, the Gospels track the growing hostility of the Jewish religious leaders to Jesus throughout his public ministry, with his arrival in Jerusalem and his challenges to the temple order as a breaking point in the view of the Synoptic Gospels (for John, Jesus's prophetic cleansing of the temple comes at the beginning of Jesus's mission). The paradoxical opposition to Jesus on the part of the people he came to save becomes one of the focal points of the Gospels, as the rejection of the prophets was a motif of the Old Testament. The Gospels of Luke and John ascribe the ultimate force leading to Jesus's condemnation as the very embodiment of evil, Satan, even though carried out through human agency; both Luke and John describe Satan "entering into Judas" (see Luke 22:3; John 13:27). In any case, the Gospels affirm in various ways the conviction that through his passion and crucifixion, Jesus experienced the raw reality of mortality and death, which, from the Bible's point of view, is the ultimate result of human sin.

Jesus's comportment during his sufferings fits this religious perspective. In Gethsemane on the eve of his death, Jesus prays for deliverance but, even more emphatically, affirms his faithfulness to God's will. At his preliminary hearing before the Jewish leaders, he is unjustly accused of threats against the Temple and in the trial before Pilate the Roman procurator, his opponents accuse him of rebellion, but in both instances, like the Suffering Servant of Isaiah's account, Jesus remains mostly silent. Luke's passion narrative emphasizes Jesus's exemplary behavior: forgiving his enemies and showing compassion to a fellow condemned criminal. In all Four Gospels Jesus's final words are a prayer: the first verse of Psalm 22 ("My God, my God, why have you forsaken me?") in Mark and Matthew; in Luke, Jesus prays Psalm 31 ("Father, into your hands I commend my spirit"); in John, Jesus declares that he has

---

[19] It should be noted that later Christian interpretation of Jewish responsibility became a prime cause for Christian anti-Semitism. No matter how the Gospels may be interpreted, it is completely illegitimate to assign collective guilt for the death of Jesus to the Jewish people.

completed his God-given mission of revealing God's love for the world ("It is finished"; 19:30; see 13:1).

Resurrection

While the crucifixion of Jesus represents an emphatic "no" to Jesus and his cause, the Gospels present his resurrection as God's thunderous "yes" to Jesus and his mission. This view of resurrection as the vindication of Jesus is found in some of the speeches of Peter, Paul, and Stephen in the Acts of the Apostles (see, e.g., Acts 2:36; 4:10–11). In the Gospels, the resurrection is portrayed both through the discovery of the empty tomb and through appearances of the Risen Jesus to his disciples. Mark's Gospel sets the pattern for the empty tomb tradition (see Mark 16:1–8). After the conclusion of the Jewish Sabbath, three women come to the tomb to anoint Jesus's body with spices in the manner of a proper Jewish burial (a burial had been done in haste two days earlier because of the impending Sabbath rest). They discover that the great stone sealing the entrance to the tomb has been rolled back and the tomb itself is empty. A heavenly messenger (described by Mark as a "young man dressed in a white robe") explains what has taken place: "Do not be alarmed; you are looking for Jesus of Nazareth, who was crucified. He has been raised; he is not here. Look, there is the place they laid him" (Mark 16:6). The women are instructed to tell the disciples that the Risen Christ has gone ahead of them to Galilee, where they will see him. The disciples who had abandoned him at the moment of his arrest and trial are to be reinstated in their mission through the initiative of the Risen Jesus. The other evangelists also include scenes of the discovery of the empty tomb, each with their own nuances. John, for example, has Mary Magdalene be the one to first discover the empty tomb and then alert Peter and the Beloved Disciple (see John 20:1–10).

The resurrection appearances referred to both in the Gospels and in Paul (see 1 Cor 15:1–11) are more important for the New Testament affirmation of the resurrection than the tradition about an empty tomb, which in itself can have an ambiguous meaning. Even in the accounts of Matthew and John, a possible alternate explanation is mentioned. In Matthew, the opponents of Jesus circulate the rumor that Jesus's own disciples came and took his body from the tomb (see Matt 27:62–66; 28:11–16), which, Matthew notes, was a false story still in circulation "to this day" (Matt 28:15). In John's account, Mary Magdalene speculates that the gardener of the place where Jesus's tomb was located had taken Jesus's body away (John 20:15). Only coupled with the resurrection appearances does the full meaning of the empty tomb strike home.

The original ending of Mark's Gospel refers to a future encounter between the Risen Jesus and his disciples but does not narrate it (see Mark 16:7). The other Gospels, however, describe various appearances, each with its own nuance. Matthew briefly notes the appearance of Jesus to the women who come to the tomb for the anointing (Matt 28:9–10) and in a climactic scene on a mountaintop where the Risen Christ appears to the "eleven" (absent Judas; Matt 28:16–20). Luke uniquely describes the appearance of Jesus to the two disciples on the road to Emmaus, where they ultimately recognize him "in the breaking of the bread" (Luke 24:13–35). When they return to Jerusalem, they learn from the other disciples that Jesus had already appeared to Simon Peter (Luke 24:34), and, at that moment, the Risen Jesus appears to the whole assembly of disciples (Luke 24:36–49). Luke's account concludes with the ascension of the Risen Jesus to heaven (Luke 24:50–53). In John, there are a series of encounters: first to Mary Magdalene outside Jesus's empty tomb (John 20:11–18), which she reports to the disciples. This is followed by an appearance of Jesus to the disciples who were gathered in a locked room "for fear of the Jews," and then a week later, another appearance which includes the encounter with Thomas who had been absent for the previous appearance and raised doubts about the disciples' testimony (John 20:26–29). John 21, which appears to be something of an appendix to the body of the Gospel, depicts a final appearance of the risen Jesus to his disciples at the Sea of

Galilee—a remarkable story in which Jesus prepares breakfast for the disciples (John 21:1–24).

As we noted earlier, another important testimony about appearances of the Risen Christ is found in Paul's First Letter to the Corinthians. He prefaces his explanation of the resurrection in response to the questions raised by some in Corinth by first recalling a series of resurrection appearances about which he had been informed:

> For I handed on to you as of first importance what I in turn had received: that Christ died for our sins in accordance with the scriptures, and that he was buried, and that he was raised on the third day in accordance with the scriptures, and that he appeared to Cephas, then to the twelve. Then he appeared to more than five hundred brothers and sisters at one time, most of whom are still alive, though some have died. Then he appeared to James, then to all the apostles. Last of all, as to one untimely born, he appeared also to me. For I am the least of the apostles, unfit to be called an apostle, because I persecuted the church of God. But by the grace of God I am what I am, and his grace toward me has not been in vain. On the contrary, I worked harder than any of them—though it was not I, but the grace of God that is with me. (1 Cor 15:3–10)

Several motifs run through these appearance stories. First, they testify to the victory of Christ over death; the Jesus who was crucified is now alive and present. Most of the stories emphasize continuity between the Risen Christ and the Jesus of Nazareth known to his disciples: in Luke's and John's accounts he shares food with the disciples (Luke 24:30, 41–43; John 21:9–14) and also shows them the wounds of his crucifixion (Luke 24:40; John 20:27). At the same time, the accounts acknowledge that resurrection is not "resuscitation"; Jesus does not simply return to the mode of his existence before his death but appears to be transformed into a new mode of life. The Risen Jesus appears and vanishes without warning (see, e.g., Matt 28:9 "suddenly"; Luke 24:31) and the witnesses at first do not recognize the Risen Jesus (Luke 24:16, 36–37; John 20:14, 26; 21:4).

Most of the resurrection accounts also include a commissioning of the disciples. The promised encounter of the Risen Jesus with his disciples in Mark's Gospel (16:7) implies that the bond between Jesus and his followers, broken through their desertion and Peter's denial, will be resumed. This is made explicit in Matthew's account of the appearance of the Risen Christ in Matt 28:16–20: the Risen and exalted Christ appears to his eleven apostles on a mountaintop in Galilee and commissions them to proclaim the gospel "to all nations." In Luke, as the Risen Christ ascends to heaven, he instructs the disciples to remain in Jerusalem for the promised Spirit who will propel them on their mission "to the ends of the earth," preparing for the outbreak of the early Christian mission to be described in the Acts of the Apostles (Luke 24:46–49; Acts 1:8). In the appearance story of John 20:19–23, the Risen Jesus commissions the disciples, "As the Father has sent me, so I send you" (a commission already anticipated in John 17:18). In the evocative story of Jesus's appearance to the disciples over breakfast on the shore of the Sea of Galilee, Jesus draws from Peter, who had denied his master, a threefold confession of his love and commands him to "feed my lambs," "tend my sheep" (John 21:15–19).

Finally, the resurrection of Jesus is portrayed in the New Testament in general as a turning point in human history. The Jewish roots of "resurrection" already bear this imprint; the resurrection of the just was understood by many Jews at the time of Jesus as an event that would mark the final day of the Lord, the culmination of human history. Matthew's Gospel moves in this direction by noting cosmic signs anticipated for the end time taking place at the moment of Jesus's death and resurrection: the dramatic tearing of the temple veil, the earthquake, the splitting of the rocks and opening of the graves, and the resurrection of the "holy ones" at the moment of Jesus's death (Matt 27:51–53), along with an "earthquake" and the presence of "an angel of the Lord" whose appearance "was like lightening, and his clothing white as snow" accompanying the moment of Jesus's resurrection (Matt 28:2–3). As we will note, Paul, too, sees the death and resurrection of Jesus as the advent of the new "Adam" who reverses the sentence of death inflicted on humanity by the sin of the first Adam (see Rom 5:15–21).[20] For the First Letter of Peter, the resurrection of Jesus gives humanity a "new birth into a living hope" (1 Pet 1:3), a definitive revelation ". . . into which angels long to look!" (1 Pet 1:12). From the perspective of the New Testament, history continues but now in a new mode, with the radical power of death broken and the future salvation of humanity secured.

More than any other set of events portrayed in the gospel narratives, the resurrection of Jesus, as the ultimate triumph over death, seals the New Testament affirmation of Jesus's unique identity and his inherent holiness and sacred character. From the Gospel of John's cosmic perspective, the death and resurrection are the final "exaltation of Jesus" and his triumphant return to his Father. In predicting the death and resurrection of Jesus, John's Gospel draws on the haunting symbolism of the "lifting up of the serpent" by Moses in the story of Numbers 21:1–9. In punishment for the people's rebellion and sin during their desert trek, God had sent a plague of poisonous serpents to inflict them. Moses pleads with God for their deliverance and his prayer prevails. God instructs Moses to "lift up" on a pole a bronze image of the very serpents that torment them and, if they gaze on that image, God promises to heal them. Three times in the Gospel, Jesus himself speaks of his impending death and resurrection as a "lifting up" in the manner of Moses's lifting up the serpent in the desert as a paradoxical sign of healing (see John 3:14; 8:28; 12:32). So, too, the Gospel of John affirms in its unique way the deep conviction of the entire New

---

[20] See Chapter 5.

Testament that the death and resurrection reveal both Jesus's divine power to heal and his status as the unique Son of God.

Conclusion

Even a partial survey of the Four Gospels illustrates their profound description of Jesus as one whose origin is in God and whose very being embodies the divine presence. Jesus's life and mission, including its climactic expression in his death and resurrection, define what it means to be holy and sacred. We have considered some of the multiple ways in which the evangelists build that portrait of Jesus's sacred character: his origin in the very life of God; the profound connection of Jesus with the promises of the Old Testament Scriptures; the depth of Jesus's intimacy with God; the profusion of religious titles ascribed to Jesus in a new mode; the power of his teaching and healing; and, above all, the climax of Jesus's triumph over death as a turning point in human history. Through the teaching and example of Jesus encountered in the Gospels, those who believe in him find their purpose and destiny.

This, of course, expressed the Christian convictions of the evangelists and those followers of Jesus who view the Gospels as "the word of God." Here we rejoin the dual perspective that we have acknowledged throughout our study of the New Testament as a "sacred text." Those who view the Gospels from a "secular" or an exclusively historical or literary perspective can also describe these same affirmations that the Gospels make about the unique identity of Jesus. But the gospel texts would not be viewed as having any inherent moral or religious authority in themselves.

Similarly, someone who personally affirms the religious authority of the biblical texts is also able to explore the historical and literary contexts in which the Gospels were composed, as well as search for what we can know about the historical circumstances of first-century Palestinian Judaism in which Jesus lived. The challenge for a scholar who is part of the community of faith is to square the theologically charged portrayal of Jesus in the Gospels with what we can know of the historical circumstances of Jesus's life. The assumption is that already inherent in the very being of the historical Jesus and his impact on his first followers were unique characteristics of holiness and charismatic power of healing and authoritative teaching that would, in the light of the resurrection and through the inspiration of the Spirit, lead to the full theological portrayals found in the post-Easter Gospels and other writings of the New Testament.

5

Jesus and Paul

Because they proclaim Jesus as the embodiment of the divine presence and the source of authentic holiness, the Four Gospels are a major reason why the New Testament is considered "sacred" by Christians. Through the Gospels, the believing Christian encounters the person of the Risen Christ who embodies that sacred reality. The same is true of the writings of Paul the Apostle, although in a manner quite different from the narrative format of the Gospels. As we noted earlier, Paul's letters form a substantial part of the New Testament writings.[1] Combined with the attention to Paul in Luke's Acts of the Apostles, the apostle stands as a colossus on the New Testament landscape.

Interest in Paul continues to absorb modern biblical scholarship. What precisely were the circumstances that prompted Paul to move from being a persecutor of Jesus's followers to an ardent proponent of the gospel?[2] Why did Paul from the outset feel compelled to proclaim Christ to the Gentile world? What was the nature of Paul's relationship with his Jewish heritage? To what degree was his theology influenced by Judaism or by Greco-Roman philosophy? What is the chronology of his life and the occasions and motivation for writing his letters? How were his letters composed and circulated to various Christian communities? These and many other such questions command the attention of contemporary Pauline studies.[3]

---

[1] See Chapter 3.

[2] Note that the term "gospel" can refer to the entirety of the Christian message as proclaimed by Paul and others as it does here, or to the written "Gospels," namely the four narratives that tell the story of Jesus.

[3] See, for example, the works of James D. G. Dunn, *The Theology of Paul the Apostle* (Grand Rapids, MI: Eerdmans, 1998); Michael J. Gorman, *Apostle of the Crucified*

The New Testament. Donald Senior, Oxford University Press. © Oxford University Press 2022.
DOI: 10.1093/oso/9780197530832.003.0006

Here, too, as has been the case throughout our study, there is an understandable divergence between those who analyze the Pauline writings from a purely historical or "secular" viewpoint and those who engage the apostle's writing from the perspective of Christian faith. Many scholars working from an exclusively historical approach stress the "discontinuity" between the exalted Christ figure who is the central focus of Paul's writings and the presumed historical reality of the first-century Galilean Jew, Jesus of Nazareth. For many, Paul should be considered the "second founder" of Christianity, one whose dramatic portrayal of Jesus as a divinely exalted figure and savior of the world completely transformed the historical reality of who Jesus actually was and laid the foundation for Christianity as a world religion. Those who also view Paul's writings as an essential part of the New Testament and therefore as sacred find in Paul an inspired grasp of the profound identity of Jesus of Nazareth, crucified and risen, and consequently view him as a privileged guide to authentic Christian life. From this viewpoint, Paul is not the "second Founder" of Christianity but one who was able to articulate for posterity the profound identity, God-given mission, and enduring significance of the First and only Founder, Jesus himself. In Paul's writings, as in the Gospels, the believing reader can encounter the sacred.

Paul's Biography

The basic components of Paul's life can be deduced both from his own letters and from corroborating details in the Acts of the Apostles. Paul himself notes his deep roots in Judaism, as he informs the Philippians, one "circumcised on the eighth day, a

---

Lord: A Theological Introduction to Paul & His Letters (Grand Rapids, MI: Eerdmans, 2nd ed., 2017); Udo Schnelle, Apostle Paul: His Life and Theology (Grand Rapids, MI: Baker Academic, 2005); Michael Wolter, Paul: An Outline of His Theology (Waco, TX: Baylor University Press, 2015).

member of the people Israel, of the tribe of Benjamin, a Hebrew born of Hebrews, as to the law, a Pharisee; as to zeal, a persecutor of the church; as to righteousness under the law, blameless" (Phil 3:5–6). Acts spells out the "zeal" Paul refers to, portraying him as a relentless persecutor of the early followers of Jesus and someone who, even as a young man, approved the execution of Stephen, the first Christian martyr (see Acts 8:1–3), a history that would continue to be an embarrassment for Paul in his later life. In Gal 1:13, Paul speaks bluntly of his former attitude: "You have heard, no doubt, of my earlier life in Judaism. I was violently persecuting the church of God and was trying to destroy it" (see also 1 Cor 15:9, "For I am the least of the apostles, unfit to be called an apostle, because I persecuted the church of God"). But, as both Paul and Luke testify, Paul would experience a profound change of heart due to a visionary encounter with the Risen Christ (see Acts 9:1–30; Gal 1:13–24)—an event, as we will note later, caused Paul to profoundly rethink his understanding of God and the dynamics of God's relationship to the world.

Although Paul traces his call to be "the apostle to the Gentiles" to his first encounter with the Risen Christ, his missionary work took some time to get on track. After spending some time in Damascus and the surrounding region of Arabia and a brief but somewhat tense visit to the leaders of the church in Jerusalem, Paul went back to his hometown of Tarsus in southern Asia Minor (Gal 1:18–2:10). According to Acts, it was Barnabas, a revered figure in the Jerusalem church, who retrieved Paul from Tarsus and brought him to Antioch (Acts 11:25–26). In this major city, the third largest in the Roman Empire at that time, there was already a community of both Jewish and Gentile Christians. Paul no doubt experienced among these Christians a deeper formation as a follower of Jesus. The presence of both Jews and Gentiles in the Christian community of Antioch probably also strengthened Paul's commitment to bring the gospel to the Gentile world.

After a year or so in Antioch, the community there commissioned Paul and Barnabas to set out on their first missionary journey, first to Cyprus and then into the heart of Asia Minor (Acts 13). Paul and his companions seemed to have followed a typical pattern when entering a new town or region. They would go first to a local synagogue and proclaim the gospel message to the congregation—a congregation often composed not only of Jews but also with some Gentile "Godfearers" who admired Judaism but did not choose to become full proselytes (the centurion in Luke 7:1–10 seems to be such a person; also Paul refers to those, who along with the children of Abraham, "fear God"; see Acts 13:11, 26). Often Paul's preaching would lead to a division of the house—some Jews and god fearers accepting his message and others taking offense at it, in some instances leading to conflict and violence. Thus developed a pattern of rejection and suffering that Paul would later incorporate into his desire to be like his crucified master.

For the next several years, Paul and his fellow missionaries (Paul never seems to have traveled alone) would travel throughout Asia Minor, Macedonia, and Achaia proclaiming the gospel message and founding local communities of Christians. Some estimate that Paul may have traveled some 10,000 miles on foot, on the sea, and perhaps occasionally on horseback or on a donkey in the pursuit of his mission. Acts traces the westward movement of Paul, from the first foray into south central Asia Minor (Acts 13), then a second journey further west that would, under divine inspiration, bring him to Macedonia (Acts 15–16), with important stops at Philippi, Thessalonica, and Berea. After another outbreak of opposition, Paul moved south to Athens, then to Corinth, and ultimately to the major city of Ephesus on the west cost of Asia Minor. A third and final missionary journey would have Paul revisit several of these communities before undertaking his final and fateful voyage to Jerusalem (Acts 18–22). There, according to Acts, a disturbance by Paul's opponents in the Jerusalem temple would lead to his being put under protective custody by Roman authorities and taken to confinement in Caesarea Maritima, the coastal city that was the seat of Roman governance in Judea. After two years, Paul's appeal as a Roman citizen to have his case heard in the imperial capital would bring him in Roman custody by ship on a dramatic sea voyage to Malta and then Italy and finally to Rome where Acts leaves Paul under house arrest (Acts 28:11–31). Acts concludes with Paul confined in Rome yet still evangelizing both Jews and Gentiles. It is presumed that sometime after this, Paul was martyred in Rome, probably under the Emperor Nero (c. 64–68 AD).

As we noted earlier, Paul's commitment to keeping in contact with the various Christian communities he had evangelized would lead to the composition of his various letters (with the exception of Rome, which Paul had not evangelized or yet visited). The circumstances of each community, the questions and concerns they raised, and Paul's reflections on his own Christian experience would shape the content and spirit of these pastoral letters. And it is from these that one must attempt to stitch together Paul's overall theological perspective. This is certainly the case with those letters that are undisputedly authored by Paul himself: Romans, 1 & 2 Corinthians, Galatians, Philippians, 1 Thessalonians, and Philemon (the latter addressed to a leader of a local house church rather than directly to a community).[4]

Paul's Theology

Our goal here is not to attempt a synthesis of Paul's entire robust and challenging theology, but to focus primarily on his portrayal of the figure of Jesus as the ultimate warrant for the sacred character of his writings. Paul's perspective was shaped by multiple factors: his

---

[4] As noted previously, there is some debate whether Paul himself or a later disciple of Paul writing in his name composed Ephesians, Colossians, 2 Thessalonians, and the Pastoral Letters of I & II Timothy and Titus. We will consider the content of these letters to Paul's overall theology later.

strong Jewish faith and the Old Testament scriptures, his absorption of the Greco-Roman culture of the world in which he lived and was educated, his formation as a Christian, and the experience and problems of the Christian communities with which he was engaged. There is no doubt that having to wrestle with the questions and problems of his fellow Christians deepened Paul's own reflection and understanding of what faith in Christ meant. But, above all, Paul's profound spiritual relationship with Jesus Christ was the defining factor for the apostle's theology.

The Starting Point: Paul's Inaugural Experience

Where should we start in sketching Paul's theology? Perhaps the best way to enter into Paul's Christology is to begin with his inaugural experience—his encounter with the Risen Christ. In emphasizing for the community of Galatia his credentials as an apostle, that is where Paul himself begins: "I want you to know, brothers and sisters, that the gospel that was proclaimed by me is not of human origin; for I did not receive it from a human source, nor was I taught it, but I received it through a revelation of Jesus Christ" (Gal 1:11–12). By a "revelation of Jesus Christ" Paul refers to his visionary encounter with Christ narrated both in Acts and by Paul himself in at least two of his letters (Gal 1:15–16; 1 Cor 15:8). The Greek word Paul uses for this "revelation" is *apokalypsis*, implying some kind of revelation coming from an outside source rather than a deduction coming from Paul's own reflections. In Acts that encounter is described by Luke in dramatic fashion (see Acts 9:1–18). Paul, as Luke vividly describes, "breathing threats and murder against the disciples," is on his way to Damascus, authorized by the High Priest in Jerusalem and the leader of the Synagogue in Damascus to arrest Christians and bring them back to Jerusalem. On the way, he is stunned by a vision of the Risen Christ and thrown to the ground. Jesus challenges Paul, "Saul, Saul, why do you persecute me?" Blind and disoriented, Paul is sent to Damascus, where the Lord had already instructed Ananias, a Christian, to heal Paul. Ananias is hesitant, given Paul's reputation: "Lord, I have heard from many about this man, how much evil he has done to your saints in Jerusalem; and here he has authority from the chief priests to bind all who invoke your name." In response, the Lord reveals Paul's destiny: "Go, for he is an instrument whom I have chosen to bring my name before Gentiles and kings and before the people Israel; I myself will show him how much he must suffer for the sake of my name."

Paul is healed when Ananias lays his hands on him, both a gesture of healing and a sign of his commissioning as an apostle. Paul himself springs into action. After staying a few days with the disciples in Damascus, Luke notes that Paul "immediately . . . began to proclaim Jesus in the synagogues, saying, 'He is the Son of God'" (Acts 9:19–20). Controversy follows Paul throughout Acts and it begins here; his Jewish opponents threaten his life and Paul must escape from Damascus somewhat ignominiously, lowered down in a basket through a hole in the city wall. Shortly after, Paul goes to Jerusalem, where the Christians there remain fearful of him until Barnabas tells the marvelous account of his conversion. Later, Paul's zealous preaching about Jesus causes some of the "Hellenists" (that is, Greek-speaking Jews) to react violently, so the members of the Jerusalem church send him off to safety in his hometown of Tarsus in southern Asia Minor (Acts 19:20–30).

This dramatic account of Paul's conversion contrasts with Paul's own reflections on his inaugural experience in his Letter to the Galatians (see Gal 1:11–24). Paul is frustrated with the Galatian community because they apparently have been persuaded by some Jewish Christians who came to their community after Paul's visit and claimed that a Gentile must first become a Jewish proselyte (i.e., accepting circumcision for men; adopting a kosher diet, etc.) before one could be a follower of Jesus. This was a position Paul rejected—believing that through faith in Christ, Gentiles had full access to Christian discipleship on a par with Jewish Christians. To bolster his response in his letter, Paul begins by asserting his apostolic credentials. His role and authority as an apostle of Jesus Christ came from a direct encounter with the Risen Christ, as the account in the Acts of the Apostles also claims.

But Paul's own reflection on that definitive moment has a much different tone than the drama in Acts about the encounter on the way to Damascus. In Galatians, Paul begins by confessing his former role as a persecutor of the church (corroborating the view of Acts): "You have heard, no doubt, of my earlier life in Judaism. I was violently persecuting the church of God and was trying to destroy it. I advanced in Judaism beyond many among my people of the same age, for I was far more zealous for the traditions of my ancestors" (Gal 1:13–14). Paul describes his turning point as a "call" from God:

> But when God, who had set me apart before I was born and called me through his grace, was pleased to reveal his Son to me, so that I might proclaim him among the Gentiles, I did not confer with any human being, nor did I go up to Jerusalem to those who were already apostles before me, but I went away at once into Arabia, and afterwards I returned to Damascus. (Gal 1:15–17)

There are several striking features in Paul's description of this experience. In speaking of God who "had set me apart before I was born," Paul may be alluding to the way the Old Testament figures, Jeremiah and Isaiah, spoke of their prophetic vocations. Jeremiah speaks of his prophetic destiny as a primordial call from God: "Before I formed you in the womb I knew you, and before you were born I consecrated you; I appointed you a prophet to the nations" (Jer 1:4–5). Isaiah, too, speaks of a prophetic call before he was born: "The Lord called me before I was born, while I was in my mother's womb he named me . . ." (Isa 49:1, 5). In both of these Old Testament passages, the universal horizon of their prophetic missions is stated: Jeremiah is appointed to be a "prophet to the nations" and in Isaiah, God also expands the horizon of the prophet's mission: "It is too light a thing that you should be my servant to raise up the tribes of Jacob and to restore the survivors of Israel; I will give you as a light to the nations, that my salvation may reach to the end of the earth" (Isa 49:6). In Galatians, Paul, too, traces his call to go to the Gentiles to the very moment of his call from God: "God . . . was pleased to reveal his Son to me, so that I might proclaim him among the Gentiles" (Gal 1:15).

Notice, too, that Paul describes this experience with the same word used in Acts: "God . . . was pleased to reveal (*apokalypsai*) his Son to me." In both instances Paul refers to this "revelation" as a unique experience breaking in on him from the outside. In Paul's listing of resurrection appearances in 1 Cor 15:3–11, he notes that he was the last in line but that the Risen Christ also "was seen" or "appeared" to him. Here Paul uses the passive voice of the verb "to see," stressing that his encounter with the Risen Christ was an experience that originated with God and not from Paul's own musings.

Luke and Paul himself describe this inaugural encounter with the Risen Christ in different literary modes. Luke's account emphasizes a sharp and rapid turn in Paul's experience, from being an overly zealous persecutor of Jesus's followers to becoming an ardent proclaimer of the gospel. Paul's own reflection in Galatians on this moment describes it as a "call" or vocation, an awakening of a God-given destiny that was his from the first moment of his existence. Nevertheless, there are important convergences in the two accounts. Both are triggered by an encounter or "revelation" of the Risen Jesus that profoundly effects Paul, changing in dramatic fashion the trajectory of his life and thought. Both Luke and Paul himself trace the beginning of his vocation as an apostle to the Gentiles to this very moment. Paul did not gradually take on this role later in his Christian experience, even if he did in fact learn more about what was entailed. But from the very outset, Paul reminds the Galatians, he was called by God to preach the gospel to Gentiles (as well as Jews).

Equally important is the fact that Paul apparently had not met Jesus of Nazareth in person; his first encounter is with the Risen Jesus who has triumphed over death, death by crucifixion. The "surprise" for Paul was not the possibility of resurrection—as a Pharisee (see Phil 3:5) Paul would believe that at the final judgment, God would raise the just who had died to a new life, a common conviction of the Pharisee party (see, e.g., Act 23:6–10, where Luke notes that the Pharisees, contrary to the Sadducees, another major faction, believed in resurrection). What was confounding for Paul must have been the realization that the Risen Christ was also the *crucified* Christ. How could one who was a condemned criminal, a threat to public order, an agitator who had endangered the Jewish Passover pilgrims by his actions in the Temple, one who suffered the most ignominious form of capital punishment and hung on a cross naked for all to witness—how could this one be the Chosen of God, the Messiah, the beloved Son of God claimed by Christian faith?

The fundamental reality of a Crucified and Risen Christ—a reality that now because of his own experience he could not deny—is what would transform Paul in a radical way. This awareness of God working through the Crucified and Risen Christ permeates all of Paul's letters and is the fundamental key to his theology. This would lead Paul, not to reject his religious heritage, but to view it in a new way. Paul was confronted with the paradox of how the God of Israel works in the world—in a way far different from human calculation. God does not use overwhelming power to make his presence felt but works through what humans often calculate as "weakness": acts of selfless service, a spirit of reconciliation and forgiveness, giving one's life for the sake of others. Paul wrestles with this "divine logic" in the opening chapter of his First Letter to the Corinthians. Learning that some of the house churches in Corinth were quarreling with each other, Paul turns to his proclamation of the crucified Christ: "For Jews demand signs and Greeks desire wisdom, but we proclaim Christ crucified, a stumbling block to Jews and foolishness to Gentiles, but to those who are called, both Jews and Greeks, Christ the power of God and the wisdom of God. For God's foolishness is wiser than human wisdom, and God's weakness is stronger than human strength" (1 Cor 1:22–25).

While this profound realization is a turning point for Paul, it was also not without continuity with the God of the Hebrew Scriptures, the God Paul the Jew worshipped all his life. The awesome God of Israel also embraced the poor and the outcasts with a particular love. As Deuteronomy reminded Israel, its choice as God's people was not because of its prowess or accomplishments but because it was "the least" of nations (Deut 7:7). A constant motif running through the Scriptures is that God favors the "widow, the orphan, and the stranger"—each representative of the vulnerable and powerless people that God cares for. Thus, the realization that God would work through a crucified and powerless Messiah as judged by human standards already had echoes in the Old Testament.

Paul and the Crucified Christ

One of the most evident consequences for Paul of his visionary inaugural encounter was an intense and lifelong spiritual relationship with Jesus Christ. This relationship became the center and driving force of his life. A couple of quotations from his letters illustrate this. In writing to the church at Philippi, a community that Paul evidently favored, the apostle considers his relationship with Christ more precious than anything else in his life, even his deep and lasting bond with his Jewish heritage:

> Yet whatever gains I had, these I have come to regard as loss because of Christ. More than that, I regard everything as loss because of the surpassing value of knowing Christ Jesus my Lord. For his sake I have suffered the loss of all things, and I regard them as rubbish, in order that I may gain Christ and be found in him, not having a righteousness of my own that comes from the

law, but one that comes through faith in Christ, the righteousness from God based on faith. I want to know Christ and the power of his resurrection and the sharing of his sufferings by becoming like him in his death, if somehow I may attain the resurrection from the dead. (Phil 3:7–11)

Paul continues by affirming that growing in his relationship with Christ is the goal of his entire life, and he urges his fellow Christians at Philippi to do likewise. Paul was not hesitant in asserting that his own spiritual life should become the pattern for the lives of those he addresses in his letters, as in 1 Cor 11:1, where he tells the Corinthians, "Be imitators of me as I am of Christ." Such exhortations no doubt were one of the major reasons Paul's letters were treasured by subsequent Christian communities.

Not that I have already obtained this or have already reached the goal; but I press on to make it my own, because Christ Jesus has made me his own. Beloved, I do not consider that I have made it my own; but this one thing I do: forgetting what lies behind and straining forward to what lies ahead, I press on toward the goal for the prize of the heavenly call of God in Christ Jesus. Let those of us then who are mature be of the same mind; and if you think differently about anything, this too God will reveal to you. Only let us hold fast to what we have attained. Brothers and sisters, join in imitating me, and observe those who live according to the example you have in us. For many live as enemies of the cross of Christ; I have often told you of them, and now I tell you even with tears. Their end is destruction; their god is the belly; and their glory is in their shame; their minds are set on earthly things. But our citizenship is in heaven, and it is from there that we are expecting a Savior, the Lord Jesus Christ. He will transform the body of our humiliation that it may be conformed to the body of his glory, by the power that also enables him to make all things subject to himself. Therefore, my brothers and sisters, whom I love and long for, my joy and crown, stand firm in the Lord in this way, my beloved. (Phil 3:12–4:1)

Paul's ardent love for Christ is evident in these passages from the Letter to the Philippians. Every other aspect of his life he considers "rubbish" compared to his relationship with Jesus Christ. Throughout his letters Paul uses a phrase that captures the intensity of this relationship for him. He speaks of being "in Christ," of being immersed in Christ, or of Christ being "in him" over 170 times in his letters. A famous passage from his Letter to the Galatians reflects this: "I have been crucified with Christ; and it is no longer I who live, but it is Christ who lives in me. And the life I now live in the flesh I live by faith in the Son of God, who loved me and gave himself for me" (Gal 2:19–20).

Paul's relationship with Christ was not generic but had a specific content and meaning. For Paul, as with the entire New Testament, the heart of Jesus's mission was revealed, paradoxically, in his death and resurrection. The condemnation that led to the death of Jesus was the outcome of his mission of healing, of confrontation with evil, of his association with those on the margins, and his bold proclamation of the "reign of God." As we noted earlier, the crucifixion of Jesus was an emphatic "no" to him and his cause on the part of those who condemned him, but, from the perspective of the New Testament, through the power of God Jesus was liberated from death and exalted to the right hand of God.[5] Because Christian faith viewed Jesus as the Messiah and the Son of God, the destiny of Jesus in overpowering the force of death revealed the destiny of all humanity.

For Paul, then, being in an intense relationship with the Crucified and Risen Christ meant that Paul, too, would experience dying and rising. He would share in the experience of Christ by being united with him. Through faith in Jesus and by the experience of baptism,

[5] See earlier Chapter 4 on Jesus and the Gospels.

Paul believed that Christians were radically liberated from death and destined for life with God. Paul speaks eloquently of this in his Letter to the Romans:

For while we were still weak, at the right time Christ died for the ungodly. Indeed, rarely will anyone die for a righteous person—though perhaps for a good person someone might actually dare to die. But God proves his love for us in that while we still were sinners Christ died for us. Much more surely then, now that we have been justified by his blood, will we be saved through him from the wrath of God. For if while we were enemies, we were reconciled to God through the death of his Son, much more surely, having been reconciled, will we be saved by his life. (Rom 5:8–10)

Paul follows this passage with his extended comparison between Adam, the first human ancestor as presented in Genesis, and Jesus, the "new" Adam representative of a redeemed and transformed humanity. Through the sin of Adam, a heritage of sin and mortality burdens all subsequent human generations. But through the death and resurrection of Jesus, the "Second Adam," that is, the new representative human being and Son of God, the heritage of sin and death is definitively broken.

Paul returns to this fundamental dynamic in his relationship to the crucified and Risen Christ in a later passage in Romans:

Therefore we have been buried with him by baptism into death, so that, just as Christ was raised from the dead by the glory of the Father, so we too might walk in newness of life. For if we have been united with him in a death like his, we will certainly be united with him in a resurrection like his. We know that our old self was crucified with him so that the body of sin might be destroyed, and we might no longer be enslaved to sin. For whoever has died is freed from sin. But if we have died with Christ, we believe that we will also live with him. We know that Christ, being raised from the dead, will never die again; death no longer has dominion over him. The death he died, he died to sin, once for all; but the life he lives, he lives to God. So you also must consider yourselves dead to sin and alive to God in Christ Jesus. (Rom 6:5–11)

For Paul, the ultimate basis for hope was the enduring love of God revealed through the death of Jesus "for us" and his triumph over death.

Paul's View of History

Paul's conviction that God was saving the world through the death and resurrection of Jesus Christ was the lens through which the apostle viewed all of reality—not only his own personal destiny but that of the world itself. Implicit in Paul's writings is a view of history drawn from the Jewish Scriptures but now centered on Christ. The account of human origins portrayed in Genesis marks the starting point for Paul: God's creation of the universe, with the formation of the human being, male and female, at its apex. The human is unique because alone among the creatures God fashioned, the human is created "in the image and likeness" of God (Gen 1:26), able to respond to God in love and also having responsibility for creation itself. The idyllic beginning of human history takes a tragic turn with the sin of Adam and Eve and introduces a heritage of violence and alienation, spelled out in the stories of the expulsion of Adam and Eve from the Garden of Eden, the fratricide of Cain against his brother Abel, and climaxing in the flood that threatens to destroy all of creation. God relents because of Noah's innocence and God initiates a covenant with Noah and humanity, promising to restore the world and to never destroy creation again.

This basic account sets the stage for Paul's view of history. In the opening chapters of his Letter to the Romans, Paul describes the lingering plight of humanity. Gentiles could have found God in the beauty of the natural world, but their vision was clouded by the legacy of sin (see Rom 1:18–25). God's chosen people, the Jews, were blessed by the gift of the Law God entrusted to Moses. The law gave the Jews moral awareness of God's will but for them, too, the power of sin prevented them from true obedience to God's law. The end result is that all of humanity—both Gentile and Jew—is in the grip of sin: "What then? Are we (i.e., the Jews) better off? No, not at all; for we have already charged that all, both Jews and Greeks, are under the power of sin . . ." (Rom 3:9).

"Sin" for Paul was not confined to individual immoral actions but was conceived of as a "power," a legacy of infidelity, injustice, and violence that holds all humanity in its grip. Paul's famous soliloquy in Romans 7 illustrates this point:

> For we know that the law is spiritual; but I am of the flesh, sold into slavery under sin. I do not understand my own actions. For I do not do what I want, but I do the very thing I hate. Now if I do what I do not want, I agree that the law is good. But in fact it is no longer I that do it, but sin that dwells within me. For I know that nothing good dwells within me, that is, in my flesh. I can will what is right, but I cannot do it. For I do not do the good I want, but the evil I do not want is what I do. Now if I do what I do not want, it is no longer I that do it, but sin that dwells within me. So I find it to be a law that when I want to do what is good, evil lies close at hand. For I delight in the law of God in my inmost self, but I see in my members another law at war with the law of my mind, making me captive to the law of sin that dwells in my members. Wretched man that I am! Who will rescue me from this body of death? Thanks be to God through Jesus Christ our Lord! So then, with my mind I am a slave to the law of God, but with my flesh I am a slave to the law of sin. (Rom 7:14–25)

Paul speaks here not in autobiographical terms about his own experience as such but as a spokesperson for all humanity that finds itself under the power of sin and unable to break free.

For Paul, the turning point in this history of sin's domination of humanity comes with the death and resurrection of Jesus Christ. Jesus experiences the withering power of death but through the power of God breaks the grip of death and becomes the pattern of the movement from death to life for all who believe in him. Paul's comparison of the two "Adams" elaborated in Romans makes this point:

> Therefore, just as sin came into the world through one man, and death came through sin, and so death spread to all because all have sinned . . . —sin was indeed in the world before the law, but sin is not reckoned when there is no law. Yet death exercised dominion from Adam to Moses, even over those whose sins were not like the transgression of Adam, who is a type of the one who was to come. But the free gift is not like the trespass. For if the many died through the one man's trespass, much more surely have the grace of God and the free gift in the grace of the one man, Jesus Christ, abounded for the many. And the free gift is not like the effect of the one man's sin. For the judgment following one trespass brought condemnation, but the free gift following many trespasses brings justification. If, because of the one man's trespass, death exercised dominion through that one, much more surely will those who receive the abundance of grace and the free gift of righteousness exercise dominion in life through the one man, Jesus Christ. Therefore just as one man's trespass led to condemnation for all, so one man's act of righteousness leads to justification and life for all. For just as by the one man's disobedience the many were made sinners, so by the one man's obedience the many will be made righteous. (Rom 5:12–19)

The liberation from the grip of sin and death effected through the death and resurrection of Jesus also sets the pattern for the future of humanity. Paul's vision of the future is eloquently stated in chapter 8 of Romans. Paul foresees that the power of God's Spirit unleashed in the world through the death and resurrection will ultimately lead to the full redemption of all creation. This extended vision of the future comes as the summit of Paul's review of human history—its plight because of sin and its liberation through the death and resurrection of Christ:

If the Spirit of him who raised Jesus from the dead dwells in you, he who raised Christ from the dead will give life to your mortal bodies also through his Spirit that dwells in you. So then, brothers and sisters, we are debtors, not to the flesh, to live according to the flesh—for if you live according to the flesh, you will die; but if by the Spirit you put to death the deeds of the body, you will live. For all who are led by the Spirit of God are children of God. For you did not receive a spirit of slavery to fall back into fear, but you have received a spirit of adoption. When we cry, "Abba! Father!" it is that very Spirit bearing witness with our spirit that we are children of God, and if children, then heirs, heirs of God and joint heirs with Christ—if, in fact, we suffer with him so that we may also be glorified with him. I consider that the sufferings of this present time are not worth comparing with the glory about to be revealed to us. For the creation waits with eager longing for the revealing of the children of God; for the creation was subjected to futility, not of its own will but by the will of the one who subjected it, in hope that the creation itself will be set free from its bondage to decay and will obtain the freedom of the glory of the children of God. We know that the whole creation has been groaning in labor pains until now; and not only the creation, but we ourselves, who have the first fruits of the Spirit, groan inwardly while we wait for adoption, the redemption of our bodies . . .

We know that all things work together for good for those who love God, who are called according to his purpose. For those whom he foreknew he also predestined to be conformed to the image of his Son, in order that he might be the firstborn within a large family. And those whom he predestined he also called; and those whom he called he also justified; and those whom he justified he also glorified. What then are we to say about these things? If God is for us, who is against us? He who did not withhold his own Son, but gave him up for all of us, will he not with him also give us everything else? Who will bring any charge against God's elect? It is God who justifies. Who is to condemn? It is Christ Jesus, who died, yes, who was raised, who is at the right hand of God, who indeed intercedes for us. Who will separate us from the love of Christ? Will hardship, or distress, or persecution, or famine, or nakedness, or peril, or sword? As it is written, "For your sake we are being killed all day long; we are accounted as sheep to be slaughtered." No, in all these things we are more than conquerors through him who loved us. For I am convinced that neither death, nor life, nor angels, nor rulers, nor things present, nor things to come, nor powers, nor height, nor depth, nor anything else in all creation, will be able to separate us from the love of God in Christ Jesus our Lord. (Rom 8:11–39)

Thus, the pattern of Jesus's own destiny—through the power of God overcoming death and transformed into abundant and everlasting life—becomes the pattern for the ultimate future of those who believe in him. Humanity now lives "in the meantime"—that is, between the radical experience of being set free from the power of sin and the enjoyment of full life in the future with God. The residue of sin's power in the world causes lingering struggle and the need for moral vigilance, but, in Paul's view, the fundamental issue is settled.

The Fate of Israel

For Paul, the gathering of the nations to Christ belongs to this "meantime"; this is the very purpose and urgency of his own God-given commission from the first moment he encountered the Risen Christ (see his deduction in Rom 10:14–17). The will of God, Paul declares, is that all who believe will be saved: "The Scripture says, 'No one who believes in him will be put to shame.' For there is no distinction between Jew and Greek; the same Lord is lord of all and is generous to all who call on him. For 'Everyone who calls on the name of the lord shall be saved'" (Rom 10:11–13).

Yet Paul was faced with the realization that most of his fellow Jews, God's chosen people Israel, seemed not to respond to the call of the gospel as Paul had. This prompts one of the most agonizing reflections in all of Paul's letters. Despite his ardent love for Christ, he says he would be willing "to be accursed and cut off from Christ" for the sake of his own people, "my kindred according to the flesh" (see Rom 9:1–5). Wrestling with this paradox takes up the whole of chapters 9–11 of Paul's letter. Perhaps, he muses, the resistance of Israel to faith in Christ enabled the mission to the Gentiles to flourish. Or, conversely, the positive response of the Gentiles to faith in Christ may have been intended to make Israel jealous and entice Israel to come in. In any case, Paul is convinced that all Israel will be saved "for the gifts and the calling God [to Israel] are irrevocable" (Rom 11:29). Paul's final solution is the realization that the ultimate destiny of both Jews and Gentiles rests with God's infinite mercy:

> Just as you [i.e., the Gentiles] were once disobedient to God but have now received mercy because of their disobedience [i.e., Israel], so they have now been disobedient in order that, by the mercy shown to you, they too may now receive mercy. For God has imprisoned all in disobedience so that he may be merciful to all. O the depth of the riches and wisdom and knowledge of

God! How unsearchable are his judgments and how inscrutable his ways! "For who has known the mind of the Lord? Or who has been his counselor?" "Or who has given a gift to him, to receive a gift in return?" For from him and through him and to him are all things. To him be the glory forever. Amen. (Rom 11:30–36)

Thus, the panorama of Paul's view of history is complete. Its starting point is in God's creation of the universe with the human being, male and female, as its crowning moment. But the first ancestors, Adam and Eve, fall prey to the power of sin and death with dire consequences for all human history. After the devastating primeval flood, the Bible's view of human history stretches from Adam through Abraham and the patriarchs and then to Moses. Moses is God's chosen liberator, leading the people out of slavery in Egypt and receiving from God the gift of the Law to his people Israel, a consequence of the covenant God forges with Israel at Sinai. The law brings moral awareness, but the Israelites, too, like the Gentiles, fail to respond with righteousness before God, and thus humanity, Jew and Gentile, remains under the power of sin. That stranglehold is radically broken by God, who out of love for humanity sends a "second Adam, a 'new creation'" (see Gal 6:15), whose experience of death and resurrection defeats the abiding power of death and becomes the source of salvation for all who believe in Jesus Christ. Now through faith and the experience of being united with Christ's dying and rising in baptism, the followers of Jesus, both Gentile and Jew, have a destiny with God. As daughters and sons of God, they will share in the glory of God.[6]

---

[6] For Paul, the conviction that salvation was experienced through faith and not the works of the law was anticipated in the experience of Abraham, who believed in God and was obedient, prior to the giving of the Mosaic Law, and therefore becomes a prototype of the Christians who are saved by faith; see Gal 3:6–9; Rom 4:9–12.

Beyond Paul: Colossians, Ephesians, and the Pastoral Letters

As noted earlier, modern biblical scholarship has called into question whether Paul himself was the author of some of the letters traditionally assigned to him or whether they were written in his name by a later disciple of Paul.[7] The goal here is not to delve into the details of that debate. Rather, our focus will be on the portrayal of Christ in these letters, the ultimate rationale for their inclusion in the New Testament canon, and the basis for their being considered "sacred" writings.

Colossians

Both Colossian and Ephesians have a strong Christological focus and show continuity, as well as development, in comparison with Paul's undisputed letters. One striking feature of both texts is their portrayal of what could be called the "cosmic" Christ. The author of Colossians, for example, seems to quote a pre-existing Christian hymn that affirms the exaltation of the Risen Christ above all elements of the universe as well as his being the "head" of his body, the church:

> He is the image of the invisible God, the firstborn of all creation; for in him all things in heaven and on earth were created, things visible and invisible, whether thrones or dominions or rulers or powers—all things have been created through him and for him.
>
> He himself is before all things, and in him all things hold together. He is the head of the body, the church; he is the beginning, the firstborn from the dead, so that he might come to have first

---

[7] This list includes Colossians; Ephesians; 2 Thessalonians; and the Pastoral epistles 1 & 2, Timothy and Titus.

place in everything. For in him all the fullness of God was pleased to dwell, and through him God was pleased to reconcile to himself all things, whether on earth or in heaven, by making peace through the blood of his cross. And you who were once estranged and hostile in mind, doing evil deeds, he has now reconciled in his fleshly body through death, so as to present you holy and blameless and irreproachable before him. (Col 1:15–22)

The reference to Christ as the pattern of creation itself echoes the prologue of John's Gospel that also refers to Jesus, the Word of God, as the one "through whom all things came into being" (John 1:3).[8] Colossians extends that lordship of Christ to "all things in heaven and on earth . . . visible and invisible, whether thrones or dominions or rulers or powers" (Col 1:16). Greco-Roman culture was absorbed by cosmic speculation and astrology, convinced that the universe was filled with intelligent beings who controlled the movement of the stars and planets and determined the course of human destiny. In asserting the rule of Christ over these powers of the universe, Christian faith was countering the kind of fatalism that dominated popular culture. Christ's rule, in contrast to that of the cosmic powers, was benign and an expression of God's love for the world.

In that spirit, the Colossian hymn also affirms that the Risen and Exalted Christ is the "head of the body, the church" (Col 1:18). Here interpreters note a difference from Paul's reflections on the church as the "body of Christ" (see, e.g., 1 Cor 12:12–31). For Paul, the metaphor of the "body of Christ" expresses the mutual dependence of the members on each other, and particularly with the most vulnerable members. Colossians, however, emphasizes Christ's "headship" over the body. The cosmic Christ, who is "before all things and in him all things hold together," is the universal reconciling power in the universe. His cosmic power is not one of domination

---

[8] See earlier discussion.

or fear but "through him God was pleased to reconcile to himself all things, whether on earth or in heaven, by making peace through the blood of his cross" (Col 1:19–20).

Based on faith in Christ's all-embracing power to reconcile the world, the author urges the Christians of Colossae to put away fear and to avoid useless cosmic speculations that seem to be the message of other competing religious movements preying on them (see Col 2:8–23). Instead, they should concentrate on the figure of Christ:

> So if you have been raised with Christ, seek the things that are above, where Christ is, seated at the right hand of God. Set your minds on things that are above, not on things that are on earth, for you have died, and your life is hidden with Christ in God. When Christ who is your life is revealed, then you also will be revealed with him in glory. Put to death, therefore, whatever in you is earthly: fornication, impurity, passion, evil desire, and greed (which is idolatry). On account of these the wrath of God is coming on those who are disobedient. These are the ways you also once followed, when you were living that life. But now you must get rid of all such things—anger, wrath, malice, slander, and abusive language from your mouth. Do not lie to one another, seeing that you have stripped off the old self with its practices and have clothed yourselves with the new self, which is being renewed in knowledge according to the image of its creator. In that renewal there is no longer Greek and Jew, circumcised and uncircumcised, barbarian, Scythian, slave and free; but Christ is all and in all! As God's chosen ones, holy and beloved, clothe yourselves with compassion, kindness, humility, meekness, and patience. Bear with one another and, if anyone has a complaint against another, forgive each other; just as the Lord has forgiven you, so you also must forgive. Above all, clothe yourselves with love, which binds everything together in perfect harmony. And let the peace of Christ rule in your hearts, to which indeed you were called in

the one body. And be thankful. Let the word of Christ dwell in you richly; teach and admonish one another in all wisdom; and with gratitude in your hearts sing psalms, hymns, and spiritual songs to God. And whatever you do, in word or deed, do everything in the name of the Lord Jesus, giving thanks to God the Father through him. (Col 3:1–17)

Here, as in most of the New Testament writings, the author's immediate purpose is not to elaborate an abstract theology but to declare that faith in Christ and Christ's God-given power can deliver the Christians from baseless fear and lead them to a life of virtue and holiness.[9] Christ's mission of cosmic reconciliation should be reflected in the mutual love and care of the Christians among themselves.

Ephesians

Many contemporary scholars believe that Ephesians was not composed as a letter to a specific community. The reference to "the saints who are *in Ephesus*" is missing in several ancient manuscripts. The original purpose of this New Testament text may have been to serve as a summary or synthesis of major elements of Paul's message and used as a kind of circular letter among various churches. In any case, its Christology has strong similarities to that of Colossians. In Ephesians, too, the cosmic dimension of Christ's power is emphasized:

God put this power to work in Christ when he raised him from the dead and seated him at his right hand in the heavenly places, far above all rule and authority and power and dominion, and above every name that is named, not only in this age but also in

---

[9] See Chapter 6.

the age to come. And he has put all things under his feet and has made him the head over all things for the church, which is his body, the fullness of him who fills all in all. (Eph 1:20–23)

Similar to Colossians, the letter to the Ephesians emphasizes the reconciling power of Jesus's death and resurrection. Ephesians illustrates this all-encompassing reconciling power by appealing to a classic example of human alienation, namely the enmity or separation between Jews and Gentiles: The Jews were God's chosen people with whom God had forged a covenant; the Gentiles, by contrast, were "aliens . . . having no hope and without God in the world," a pessimistic view of the Gentiles that echoes Paul's even more dire view of the Gentiles' plight in his letter to the Romans, ". . . for though they knew God, they did not honor him as God or give thanks to him, but they became futile in their thinking, and their senseless minds were darkened." (See Paul's full indictment of the Gentiles in Rom 1:18–32.) Ephesians goes on to describe the reconciling impact of Christ's death and resurrection on this classic alienation:

So then, remember that at one time you Gentiles by birth, called "the uncircumcision" by those who are called "the circumcision"—a physical circumcision made in the flesh by human hands—remember that you were at that time without Christ, being aliens from the commonwealth of Israel, and strangers to the covenants of promise, having no hope and without God in the world. But now in Christ Jesus you who once were far off have been brought near by the blood of Christ for he is our peace; in his flesh he has made both groups into one and has broken down the dividing wall, that is, the hostility between us. He has abolished the law with its commandments and ordinances, that he might create in himself one new humanity in place of the two, thus making peace, and might reconcile both groups to God in one body through the cross, thus putting to death that hostility through it. So he came and proclaimed peace to you who were far off and peace to those who were near; for through him both of us have access in one Spirit to the Father. (Eph 2:11–18)

The metaphor of "those who were far off" echoes the words of Isaiah the prophet in speaking of the "nations" or Gentiles as "far off," as distinct from the Israelites who were "near" (Isa 57:19). The death (and resurrection) of Christ overcomes the power of death that had flooded the world with alienation and enmity and creates instead peace and reconciliation. The author of Ephesian uses the striking image of a "dividing wall" that had stood between Jews and Gentiles. Many commentators believe that the "dividing wall" the author has in mind was the barrier in the Jerusalem temple precincts that separated Gentiles from the interior sacred space where only Jews were permitted entry. Now that symbolic barrier is "broken down" in order to create "one new humanity in place of the two, thus making peace" and reconciling both groups to God "in one body through the cross."

Through this fundamental reconciliation, the author views the church as a community of reconciliation, a universal sign of God's reconciliation of the world:

So then you are no longer strangers and aliens, but you are citizens with the saints and also members of the household of God, built upon the foundation of the apostles and prophets, with Christ Jesus himself as the cornerstone. In him the whole structure is joined together and grows into a holy temple in the Lord; in whom you also are built together spiritually into a dwelling place for God. (Eph 2:19–22)

Paul is portrayed in the letter as one entrusted with this message of reconciliation—what Ephesians refers to as a "mystery hidden for ages in God" but now revealed in order that "through the church the wisdom of God in its rich variety might now be made known to the rulers and authorities in the heavenly places" (Eph 3:7–13).

Thus, both Colossians and Ephesians expand or at least accentuate the horizon of the role of Christ reflected in Paul's undisputed letters. The death and resurrection of Christ that broke the power of death and led to abundant new life also has an impact on the universe itself—disarming the alien powers that create enmity and threaten humanity itself. This act of universal reconciliation also amplifies the mission of the church, the Body of Christ. The mutual love and reconciliation among its members—both Jews and Gentiles—become a sign of what the world's destiny is to be. Thus, the author eloquently prays in Ephesians:

> For this reason I bow my knees before the Father, from whom every family in heaven and on earth takes its name. I pray that, according to the riches of his glory, he may grant that you may be strengthened in your inner being with power through his Spirit, and that Christ may dwell in your hearts through faith, as you are being rooted and grounded in love. I pray that you may have the power to comprehend, with all the saints, what is the breadth and length and height and depth, and to know the love of Christ that surpasses knowledge, so that you may be filled with all the fullness of God. Now to him who by the power at work within us is able to accomplish abundantly far more than all we can ask or imagine, to him be glory in the church and in Christ Jesus to all generations, forever and ever. Amen. (Eph 3:14–21)

The Pastoral Letters

We turn briefly to the last set of letters in the New Testament traditionally attributed to Paul. Many scholars today question whether Paul, in fact, wrote these letters or whether they were the work of later authors writing in Paul's name. All three of these so-called

Pastoral Letters are addressed to individuals, Timothy and Titus, who were trusted companions of Paul on his missionary journeys and cited both in Acts and in Paul's own letters. The contents of the Pastoral Letters seem to reflect a later stage in the development of the early church, a prime reason for assigning a date beyond the lifetime of Paul himself. As the early Christian community moved beyond the first generations of the followers of Jesus, concern arose about important institutional issues, such as the requirements for leadership and appropriate community structures, and the need to maintain the authentic teaching and traditions of the church in the face of doctrinal errors. All three of these letters, particularly 2 Timothy, which is more autobiographical in tone, portray Paul as handing on to Timothy and Titus his mantle as apostle and urging them to persevere in their ministry.

There are important affirmations in these letters about the identity and mission of Jesus Christ, including snatches of early Christian hymns and credal statements. For example, 1 Tim 2:5 affirms Jesus as "the one mediator between God and humankind, Christ Jesus, himself human, who gave himself a ransom for all." Another poetic quotation sums up the impact of Jesus's universal mission: "He was revealed in flesh, vindicated in spirit, seen by angels, proclaimed among Gentiles, believed in throughout the world, taken up in glory" (1 Tim 3:16).

Yet the overall content of the three letters is mostly concerned with refuting errors and urging Paul's successors to give proper attention to the leadership and stability of the church. Paul's exhortation in 2 Tim 4:1–5 is typical:

> In the presence of God and of Christ Jesus, who is to judge the living and the dead, and in view of his appearing and his kingdom, I solemnly urge you: proclaim the message; be persistent whether the time is favorable or unfavorable; convince, rebuke, and encourage, with the utmost patience in teaching. For the time is coming when people will not put up with sound doctrine, but

having itching ears, they will accumulate for themselves teachers to suit their own desires, and will turn away from listening to the truth and wander away to myths. As for you, always be sober, endure suffering, do the work of an evangelist, carry out your ministry fully.

As the purported author, Paul emphasizes his apostolic vocation, admitting as he had done in other letters, that before his conversion he had been a persecutor of the church, an admission that Paul turns into a proclamation of Christ's mission of salvation:

I am grateful to Christ Jesus our Lord, who has strengthened me, because he judged me faithful and appointed me to his service, even though I was formerly a blasphemer, a persecutor, and a man of violence. But I received mercy because I had acted ignorantly in unbelief, and the grace of our Lord overflowed for me with the faith and love that are in Christ Jesus. The saying is sure and worthy of full acceptance, that Christ Jesus came into the world to save sinners—of whom I am the foremost. But for that very reason I received mercy, so that in me, as the foremost, Jesus Christ might display the utmost patience, making me an example to those who would come to believe in him for eternal life. To the King of the ages, immortal, invisible, the only God, be honor and glory forever and ever. Amen. (1 Tim 1:12–17)

Several times in the Pastorals, Paul points to his own experience to bolster the vocations of his young successors:

Now you have observed my teaching, my conduct, my aim in life, my faith, my patience, my love, my steadfastness, my persecutions, and my suffering the things that happened to me in Antioch, Iconium, and Lystra. What persecutions I endured! Yet the Lord rescued me from all of them. Indeed, all who want to live a godly life in Christ Jesus will be persecuted. But wicked people and impostors will go from bad to worse, deceiving others and being deceived. But as for you, continue in what you have learned and firmly believed, knowing from whom you learned it, and how from childhood you have known the sacred writings that are able to instruct you for salvation through faith in Christ Jesus. All scripture is inspired by God and is useful for teaching, for reproof, for correction, and for training in righteousness, so that everyone who belongs to God may be proficient, equipped for every good work. (2 Tim 3:10–17)

The author signals the end of Paul's life, as the apostle anticipates his receiving the "crown of righteousness" that the Lord has reserved for him:

As for me, I am already being poured out as a libation, and the time of my departure has come. I have fought the good fight, I have finished the race, I have kept the faith. From now on there is reserved for me the crown of righteousness, which the Lord, the righteous judge, will give me on that day, and not only to me but also to all who have longed for his appearing. (2 Tim 4:6–8)

Thus, the Pastoral Letters throw the spotlight on Paul's own example of what it means to be an apostle, one whose life is spent in proclaiming Christ, an emphasis which confirms the rationale for the inclusion of Paul's writings in the canon and their sacred character.

Conclusion

Why were the letters of Paul circulated widely in the early Christian community, and early on considered "sacred" writing to be included in the nucleus of the New Testament canon? The reason is the same as why the Four Gospels quickly became foundational sacred texts of the early Christian community. Although different in style and context, the Gospels and Paul's letters were powerful, compelling portrayals of Jesus Christ, the center of Christian faith. Each set of texts viewed Christ through the lens of his death and resurrection, the heart of the mission of Jesus and, in the perspective of Christian faith, the act that redeemed the world. And both sets of text mediated for the believing Christian an encounter with the sacred.

Our focus to this point has been on the portrayal of Christ in both the Gospels and Paul. Still to be considered is the expected impact of this portrayal on the lives of the followers of Jesus. A fundamental conviction of the New Testament, and indeed of the Bible as a whole, is that the encounter with the divine leads to a life of holiness.

6

The Remaining New Testament Books as Sacred

As we noted at the outset, the format this study has taken is not that of a standard "Introduction to the New Testament." The goal of a New Testament introduction is to provide its readers with information on the background, literary genre, structure, and content of each New Testament book. While some of this information is supportive of this study's purpose, our focus is elsewhere: namely, why the New Testament is considered "sacred." The fundamental conviction of this study is that the reason the New Testament is considered "sacred" by Christians is because the books of the New Testament are, in effect, a "proclamation" of the core of the Christian message, offering an encounter with Jesus Christ, the embodiment of what is meant by "sacred, and, therefore, the guide and norm of a life of holiness.

We have tried to make this case in exploring the portrayal of Jesus in the Four Gospels. The Four Gospels were not intended to be historical records of Jesus's life but, as the label "gospel" implies, are announcements of "good news," offering the early Christian community and its successors an encounter with the person and mission of the crucified and Risen Christ. As we noted earlier, the Gospels are rooted in historical traditions, but simply recording history is not their ultimate purpose.[1] The same is true of Paul's letters, even though they obviously have a very different literary form than the gospel narratives. Paul's letters were not casual correspondence

[1] See Chapter 2.

The New Testament. Donald Senior, Oxford University Press. © Oxford University Press 2022.
DOI: 10.1093/oso/9780197530832.003.0007

but extensions of his own mission of proclaiming Christ, especially to the Gentiles, which he believed was his God-given vocation. Although the contents of Paul's letters were prompted by the concerns and problems of his communities in Asia Minor, Greece, and Rome and contain practical pastoral advice, their "sacredness" was recognized by his recipients because they proclaimed Christ in a vivid way. Not only Paul's words but also the example of his own life, which he freely shared, mediated for his recipients an encounter with Christ, the embodiment of the sacred and the path to holiness.

We turn now, with the same conviction, to some of the remaining New Testament books. As we noted in studying the formation of the canon, the criteria for inclusion of particular books into the framework of the "canon" are clear: they claim apostolic origin; they were received and read in the assemblies of the early Christian communities; and their contents were in harmony with the deepest and most widespread convictions of the early Christians.[2] While the nucleus of the New Testament was shaped early on in conformity with these criteria—for example, the Gospels and the letters of Paul—the rationale for the inclusion of some books remains a mystery. This is especially true of brief works such as Jude, and 2 & 3 John. Our goal here is not to consider every book of the New Testament but to make the case that in the vast majority of them, their proclamation of Christ is central and defining.

The books we will focus on this chapter include Hebrews, James, 1 Peter, 1 John, and Revelation, taken in the order in which they appear in the canon. Hebrews comes first because early on it was considered by many ancient authors as one of Paul's letters. However, it was clear even to early observers that it has a style and theological perspective quite different from Paul's undisputed letters. The next letters we will consider—James, 1 Peter, 1 John—are three of what have been dubbed the "catholic epistles"—"catholic"

[2] See Chapter 3.

in the sense that they are addressed not to a specific community but intended for a wider audience.[3] And finally, in a category and style all its own, we will consider the concluding book of the New Testament, the book of Revelation. As we have noted several times during our study, the books of the New Testament have a striking diversity in style and perspective. That will be very evident in the books we now turn to. But, at the same time, through all the New Testament books there is a commanding unity—a unity grounded in their focus on the figure of Jesus Christ. It is that varied but unifying portrayal found in these books which will command our attention.

The Letter to the Hebrews

The Letter to the Hebrews has a unique style and literary form. Although traditionally called a "letter," it has few of the usual marks of an actual letter. There is no opening greeting, and the closing farewell seems contrived and may have been added at a later point to give the appearance of a letter (see Heb 13:22–25). Although the title indicates that it is directed to the "Hebrews," it is not known for sure where it was composed or to whom it is addressed. The closing lines declare that "those from Italy send you greetings" (13:24), suggesting to some that it is addressed to Christians in Rome, perhaps from Alexandria, a center of Hellenistic Judaism as well as Jewish Christianity. The sophisticated Greek of the text and its use of an elaborate temple metaphor might indicate that the letter originated in the Jewish Christian community of that city.

---

[3] In addition to the three texts we will study, 2 Peter, 2 & 3 John, and Jude are also counted among the "catholic" epistles. Note that 2 & 3 John are, in fact, addressed to individuals and that 1 Peter is intended for several specific communities in north central Asia Minor. So the description "catholic" in the sense of addressed to a wide and undetermined audience is relative in their case.

In any case, it is clear from the contents of Hebrews that it was meant as an exhortation to Christians to remain faithful to their calling at a time when their fervor seemed to be flagging. The author recalls an earlier time when the recipients had

> . . . endured a hard struggle with sufferings, sometimes being publicly exposed to abuse and persecution, and sometimes being partners with those so treated. For you had compassion for those who were in prison, and you cheerfully accepted the plundering of your possessions, knowing that you yourselves possessed something better and more lasting. Do not, therefore, abandon that confidence of yours; it brings a great reward. For you need endurance, so that when you have done the will of God, you may receive what was promised. (Heb 10:12–36)

He urges his fellow Christians to "lift your drooping hands and strengthen your weak knees, and make a straight path for your feet, so that what is lame may not be put out of joint, but rather be healed" (12:12–13).

Jesus the Word of God

To enflame their lagging faith, the author urges the recipients of his letter "to fix their eyes on Jesus, the pioneer and perfecter of our faith" (Heb 12:2). This is the prevailing strategy of the entire letter. Inviting them to consider in a deeper way the identity of Jesus and his work of salvation on their behalf is the current that runs throughout Hebrews. To portray Jesus in a fresh way, the author draws on the theology of the Word of God founded on the Jewish Scriptures and also fashions an elaborate metaphor of Jesus as the eternal High Priest, offering the perfect sacrifice within the heavenly Temple of God, a portrayal unique within the New Testament. The author accuses his audience of becoming "dull in understanding" (5:11), of needing to be fed on "milk not solid food" (5:112). He challenges them to advance in their understanding beyond the basics through the imaginative teaching about Christ he will provide: ". . . leaving behind the basic teaching about Christ, and not laying again the foundation: repentance from dead works and faith towards God, instructions about baptisms, laying on of hands, resurrection of the dead and eternal judgment" (Heb 6:1–2).

That imaginative teaching about Christ is found in several of the major motifs of Hebrews. The opening chapter portrays Jesus in exalted terms as God's Word. Just as God spoke to the ancestors of God's people through the prophets, now "in these last days, he has spoken to us by a Son, whom he appointed heir of all things, through whom he also created the worlds" (Heb 1:1–2), language reminiscent of the prologue of John's Gospel. The author leaves little doubt about the exalted, indeed, divine status of the Son: "He is the reflection of God's glory and the exact imprint of God's very being, and he sustains all things by his powerful word." Having accomplished his God-given mission, "[Jesus] sat down at the right hand of the majesty on high, having become as much superior to angels as the name he has inherited is more excellent than theirs" (1:3–4). Because of this exalted status, it is essential to hear the Son's word and to be responsive to it (2:1).

Jesus the High Priest

Hebrews' most distinctive portrayal of Christ and his mission is as the eternal High Priest. Here the influence of platonic philosophy, which was widespread in the Greco-Roman world of the first centuries, comes into play. Platonism in general saw the material world as a reflection or shadow of the real and ideal heavenly world. The author of Hebrews applies this framework to the Temple. The earthly sanctuary of the Jerusalem Temple (probably already destroyed at the time Hebrews was composed, after 70 AD), was only a pale reflection of the heavenly sanctuary. From this framework the author constructs an elaborate metaphor to illustrate the identity of Jesus as the perfect and eternal high priest and his death and resurrection as the ultimate and fully effective sacrifice that atones for the sins of the world.

Jesus as the perfect "High Priest" partakes of both the human and divine world. Like all priests he is chosen from among humans and understands their experience:

> Every high priest chosen from among mortals is put in charge of things pertaining to God on their behalf, to offer gifts and sacrifices for sins. He is able to deal gently with the ignorant and wayward, since he himself is subject to weakness; and because of this he must offer sacrifice for his own sins as well as for those of the people. And one does not presume to take this honor, but takes it only when called by God, just as Aaron was. (Heb 5:1–4)

In emphasizing the humanity of Jesus, the author seems to evoke the anguished prayer of Jesus on the eve of his death found in the Synoptic Gospels and echoed in John's Gospel as well:

> In the days of his flesh, Jesus offered up prayers and supplications, with loud cries and tears, to the one who was able to save him from death, and he was heard because of his reverent submission. Although he was a Son, he learned obedience through what he suffered; and having been made perfect, he became the source of eternal salvation for all who obey him . . . (Heb 5:7–9; see also Mark 14:32–42; Matt 26:36–46; Luke 22:39–46; John 12:27–28)

The same elaborate metaphor allows Hebrews to understand in a new way the effects of Jesus's death and resurrection. As High Priest, Jesus offers the perfect sacrifice, his own life, which becomes the sacrifice that destroys death once and for all and gains access to God. Throughout, the author contrasts the perfect priesthood of

Jesus with the "shadow" reality of the priesthood exercised in the Jerusalem Temple.

> For it was fitting that we should have such a high priest, holy, blameless, undefiled, separated from sinners, and exalted above the heavens. Unlike the other high priests, he has no need to offer sacrifices day after day, first for his own sins, and then for those of the people; this he did once for all when he offered himself. For the law appoints as high priests those who are subject to weakness, but the word of the oath, which came later than the law, appoints a Son who has been made perfect forever. Now the main point in what we are saying is this: we have such a high priest, one who is seated at the right hand of the throne of the Majesty in the heavens, a minister in the sanctuary and the true tent that the Lord, and not any mortal, has set up. For every high priest is appointed to offer gifts and sacrifices; hence it is necessary for this priest also to have something to offer. Now if he were on earth, he would not be a priest at all, since there are priests who offer gifts according to the law. They offer worship in a sanctuary that is a sketch and shadow of the heavenly one; for Moses, when he was about to erect the tent, was warned, "See that you make everything according to the pattern that was shown you on the mountain." But Jesus has now obtained a more excellent ministry, and to that degree he is the mediator of a better covenant, which has been enacted through better promises. (Heb 7:26–8:6)

Pulsing through Hebrews' reflection on Jesus and his work of redemption is a sense that Jesus is out in front, leading the community to its new life. Jesus is the "pioneer" of humanity's salvation (2:10; 12:2). He is the "forerunner" (6:19–20) who goes through the veil of the Heavenly Temple and enters first, on our behalf, into the inner heavenly sanctuary (where God dwells). The heart of all of this is the efficacy of Jesus's death and resurrection which the author perceives as the ultimate sacrifice that breaks the bonds of death and makes life—that is, entrance into the realm of God—possible:

> For Christ did not enter a sanctuary made by human hands, a mere copy of the true one, but he entered into heaven itself, now to appear in the presence of God on our behalf.
>
> Nor was it to offer himself again and again, as the high priest enters the Holy Place year after year with blood that is not his own; for then he would have had to suffer again and again since the foundation of the world. But as it is, he has appeared once for all at the end of the age to remove sin by the sacrifice of himself. And just as it is appointed for mortals to die once, and after that the judgment, so Christ, having been offered once to bear the sins of many, will appear a second time, not to deal with sin, but to save those who are eagerly waiting for him. (9:24–28)

Words of Encouragement

The realization that Jesus the "High Priest" has offered the perfect sacrifice in laying down his life for sinners provides the basis for hope and perseverance which commands the latter part of the letter and reveals its purpose:

> Therefore, my friends, since we have confidence to enter the sanctuary by the blood of Jesus, by the new and living way that he opened for us through the curtain (that is, through his flesh), and since we have a great priest over the house of God, let us approach with a true heart in full assurance of faith, with our hearts sprinkled clean from an evil conscience and our bodies washed with pure water. Let us hold fast to the confession of our hope without wavering, for he who has promised is faithful. And let us consider how to provoke one another to love and good deeds,

not neglecting to meet together, as is the habit of some, but encouraging one another, and all the more as you see the Day approaching. (10:19–25)

Hebrew's main purpose—encouraging the recipients to remain hopeful and to persevere in faith—commands the concluding section of the letter (Hebrews 11–13). The example of Jesus recalls the faith of generations of ancestors, beginning with Abel, Enoch, and Noah and extending through Abraham and Moses and the great heroes of the Old Testament (Hebrews 11). This "cloud of witnesses" leads to Jesus himself, who is again described in dynamic terms as the one who leads the Christians through their final race:

Therefore, since we are surrounded by so great a cloud of witnesses, let us also lay aside every weight and the sin that clings so closely, and let us run with perseverance the race that is set before us, looking to Jesus the pioneer and perfecter of our faith, who for the sake of the joy that was set before him endured the cross, disregarding its shame, and has taken his seat at the right hand of the throne of God. Consider him who endured such hostility against himself from sinners, so that you may not grow weary or lose heart. (12:1–3)

The letter concludes with a vision of paradise, the encounter with the Risen and Exalted Christ:

But you have come to Mount Zion and to the city of the living God, the heavenly Jerusalem, and to innumerable angels in festal gathering, and to the assembly of the firstborn who are enrolled in heaven, and to God the judge of all, and to the spirits of the righteous made perfect, and to Jesus, the mediator of a new covenant, and to the sprinkled blood that speaks a better word than the blood of Abel. (12:22–24)

All of this is to have an impact on the lives of those who follow Christ. This is the point of the final words of the Letter (13:1–21) with its long list of directives to the recipients, summed up in the command: "Let mutual love continue . . ." (13:1). The self-sacrifice and love of the Crucified and Risen Christ, now at the right hand of God, becomes the pattern for a Christian life of holiness.

Conclusion

The Letter to the Hebrews clearly illustrates the dynamic that characterizes virtually all the books of the New Testament. The letter's portrayal of Jesus and the saving power of his death and resurrection is not intended as abstract theological speculation but as a means of enkindling the faith and perseverance of its recipients. The letter's reflections on the sacrifice of Jesus the High Priest and its recall of the faith of the "cloud of witnesses" is a proclamation of the gospel.

For some interpreters, Hebrews represents a brand of "successionist" theology that appears to acclaim Christianity at the expense of Judaism. The sacrifice of Christ and his entrance into the heavenly sanctuary contrast with and render obsolete the repetition and ineffectual liturgy of the Jerusalem Temple. While the elaborated metaphor of Jesus as High Priest does imply an advance beyond the sacrificial system of the Jerusalem Temple, the Letter's intent need not be seen as a disregard or disparagement for the Jewish heritage of Christianity. Some have suggested that in fact the author may be responding to the sadness experienced by Jewish Christians regarding the brutal destruction of the Temple in 70 AD. The Acts of the Apostles affirms that the Jerusalem Christians continued to worship daily in the Temple, a temple also revered by Jesus as "my father's house" (Luke 2). The Jewish Christian author of Hebrews may be consoling his community who revered the Temple and mourned its loss, by affirming that God had now provided an eternal and perfect temple in the person and mission of Jesus.

While it took some time for Hebrews to be fully accepted into the New Testament canon, it is clear that its proclamation of Christ as the source of Christian hope and the pattern for Christian holiness is the basis for its status as a "sacred" text.

The Letter of James

Like Hebrews, the Letter of James is not a letter in the proper sense of the term but an exhortation dressed in some of the trappings of a letter, much like the form of a "open letter" seen in publications today. It is addressed to "the twelve tribes in the dispersion"—a phrase that reflects the strong Jewish Christian characteristics of this text and may refer literally to Jewish Christians living outside of Palestine (i.e., in the "dispersion" or "diaspora," a term used in Judaism itself for Jews living outside the homeland), or it could be meant metaphorically for all Christian communities generally, signifying they are members of God's people away from their ultimate true heavenly home (see a similar metaphorical usage in 1 Peter 1:1, "to the exiles of the Dispersion in Pontus, Galatia, Cappadocia, Asia, and Bithynia").

The date and authorship of this text are also debated. The "James" who claims authorship is unlikely to be one of the two apostles who bore that name (i.e., James, son of Zebedee, and James, son of Alphaeus; see Matt 10:2–4), since nowhere in the letter does the author claim this unique and honored role. Instead, he identifies himself as "a servant of God and of the Lord Jesus Christ" (Jas 1:1). More likely the James of this letter is the leader of the Jerusalem church mentioned in the Acts of the Apostles (see especially Acts 15:13–21; 21:18) and referred to by Paul as one of the leading figures in Jerusalem (Gal 2:9, 12). The first-century Jewish Josephus mentions this James, noting his violent death around 62 AD.[4] Many scholars question whether this James was the actual author of the Letter; it is written in elegant Greek and would have to be composed in the late 50s or early 60s if he were the author. Most likely it is a text composed later in the first century by someone writing in James's name. In any case, it bears the strong imprint of Jewish ethical traditions now incorporated into a Christian context.

Christian Conduct

In some ways, James is an exception to the case we are trying to make about the rationale for considering the books of the New Testament "sacred." The focus of its content is not directly on the figure of Christ as such but on the ethical conduct that should characterize a follower of Jesus. In fact, explicit reference to "Jesus" appears only twice in the entire text (Jas 1:1; 2:1), along with reference to the Parousia or second coming of Christ (i.e., "the coming of the Lord"; see Jas 5:7, 8). But early in the letter the author affirms a key principle that governs the entirety of his ethical exhortations; urging that when the Christians gather in assembly (literally in the "synagogue" see Jas 2:2) there be no favoritism shown the rich at the expense of the poor; he asks this question: "My brothers and sisters, do you with your acts of favoritism really believe in our glorious Lord Jesus Christ?" (Jas 2:1). An urgent assumption of James is that true faith in Christ must be expressed in action: "What good is it, my brothers and sisters, if you say you have faith but do not have works?" (Jas 2:14). James concludes: "For just as the body without the spirit is dead, so faith without works is also dead" (Jas 2:26). Some interpreters believe that here James is opposing the Pauline emphasis on faith rather than works as the means of salvation. But Paul, too, asserted ". . . the only thing that counts is faith working

---

[4] Josephus, *Antiquities of the Jews*, Book 20, Chapter 9, 1.

through love" (Gal 5:6)—a principle that James would completely endorse. There is no clear evidence that James is writing as an explicit corrective to Paul's views.

Care for the Poor

There are several specific ethical challenges the author refers to, along with general exhortations to avoid "worldliness" and embrace integrity and holiness. Prime among these is care for the poor as opposed to favoritism of the rich. The Letter's insistence on care for the poor surely derives from the Old Testament itself, with its characteristic call for care for the "widow, the orphan, and the stranger" (see, among many examples, Exod 22:21–24; Deut 10:18; 24:17–18; 26:12; 27:19). "Listen, my brothers and sisters. Has not God chosen the poor in the world to be rich in faith and to be heirs of the kingdom that he has promised to those who love him?" (Jas 2:5). And here the letter reflects Jesus's own teaching emphasized in the Gospels as "good news for the poor"—itself with deep roots in Jesus's Jewish heritage (see, e.g., Matt 25:31–46; Luke 4:18). For James, care for the poor is a response to the commandment that is bound together with love of God, a characteristic emphasis of Jesus himself: "You do well if you really fulfil the royal law according to the scripture, 'You shall love your neighbor as yourself'" (Jas 2:8; see Matt 22:4–40).

Christian Speech

A second ethical concentration of James is the damage that can be done through slander and vicious language, particularly when directed against a fellow Christian. This is one of the characteristic teachings of this New Testament letter, an exhortation about the dangers of the tongue that takes up almost the entirety of chapter 3.

Here, too, integrity is at stake: "How great a forest is set ablaze by a small fire? And the tongue is a fire . . . With it we bless the Lord and Father, and with it we curse those who are made in the likeness of God. From the same mouth come blessing and cursing. My brothers and sisters, this ought not to be so" (Jas 3:5, 6, 9–10). James is particularly concerned about "speaking evil" against a fellow Christian: "Do not speak evil against one another, brothers and sisters" (Jas 4:11), an exhortation that also echoes Jesus's teaching in the Sermon on the Mount (see Matt 5:22).

Care for the Sick

The Letter concludes with a famous passage about anointing and healing the sick, which Roman Catholic and Orthodox Christians claim as a biblical basis for the sacrament of anointing.

> Are any among you suffering? They should pray. Are any cheerful? They should sing songs of praise. Are any among you sick? They should call for the elders of the church and have them pray over them, anointing them with oil in the name of the Lord. The prayer of faith will save the sick, and the Lord will raise them up; and anyone who has committed sins will be forgiven. Therefore confess your sins to one another, and pray for one another, so that you may be healed. The prayer of the righteous is powerful and effective. (Jas 5:13–16)

Here again a characteristic of Jesus's mission portrayed in the Gospels stands as a background for James. Each of the Gospels emphasizes Jesus's power to heal. In fact, each of the main concerns of the letter reflects Jesus's teaching and example—which in turn stands in harmony with Jewish ethical traditions. Care for the poor and warnings about the moral corrosion that wealth can bring; love for the neighbor that avoids abusive speech toward a brother or sister; the healing power of prayer and touch; a call for integrity and avoidance of religious hypocrisy; faith in God expressed in action not simply in words.

Unlike the gospel portrayals, or Paul's ardent personal testimony, or the exalted temple metaphor of Hebrews, one does not encounter in James direct proclamation about the figure of Jesus. What one does encounter is a series of exhortations that connect directly with Jesus's own teaching and claim his authority as Messiah and Lord (i.e., "James, a servant of God and of the Lord Jesus Christ," Jas 1:1). In this sense, the sacredness of Jesus leads to a life of integrity and holiness, a justification for including the Letter of James within the canon as a sacred text.[5]

The First Letter of Peter

The First Letter of Peter is one of the most beautiful and elegant books of the New Testament, not so much due to its literary style but because of its rich theological and pastoral message. As with many of the New Testament writings, there is considerable debate in modern biblical scholarship about 1 Peter's origin and context. Although the letter itself claims Peter as its author in its opening line—"Peter, an apostle of Jesus Christ"—many scholars question whether Peter himself was the actual author. The letter is written in polished Greek and seems to reflect circumstances of a period later than the apostle's lifetime. There is no reference at all to the debate about the Gentile mission that was a major concern of Paul's writings and reflected in the Four Gospels. In the Acts of the Apostles Peter plays a major role in the opening to the Gentiles, but none of that is reflected in the Letter of Peter (see Acts 10–11).

---

[5] It took some time for this step to be made. We will look further at the connection between the characteristic ethical exhortations of the New Testament as part of the foundation for its claim to be "sacred"; see Chapter 7.

Some have suggested that it may have been composed in the last quarter of the first century by a "Petrine group" of church leaders writing from Rome, the imperial capital and where, we know, there was a significant Christian community.[6] Peter's name is invoked as a leading figure of the early church. The evangelists portray Peter as among the first disciples to be called by Jesus and serving as their leader and spokesperson. He is cited in the Gospels, Acts, and in Paul's letters as one of the first witnesses to the resurrected Christ; presented in the early chapters of Acts as apostolic witness and leader of the Jerusalem church; as mediator of Gentile mission (Acts 10–11); and in a decisive role at the Council of Jerusalem (Acts 15:1–29). Paul's contention with Peter in Antioch (see Gal 2:11–14) also shows the importance of Peter as a mediator between the Jewish and Gentile wings of the early church. 1 Peter's assumption that "Peter" could offer counsel from Rome to churches in Asia Minor harmonizes with this leading role of Peter in these other New Testament writings.

The letter identifies itself as coming from "your sister church in Babylon" (1 Pet 5:13), a term used in early Christian literature to refer to Rome and its excesses (see Rev 17:5) and in some Jewish texts from this period such as 4 Ezra and 2 Baruch. It seems, then, that the author assumes a certain authority, enabling him to offer advice and encouragement to a series of Christian communities in north central Asia Minor: Pontus, Galatia, Cappadocia, Asia, and Bithynia (1 Pet 1:1). In the early second century, we know that the author of 1 Clement wrote from Rome to the church at Corinth with the same sense of authority.

The letter refers to the recipients as "exiles of the diaspora" (1 Pet 1:1) and as "aliens and exiles" (2:11). There is a question whether the author uses such designations in a spiritual or symbolic sense,

---

[6] On this, see John H. Elliott, *A Home for the Homeless: A Sociological Exegesis of I Peter, Its Situation and Strategy* (Philadelphia: Fortress, 1981); also, *I Peter. A New Translation with Introduction and Commentary* (The Anchor Bible; New York: Doubleday, 2000); Donald Senior, C.P, *1 Peter* (Sacra Pagina; Collegeville, MD: Liturgical Press, 2003).

that is, the Christians are "exiles" on earth from their true home in heaven (see also Jas 1:1), or whether, additionally, the Christians in these regions are, in fact, "aliens" or newly established migrants. The Greek term translated as "aliens" is literally *paroikous*, that is, "apart from home." This more sociological sense of "aliens and exiles" may explain the letter's concern about harassment experienced by the Christians from their neighbors (see 1 Pet 2:12; 3:14–16) and the threat of possible outright persecution (see 1 Pet 4:12–19). This precarious circumstance helps explain the author's focus on encouragement, on his appeal that the Christians give witness to their faith by good conduct, and by the frequent reference to the sufferings of Christ as an inspiration for what the Christians have to endure—all key components of the letter we will consider.

Our interest here is not to provide a comprehensive commentary on 1 Peter but to identify the primary reasons for its evaluation as a "sacred" text and therefore its ultimate inclusion in the New Testament canon. Here, as with the other books of the New Testament we have considered, the power of its proclamation of Christ and the Christian gospel provides that rationale.

Focus on the Resurrection

The heart of 1 Peter's encouragement of its recipients is to recall the basis for Christian hope—the resurrection of Jesus Christ from the dead. As in the gospel narratives and in the writings of Paul, Hebrews, and the other New Testament texts we have considered, the death and resurrection stand at the heart of the Christian message. That is the opening line of the letter and its fundamental rationale:

Blessed be the God and Father of our Lord Jesus Christ! By his great mercy he has given us a new birth into a living hope through the resurrection of Jesus Christ from the dead, and into an inheritance that is imperishable, undefiled, and unfading, kept in heaven for you, who are being protected by the power of God through faith for a salvation ready to be revealed in the last time. (1 Pet 1:3–4)

The author emphasizes that this moment of salvation which the Christians experience is something the Old Testament prophets spoke of and longed to see (1 Pet 1:10–12). But it is the Christians who now are privileged to experience this salvation brought about through the death and resurrection of Christ:

You know that you were ransomed from the futile ways inherited from your ancestors, not with perishable things like silver or gold, but with the precious blood of Christ, like that of a lamb without defect or blemish. He was destined before the foundation of the world, but was revealed at the end of the ages for your sake. Through him you have come to trust in God, who raised him from the dead and gave him glory, so that your faith and hope are set on God. (1 Pet 1:18–21)

Their faith in the crucified and risen Christ is the basis for the church itself and its standing before God. 1 Peter draws on a collage of Old Testament images and texts to extol the church. Remarkably, the author absorbs this Old Testament heritage effortlessly and un-apologetically; there is no implied polemic that these no longer belong to Israel nor any explicit reference to the church's "fulfilling" the promises first made to Israel. In a famous passage the author describes the church as the new and living temple:

Come to him, a living stone, though rejected by mortals yet chosen and precious in God's sight, and like living stones, let yourselves be built into a spiritual house, to be a holy priest-hood, to offer spiritual sacrifices acceptable to God through Jesus Christ. For it stands in scripture: "See, I am laying in Zion a stone, a cornerstone chosen and precious; and whoever believes in him will not be put to shame." (1 Pet 2:4–6)

Likewise, the Christians are the people of God, laden with titles of honor formerly applied to Israel itself:

But you are a chosen race, a royal priesthood, a holy nation, God's own people, in order that you may proclaim the mighty acts of him who called you out of darkness into his marvelous light. Once you were not a people, but now you are God's people; once you had not received mercy, but now you have received mercy. (1 Pet 2:9–10)

The Sufferings of Christ

A characteristic emphasis of 1 Peter is its focus on the sufferings of Christ, first of all as essential to understanding Christ's triumph over death and its outcome in resurrection. But Christ's suffering and triumph over suffering are also the inspiration for the followers of Jesus to endure the sufferings imposed on them—not only in the communities addressed by the letter but in the fellowship of sufferings endured by "your brothers and sisters throughout the world" (1 Pet 5:9). This focus runs through the whole letter. Particularly vulnerable in the community are slaves, especially those treated harshly by unjust masters, and the wives of non-Christians husbands whom society expected would conform to the religious preferences of their husbands. For slaves who suffer abuse, 1 Peter lifts up the example of the suffering Jesus, who did not retaliate against violence but responded with forbearance and integrity.

For it is a credit to you if, being aware of God, you endure pain while suffering unjustly. If you endure when you are beaten for doing wrong, what credit is that? But if you endure when you do right and suffer for it, you have God's approval. For to this you have been called, because Christ also suffered for you, leaving you an example, so that you should follow in his steps. "He committed no sin, and no deceit was found in his mouth." When he was abused, he did not return abuse; when he suffered, he did not threaten; but he entrusted himself to the one who judges justly. He himself bore our sins in his body on the cross, so that, free from sins, we might live for righteousness; by his wounds you have been healed. (1 Pet 2:18–24)

The wives of non-Christian husbands are to "win them [i.e., their pagan husbands] over" by their good example. Their "adornments" are not to be their hairstyles or gold ornaments but their "inner self with the lasting beauty of a gentle and quest spirit, which is very precious in God's sight" (1Pet 3:1–6).

Modern readers will be struck by the culturally bound view of the letter which does not challenge the basic injustice of slavery and seems to view women in a purely passive role, even judging them as the "weaker" sex, while conceding that they are "co-heirs" with their husbands "of the gracious gift of life" (1 Pet 3:7).

The Community's Witness

Although these two groups within the community were especially vulnerable because of social status, in fact, the entire community is to give a witness in the manner of the suffering Christ. Here again, the letter's fundamental Christology sets the pattern for both the inner life of the community and its public witness to the world around it:

Finally, all of you, have unity of spirit, sympathy, love for one another, a tender heart, and a humble mind. Do not repay evil for evil or abuse for abuse; but, on the contrary, repay with a blessing. It is for this that you were called—that you might inherit a blessing. For "Those who desire life and desire to see good days, let them keep their tongues from evil and their lips from speaking deceit; let them turn away from evil and do good; let them seek peace and pursue it. For the eyes of the Lord are on the righteous, and his ears are open to their prayer. But the face of the Lord is against those who do evil." Now who will harm you if you are eager to do what is good? But even if you do suffer for doing what is right, you are blessed. Do not fear what they fear, and do not be intimidated, but in your hearts sanctify Christ as Lord. Always be ready to make your defense to anyone who demands from you an accounting for the hope that is in you; yet do it with gentleness and reverence. Keep your conscience clear, so that, when you are maligned, those who abuse you for your good conduct in Christ may be put to shame. For it is better to suffer for doing good, if suffering should be God's will, than to suffer for doing evil. For Christ also suffered for sins once for all, the righteous for the unrighteous, in order to bring you to God. He was put to death in the flesh, but made alive in the spirit ... (1 Pet 3:8–18)

Despite the harassment the Christians have endured from the surrounding culture as "aliens and exiles," they do not attempt to respond in kind but with the quality of their lives and the witness of their testimony of hope. This is one of the remarkable qualities of this New Testament book.

The letter's proclamation of Christ and his example is to suffuse the lives of the Christians and make them holy:

Above all, maintain constant love for one another, for love covers a multitude of sins.

Be hospitable to one another without complaining. Like good stewards of the manifold grace of God, serve one another with whatever gift each of you has received. Whoever speaks must do so as one speaking the very words of God; whoever serves must do so with the strength that God supplies, so that God may be glorified in all things through Jesus Christ. To him belong the glory and the power forever and ever. Amen. (1 Pet 4:8–11)

Conclusion

Why is the First Letter of Peter considered "sacred"? Obviously not because of its biographical information about the apostle Peter— of which there is virtually none.[7] Instead, this letter is sacred to Christians because of its compelling proclamation of the gospel, that is, the death and resurrection of Jesus Christ, and the significance of this act of salvation for the nature of the church, as the pattern for the holiness of its members and their mission of witness to the world.

The First Letter of John

Another of the so-called catholic epistles is the First Letter of John. As was the case with Hebrews and James, it has few characteristics of an actual letter and is more of a manifesto of the author to encourage and instruct a community, or more likely, a series of communities to which it was sent. There is no mention of any specific recipient at the outset of the text and no specific greetings at its conclusion. There has been considerable debate about the authorship of the letter and its relationship to the Gospel of John. Particularly in the case of 1 John (as distinct from 2 & 3 John), the

---

[7] The Second Letter of Peter, which is dated by virtually all scholars as composed late in the first or early second century and not authored by the historical Peter, has one "autobiographical" note, referring to Peter's witness of the transfiguration: "We ourselves heard this voice come from heaven, while we were with him on the holy mountain" (2 Pet 1:18).

style of language and the content, including the qualities ascribed to Christ, are strongly reminiscent of the Gospel of John, for example, the emphasis on "light" (1 John 1:5–10), on "truth" (2:8), and on the seductions of the "world" (2:15). Also 1 John has a sharp "dualistic" tone, with clear contrasts emphasized between "light" and "darkness," "truth and falsehood," "fidelity" and "betrayal"— not unlike similar perspectives in the Gospel of John. Whether or not the letter was written by the same author of the Gospel, they both share a similar perspective and literary style.

There is also speculation about the dating of 1 John. Was it composed before or after the Gospel? Raymond E. Brown, one of the major commentators on the Johannine literature, suggests that the letter came after the Gospel was composed, even if the Gospel itself may have undergone some final editing later in the first century after the letter.[8] One notable comparison that supports this is that in the Gospel of John, the opponents of Jesus are frequently labeled as "the Jews" and there are sharp clashes between Jesus and the Jewish religious leaders throughout the narrative, plus a suggestion that followers of Jesus were being expelled from the synagogue (see John 9:22). But in the First Letter of John there is no mention of this tension; now the tension is between the author and fellow Christians who have gone astray and apparently separated themselves from the community (see, e.g., 1 John 2:19). This intra-Christian polemic commands even more intensely the focus of the Second and Third Letters (see 2 John 7–11: 3 John 9–10).

---

[8] See Raymond E. Brown's succinct statement about the authorship of the Johannine letters in his *Introduction to the New Testament*, pp. 383–405, a synthesis of positions elaborated in his full-length commentary, *The Epistles of John* (The Anchor Bible; New York: Doubleday, 1982).

Jesus the Incarnate Word

A central reason for this division in the community is that some Christians had called into doubt the humanity of Jesus. While the Gospel of John presents Jesus as an exalted and transcendent figure—the Word of God—there is also a strong emphasis on the authentic humanity of Jesus: "The Word became flesh and dwelt among us" (John 1:14). This bedrock claim of the Gospel would be declared a formal doctrine of Christianity at the Council of Chalcedon in 451 AD but was already asserted in a variety of ways in the New Testament, none more firmly than in the Gospel of John (see also the final acclamation of Thomas: "My Lord and My God" in John 20:28). This same conviction runs through the Letters of John. The author of 1 John lays out the choice in stark terms:

> Beloved, do not believe every spirit, but test the spirits to see whether they are from God; for many false prophets have gone out into the world. By this you know the Spirit of God: every spirit that confesses that Jesus Christ has come in the flesh is from God, and every spirit that does not confess Jesus is not from God. (1 John 4:1–3)

The Second Letter of John is equally severe on this:

> Many deceivers have gone out into the world, those who do not confess that Jesus Christ has come in the flesh; any such person is the deceiver and the antichrist! Be on your guard, so that you do not lose what we have worked for, but may receive a full reward. Everyone who does not abide in the teaching of Christ, but goes beyond it, does not have God; whoever abides in the teaching has both the Father and the Son. Do not receive into the house or welcome anyone who comes to you and does not bring this teaching; for to welcome is to participate in the evil deeds of such a person. (2 John 7–11)

At stake was belief in the Incarnation, the Christian doctrine that Jesus Christ was both divine and human. In the second century there would be a number of controversies about this, with some such as the Docetists and other Gnostic groups, affirming the divinity of Christ but denying that he was truly human—only taking on the form of a human. Some scholars believe that the conflict standing behind the Johannine Letters was an early phase of this fundamental controversy.

While the Gospel of John affirmed the traditional teaching of Jesus's authentic humanity, later members of the Johannine communities began to question this. Thus, the author of 1 John affirms at the outset of the letter that his teaching (about the human nature of Jesus) was the authentic tradition:

> We declare to you what was from the beginning, what we have heard, what we have seen with our eyes, what we have looked at and touched with our hands, concerning the word of life—this life was revealed, and we have seen it and testify to it, and declare to you the eternal life that was with the Father and was revealed to us—we declare to you what we have seen and heard so that you also may have fellowship with us; and truly our fellowship is with the Father and with his Son Jesus Christ. We are writing these things so that our joy may be complete. (1 John 1:1–4; see also 2:7, 24; 3:11)

The Love Command

Of particular importance for the author of 1 John is Jesus's teaching of the "love command"—a central emphasis of John's Gospel as well. In the letter the author, in effect, condenses the very essence of Jesus's mission and the requirements of discipleship from the Johannine point of view. Jesus is the embodiment of God's love for the world and is sent into the world to proclaim this message of love.

Those who are "children of God" obey God's command, expressed in love for one another. In one of the letter's most frequently quoted passages, this teaching is eloquently stated:

> Beloved, let us love one another, because love is from God; everyone who loves is born of God and knows God. Whoever does not love does not know God, for God is love. God's love was revealed among us in this way: God sent his only Son into the world so that we might live through him. In this is love, not that we loved God but that he loved us and sent his Son to be the atoning sacrifice for our sins. Beloved, since God loved us so much, we also ought to love one another. No one has ever seen God; if we love one another, God lives in us, and his love is perfected in us. By this we know that we abide in him and he in us, because he has given us of his Spirit. And we have seen and do testify that the Father has sent his Son as the Savior of the world. God abides in those who confess that Jesus is the Son of God, and they abide in God. So we have known and believe the love that God has for us. God is love, and those who abide in love abide in God, and God abides in them. (1 John 4:7–16; reaffirmed in 1 John 5:1–12)

And here we encounter another deep pattern of the New Testament writings: the essential connection between God's love manifested in Jesus and the qualities that the followers of Jesus are to exemplify. If one can sum up the life of Jesus as loving self-sacrifice for others, then this is also to be the pattern of Christian existence.

Conclusion

Although the First Letter of John (as well as the Second and Third Letters) stood originally on the perimeters of the New Testament canon and some early church leaders questioned its canonical status, it eventually was counted among the "sacred" and canonical books of the New Testament. While its claim to apostolic authorship no doubt was an important consideration, its content also fits under the category of the "rule of faith." The letter affirms that the encounter with God through Jesus is decisive for Christian faith. At the same time, as many of the later New Testament writings do, it strongly rejects views that would blunt or distort this central teaching. At its heart, 1 John is not about information but proclamation. The author proclaims to his recipients the gospel that was true and compelling, "from the beginning."

The Book of Revelation

The book of Revelation serves as the conclusion of the New Testament and remains one of its most distinctive and challenging books. The title "Revelation" comes from the first word of the book which claims it is a "revelation of Jesus Christ;" the term "revelation" in Greek is *apocalypsis*, explaining the traditional title for the book, "The Apocalypse." The book presents itself as testimony about a great "vision" or "revelation" of Jesus Christ given to "John," who seems to be in exile on the Mediterranean island of Patmos (1:1–2, 9). Unlike many early commentators, most scholars today surmise that this "John" is not the same apostolic John which tradition identified as the author of the Gospel of John and the Johannine letters. "John the Seer" or "John the Divine," as he is called, writes in a very different style and with a different theological perspective than the other Johannine materials we have considered.

It seems that the John of the Apocalypse was a leader of the early church in western Asia Minor late in the first century during a time of persecution by Roman authorities. While in exile on this penal island he writes to several churches, testifying to his remarkable vision and determined to both encourage and challenge his fellow Christians. The letter is a mixture of literary forms. The author himself speaks of it as a "word of prophecy" (1:3), expressed especially like the great Israelite prophets in the sharp corrections and challenges he poses for his fellow Christians. Chapters 2 and 3 take the form of letters written to the Christian communities in seven major cities in the western region of the Roman province of Asia: Ephesus, Smyrna, Pergamum, Thyatira, Sardis, Philadelphia, and Laodicea. Each is a mixture of admonition, some praise, and sharp warnings. Most of the book takes the form of "apocalyptic" writing, revealing the dramatic content of the author's vision. Here the author employs the vivid and often enigmatic symbolism of Jewish apocalyptic writings such as those of the book of Daniel or Enoch, which report on heavenly visions and use vivid symbols and snatches of Greco-Roman mythology to proclaim its message.

Rome as the Beast

Dominant in the letter is the powerful and seductive threat posed by the Roman Empire. The idolatrous claims of divine status for the Emperor and the severely oppressive economic exploitation of the Roman Empire and its impact on the poor lead the author to consider the Empire as demonic.[9] The Empire is represented by a fearsome beast, intent on destroying God's people and wreaking havoc on earth. This "beast" blasphemes God and God's name and is permitted "to make war on the saints." It is given "authority over every tribe and people and language and nation, and all the inhabitants of the earth will worship it" (Rev. 13:7–8). Particularly strong is Revelation's critique of the economic havoc the "beast"

[9] Francis Moloney challenges the dominant role of Roman persecution as the underlying issue of Revelation. He asserts that the victory of the Risen Christ over the forces of death—a triumph anticipated from the beginning of time is the fundamental message of Revelation. Roman oppression and economic exploitation are simply an illustration of the symptoms of evil and death over which Christ triumphs; see Francis J. Moloney, SDB, *The Apocalypse of John: A Commentary* (Grand Rapids: Baker Academic, 2020).

wreaks on the poor through its economic exploitation. Chapters 17 and 18 describe in vivid detail God's final judgment against the destructive economic network of the Empire, as an avenging Angel cries out:

"Fallen, fallen is Babylon the great! It has become a dwelling place of demons, a haunt of every foul spirit, a haunt of every foul bird, a haunt of every foul and hateful beast.

For all the nations have drunk of the wine of the wrath of her fornication, and the kings of the earth have committed fornication with her, and the merchants of the earth have grown rich from the power of her luxury . . ." And the kings of the earth, who committed fornication and lived in luxury with her, will weep and wail over her when they see the smoke of her burning; they will stand far off, in fear of her torment, and say, "Alas, alas, the great city, Babylon, the mighty city! For in one hour your judgment has come." And the merchants of the earth weep and mourn for her, since no one buys their cargo anymore, cargo of gold, silver, jewels and pearls, fine linen, purple, silk and scarlet, all kinds of scented wood, all articles of ivory, all articles of costly wood, bronze, iron, and marble, cinnamon, spice, incense, myrrh, frankincense, wine, olive oil, choice flour and wheat, cattle and sheep, horses and chariots, slaves—and human lives. "The fruit for which your soul longed has gone from you, and all your dainties and your splendor are lost to you, never to be found again!" The merchants of these wares, who gained wealth from her, will stand far off, in fear of her torment, weeping and mourning aloud, "Alas, alas, the great city, clothed in fine linen, in purple and scarlet, adorned with gold, with jewels, and with pearls! For in one hour all this wealth has been laid waste!" And all shipmasters and seafarers, sailors and all whose trade is on the sea, stood far off and cried out as they saw the smoke of her burning, "What city was like the great city?" And they threw dust on their heads, as they wept and mourned, crying out, "Alas, alas, the great city, where all who had ships at sea grew rich by her wealth! For in one hour she has been laid waste." (Rev 18:2-17)

Unlike the perspectives of Paul in Romans 12 which called for respect for legitimate civic authority or 1 Peter (1 Pet 2:13-17) that also advised respect for imperial authority and a stance of good conduct as a witness to the wider world, the author of Revelation rejects all compromise with a system that it views as inherently evil and opposed to the Christian faith. Thus, any form of accommodation on the part of the churches he addresses is condemned, including the practice of eating meat that had been offered in pagan rituals—a practice Paul permitted as long as it did not offend fellow Christians who had "weak" consciences (compare 1 Cor 8:1-13 and Rev 2:14, 20).

The Lamb That Was Slain

Standing in opposition to the Roman Empire—the "beast" and the corrupt "Babylon"—is the figure of the Risen and Exalted Christ, presented consistently in Revelation as the "Lamb that was slain." The lamb of sacrifice, a seemingly vulnerable character, becomes the one who through the sacrifice of his life conquers the demonic power of the beast:

> Then one of the elders said to me, "Do not weep. See, the Lion of the tribe of Judah, the Root of David, has conquered, so that he can open the scroll and its seven seals." Then I saw between the throne and the four living creatures and among the elders a Lamb standing as if it had been slaughtered, having seven horns and seven eyes, which are the seven spirits of God sent out into all the earth. He went and took the scroll from the right hand of the one who was seated on the throne. When he had taken the scroll, the four living creatures and the twenty-four elders fell before

the Lamb, each holding a harp and golden bowls full of incense, which are the prayers of the saints. They sing a new song: "You are worthy to take the scroll and to open its seals, for you were slaughtered and by your blood you ransomed for God saints from every tribe and language and people and nation; you have made them to be a kingdom and priests serving our God, and they will reign on earth." Then I looked, and I heard the voice of many angels surrounding the throne and the living creatures and the elders; they numbered myriads of myriads and thousands of thousands, singing with full voice, "Worthy is the Lamb that was slaughtered to receive power and wealth and wisdom and might and honor and glory and blessing!" Then I heard every creature in heaven and on earth and under the earth and in the sea, and all that is in them, singing, "To the one seated on the throne and to the Lamb be blessing and honor and glory and might forever and ever!" And the four living creatures said, "Amen!" And the elders fell down and worshiped. (Rev 5:5–14)

The image of Christ as a "lamb" is already found in the Gospel of John where John the Baptist acclaims Jesus as "the lamb of God who takes away the sin of the world" (John 1:29; see also 1:36). Later in the Gospel, John will align the moment of Jesus's crucifixion with the time when the Passover lambs were slain in the temple (see John 19:14), another possible connection with this motif. In Revelation the portrayal of Jesus as the "lamb that was slain" leaves no doubt that the author is evoking the Passover ritual as a means of affirming the atoning power of Christ's death. But, additionally, pitting the figure of a lamb over against a ravenous beast points to another level of symbolism—the brute and violent power of the Roman Empire is overcome by the witness of love and justice exemplified by Christ and his followers. Thus, the symbolism of the "lamb" defangs the toxic power of the beast; the "saints" redeemed by Christ's triumph over the power of death come "from every tribe and language and people and nation" and become "a kingdom and priests serving our God" and "they will reign on earth" (Rev 5:9–10).

That final triumph is described in the conclusion to Revelation. The vison of the Seer draws to a close with a vision of "a new heaven and a new earth" that replaces the former realm of suffering and injustice. In its midst is the new Jerusalem, a city transformed:

> Then I saw a new heaven and a new earth; for the first heaven and the first earth had passed away, and the sea was no more. And I saw the holy city, the new Jerusalem, coming down out of heaven from God, prepared as a bride adorned for her husband.
>
> And I heard a loud voice from the throne saying, "See, the home of God is among mortals. He will dwell with them; they will be his peoples, and God himself will be with them; he will wipe every tear from their eyes. Death will be no more; mourning and crying and pain will be no more, for the first things have passed away." And the one who was seated on the throne said, "See, I am making all things new." (Rev 21:1–4)

The author describes this new Jerusalem as incredibly beautiful and richly adorned, perhaps consciously comparing it to the famously opulent villas of the imperial court, whose excesses and injustice are now replaced by the new Jerusalem, a place where God dwells and where is life is vibrant (see the extended description in Rev 21:9–22:5). It is important to note that the author's vision is not that of a "heavenly" or purely spiritual Jerusalem but of a renewed and earthly Jerusalem. The "holy city, the new Jerusalem, *comes down* out of heaven from God . . . " (Rev. 21:3). Thus, the apocalyptic vision of this New Testament foresees a transformation and renewal of the earth, from being a place of terror and exploitation under the Beast, to a place of justice and light ruled by the Lamb of God:

Nothing accursed will be found there anymore. But the throne of God and of the Lamb will be in it, and his servants will worship him; they will see his face, and his name will be on their foreheads. And there will be no more night; they need no light of lamp or sun, for the Lord God will be their light, and they will reign forever and ever. (Rev 22:3–5)

It not surprising that the dramatic and often enigmatic apocalyptic symbolism that runs through the book of Revelation has triggered a variety of interpretations over the centuries. For some, more fundamentalist, interpretations, its code-like predictions have been taken as predictors of future events that will lead to the end of the world. Most contemporary scholars see the original goal of Revelation not as a prediction of future events but as a coded critique of the excesses of the Roman Empire and a call for fidelity, courage, and perseverance on the part of the Christians to whom the book was addressed. One author, Elizabeth Fiorenza, has made an interesting comparison to Martin Luther King's famous "Letter from a Birmingham Jail."[10] At a time of crisis, Dr. King wrote a text that had a threefold component: (1) naming the "beast," which was systemic racism; (2) describing a future world of justice; and (3) encouraging his followers to persevere and not lose hope. Those same fundamental components mark the book of Revelation, Fiorenza noted the following: (1) the "beast" was the destructive power of the Roman Empire; (2) the vision of a "new heavens and a new earth" with the New Jerusalem as its center is the world of justice and peace that the victory of Christ would make possible; and (3) the author exhorts the churches not to compromise but to persevere and remain faithful.

While this analysis of the immediate strategy of the book of Revelation is persuasive, it is also important to note that the

---

[10] Elisabeth Schüssler Fiorenza, *Revelation. Vision of a Just World* (Proclamation Commentaries; Minneapolis, MN: Fortress Press, 1991), pp. 10–12.

foundation for this is the author's proclamation of Christ as the "Lamb who was slain" and is now triumphant. At the heart of Revelation's message is one that is found in virtually every New Testament book, namely the triumph over the power of death effected thought the death and resurrection of Jesus Christ. In the case of Revelation, that proclamation is cloaked in the strange language and symbols of an apocalyptic vision, but the fundamental content and purpose of the book align with the Gospels, Paul's writings, and most of the other New Testament texts we have considered. In this case, too, the Christology of the book is the foundation for its ethical message. The courage and faithful perseverance of the persecuted Christians addressed by John the Seer are to take their inspiration from the fidelity and courage of the Crucified and Risen Christ. Just as Jesus had faced the menacing power of Rome and triumphed; so, too, would the Christians of Asia Minor.

It is here, in what we could call the fundamental pastoral theology of Revelation, we find its timeless message for Christians and the reason it was ultimately judged to be "sacred" and an integral part of the New Testament. By its place at the end of the canonical sequence, the book of Revelation does serve as a "predictor" of the future. Not the future in the sense that its contents reveal a calendar of specific future historical events that will usher in the end of the world, but the "future" in the sense that fundamental Christian hope believes in the ultimate triumph of God over the forces of death and in that, the renewal of humanity and of creation itself.[11]

---

[11] On this see Ryan Leif Hansen, *Silence and Praise. Rhetorical Cosmology and Political Theology in the Book of Revelation* (Minneapolis, MN: Fortress, Press, 2014).

Conclusion

Like the Gospels and the Pauline literature, the New Testament books we have considered here were all judged to be "sacred" by early Christianity, even though in some cases it took a while for that judgment to be universally accepted. For the ones we have considered, no doubt the criterion of "apostolic origin" was at work. Hebrews was associated by many with Paul the Apostle; James was believed either to be the apostle James or, at least, the James of Jerusalem and the "brother of the Lord" closely associated with the apostles; 1 Peter was attributed to Peter the Apostle, even if modern scholarship doubts that probability; and the Letters of John and the book of Revelation were linked with the apostle John.

Even if this purported apostolic link paved the way for these texts to be included in the canon, examination of their contents shows that another and perhaps deeper instinct was also at work. Each of these New Testament texts in its own distinctive way proclaims the "gospel" of Jesus Christ, presenting him as both the revealer of the Divine and as its embodiment. The death and resurrection of Christ and the significance of this for all human destiny form the basic message of these biblical texts and lay the foundation for the ethical demands they propose. In this lies the judgment that for Christians they are sacred texts.

If Christology is fundamental to the sacredness of New Testament books, then so, too, is the guide they offer for Christian holiness, both for the individual follower of Jesus and for the community formed in his name. It is to this dimension of the "sacredness" of the New Testament we now turn.

7

Christian Holiness and the Sacredness of the New Testament

The Gospels and Paul

Scanning the New Testament to learn the reason Christians consider it "sacred" has led to the realization that the primary function of the books of the New Testament is to proclaim the unique identity and profound religious significance of Jesus Christ, whom Christian believers hold as the embodiment of the divine presence in the world. The Four Gospels proclaim that message through biographical narratives whose purpose is not simply to inform their Christian readers about the history of Jesus of Nazareth but to proclaim the present spiritual reality of the crucified and risen Christ. The letters of Paul to early Christian communities in Asia Minor, Macedonia, Achaia, and Rome were intended not simply to keep in touch or to respond to their concerns and questions but ultimately to extend to his fellow Christians his missionary proclamation of the person of Jesus Christ as the redeemer of the world. Letters such as Colossians or Ephesians, perhaps written in Paul's name beyond his lifetime, share in the same purpose—now extending Christian proclamation of Jesus to incorporate his significance for the universe itself. New Testament books as diverse in literary form and context as the Letter to the Hebrews, or the Letter of James, or 1 Peter, or 1 John, or the book of Revelation—each in their way can also be described as fostering in their recipients an encounter with the person, mission, and teaching of Jesus.

The New Testament. Donald Senior, Oxford University Press. © Oxford University Press 2022.
DOI: 10.1093/oso/9780197530832.003.0008

It is because of this intense focus on the both earthly and transcendent figure of Jesus as viewed by Christian faith that the New Testament books have a "sacred" character for the community of faith. But like any proclamation or preaching, these New Testament portrayals of Jesus are not abstract or speculative. As one author put it, the books of the New Testament are not the equivalent of a first-century academic theological seminar. The purpose of their proclamation is to compel the recipients of their words to respond to what they hear, to transform their lives, and to discover the path to individual and communal holiness. The concluding words of chapter 20 of John's Gospel make explicit what is implicit in all of the New Testament writings: "Now Jesus did many other signs in the presence of his disciples, which are not written in this book. But these are written so that you may come to believe that Jesus is the Messiah, the Son of God, and that through believing you may have life in his name" (John 20:30–31).

One of the criteria for the inclusion of the diverse books of the New Testament into the canon was their widespread "reception" by the communities of the early church. "Reception" in this context did not mean simply agreeing to receive these texts or even allowing them to be read in the assemblies of these communities, although the latter was a very important endorsement of any text sent to a community. A prior "condition" for their full and widespread acceptance was the transformative impact these readings had on the lives of the Christians who encountered them. The content of these writings—bolstered by their assumed apostolic origin—inspired, challenged, and instructed the recipients on how to lead a life of holiness expressed in virtue and mutual love, together with their fellow believers and extending in mission out to the world around them. The New Testament writings were "sacred" because they proclaimed Christ and because that proclamation opened the path to holiness for Christians.

It is this impact of the New Testament we want to explore briefly in this chapter. As has been the case all along, the diverse literary forms and historical contexts of the individual New Testament books influence the way they have an impact on their recipients. Our goal here is not to present a full study of New Testament ethics, a task far beyond the scope of this book.[1] Instead, we will present enough examples to demonstrate that the books of the New Testament anticipate that the Christian readers will both expect and discover within these texts guidance on how to live a life of holiness.

"Following Jesus": The Gospels and the Way of Discipleship

How do the Gospels enable their readers to discover the path to holiness? The Gospels are narratives, not essays or treatises. They reveal authentic holiness through the dynamics of the story they tell—both in the example of Jesus and in the reactions of key characters in the narrative. Particularly important in this regard are the ways the Gospels portray Jesus's disciples. "Discipleship" in the sense of a "learner" (the Greek word used for disciple is *mattheteus* or "learner") was familiar to Judaism, as would-be students of the law attached themselves to learned rabbis. But the notion of discipleship in the Gospels has its own unique qualities. More than with any other characters in the Gospels, the Christian readers through the centuries have identified with the disciples of Jesus, both for the privilege of following Jesus and for the sobering example of their weaknesses and failures. Although here, too, as with the Gospels' diverse portraits of Jesus, there are different nuances in each of the evangelists' portrayals of the disciples. Our goal, however, is to

---

[1] See, for example, Richard B. Hays, *The Moral Vision of the New Testament: Community, Cross, New Creation. A Contemporary Introduction to New Testament Ethics* (San Francisco: Harper, 1996); Frank Matera, *New Testament Ethics. The Legacies of Jesus and Paul* (Louisville, KY: Westminster John Knox Press, 1996).

focus mainly on the common characteristics of discipleship found across the Four Gospels.

The Call to Discipleship in the Gospel Literature

One of the evident characteristics of discipleship in the Gospels is the fact that discipleship is a "call," not a choice, a significant difference from the disciple–master relationship in Judaism where the student would seek out a suitable master. The Synoptic Gospels present the calling of Jesus's disciples among the very first actions of his mission. For Mark, followed by Matthew, that call comes along the shore of the Sea of Galilee as Jesus encounters a group of fishermen tending their nets (see Mark 1:16–21). There is no lead-in to or preparation for their call—emphasizing that the initiative is from Jesus alone and not from the deliberation of the disciples. Jesus summons them to "come follow me and I will make you fishers of people" (Mark 1:17). Immediately, the first clusters of disciples respond (identified as "Simon and Andrew," and "James and John," two sets of brothers), leaving everything behind and following Jesus. Luke's Gospel adds a dramatic flair, having the call of the first disciples take place on the Sea of Galilee itself (see Luke 5:1–11). Despite a night of frustrated fishing, Jesus instructs the disciples to let down their nets and "put out into the deep water," and there follows an abundant catch. Peter, struck by the power of Jesus's words, falls to his knees, pleading, "Go away from me, Lord, for I am a sinful man!" But Jesus reassures him: "Do not be afraid; from now on you will be catching people." The narrator notes, "When they had brought their boats to shore, they left everything and followed him" (Luke 5:11). Other stories in the Gospels such as the call of Levi (Mark 2:13–17; designated as "Matthew" in Matthew's Gospel; Matt 9:9–13) or the examples of Bartimaeus or Zacchaeus demonstrate this same decisive commitment to following Jesus (see Mark 10:46–52; Luke 19:1–10).

Here, as in virtually all aspects of the Gospel narratives, John's Gospel takes a distinctive path. The setting for the call of the disciples is not at the Sea; rather it is at "Bethany across the Jordan" where John the Baptist was baptizing. Jesus's presence lures away some of John's disciples who seek him out (see John 1:35–42); later Jesus will also call disciples in Galilee but, again, not in the setting of the sea (John 1:43–51). Although the Johannine Jesus does not use the same words as the Synoptic accounts, there is no doubt that for John's Gospel, too, following Jesus and sharing in his mission define the essence of discipleship.

In each of these accounts, the command of Jesus points to two fundamental characteristics of discipleship. The first is "following Jesus," setting up the basic dynamic of the Christian life. To "follow Jesus" means to live by his teaching and his example. In the Old Testament, a fundamental obligation that underwrites the entire ethic of the Mosaic law is the summons of God "to be holy as I am holy" (Lev 19:2), a basic link between the character of God's own actions and the ethical requirements of those who respond to God in faith and obedience. That call to "imitate" God is found in key sayings of Jesus, such as in Matt 5:48, "Be perfect, therefore, as your heavenly Father is perfect." Luke's parallel is, "Be merciful, just as your Father is merciful" (Luke 6:36). In Christian, and especially in Catholic Christianity, this axiom becomes the equation that "imitation of Christ" is equivalent to "imitation of God."[2]

The second basic principle of discipleship is reflected in Jesus's metaphor: "And I will make you fishers of people" (Mark 1:17; Matt 4:19). In all Four Gospels, Jesus commissions his disciples to carry on the work of his own mission of proclamation of the reign of God and of healing and exorcisms (see, e.g., Mark 3:13–19; Matt 10:1–4; Luke 9:1–6). John's unique formulation makes the same equivalency, but again without the metaphor of fishing, when the Risen

---

[2] See the famous work of Thomas a Kempis, *Imitatio Christi*, one of the most popular devotional treatises in the late Middle Ages.

Jesus declares, "As the Father has sent me, so I send you" (John 20:21; see also 17:18). Jesus is defined in John's Gospel as "the one sent" from the Father and now that status is given to the disciples.

Thus, early in the gospel narratives, Jesus gathers a community of disciples, presents himself as a model for their lives of discipleship, and commissions them to share in his mission of redeeming the world.

Faith as Fundamental Response

Discipleship as portrayed in the Gospels is not an intellectual exercise but a compelling and all-encompassing relationship. Disciples are expected to conform their entire lives to following Jesus. They are to "believe" in him, that is, to entrust their lives to him and his mission. This relationship of trust and commitment defines the notion of "faith" described in the Gospels. There are numerous sayings and stories in the Gospels that spell out this required commitment on the part of the disciples. The idea of "leaving behind" one's former way of living and even to separate from one's family is stressed. So, too, "possessions" that stand in the way of one's freedom to act are to be put aside. In Luke's Gospel, for example, a series of would-be disciples are rebuffed when they place other obligations first, before following Jesus, even in the face of a sacred obligation such as burying one's father (see Luke 9:57–62). Similarly, Matthew presents the story of the rich young man who is unable to let go of his possessions in order to follow Jesus (Matt 19:16–27.). In Mark's Gospel, during their journey to Jerusalem, Peter says to Jesus, " 'Look, we have left everything and followed you.' Jesus said, 'Truly I tell you, there is no one who has left house or brothers or sisters or mother or father or children or fields, for my sake and for the sake of the gospel, who will not receive a hundredfold now in this age—houses, brothers and sisters, mothers and children, and fields, with persecutions—and in the age to come eternal life'" (Mark 10:28–30). The comprehensive nature of the commitment to discipleship is clear.

The Gospels also use other metaphors for "faith" such as perception metaphors of "seeing," "hearing," and "understanding." In Mark's account, the failure of the disciples to understand Jesus's multiplication of the loaves and his warning about the "leaven" of the Pharisees and Herod triggers his lament about their lack of faith:

> Do you still not perceive or understand? Are your hearts hardened? Do you have eyes, and fail to see? Do you have ears, and fail to hear? And do you not remember? When I broke the five loaves for the five thousand, how many baskets full of broken pieces did you collect?" They said to him, "Twelve." "And the seven for the four thousand, how many baskets full of broken pieces did you collect?" And they said to him, "Seven." Then he said to them, "Do you not yet understand?" (Mark 8:17–21)

Here, as in Jesus's warning about those who do not understand his parables (Mark 4:11–12), these perception metaphors echo the words of Isaiah 6:9–10, chastising Israel for its failure to respond.

For John's Gospel, too, "faith" in Jesus is a supreme commitment. As we noted previously, John portrays Jesus as the "Word of God," whose message of God's love for the world is expressed in both his powerful actions (i.e., his miraculous "signs" in John's terminology) and his "words" or discourses. Faith in John's account means that the disciple both "hears" and "listens' to the words of Jesus and "sees" and "understands" the meaning of his signs.

Characteristic Signs of Christian Holiness

In multiple ways the Gospels portray Jesus as the embodiment of the divine presence and the exemplar of authentic holiness. The call to believe in Jesus, to "follow after" him and to share in his mission, is the entry point into the fundamental encounter of the Christian with Jesus Christ that is the basic purpose of the Gospels. As Lee Martin McDonald notes, "It is obvious that the Gospels were not written as objective and unbiased reports about Jesus, but rather as documents written to foster the faith of Jesus' followers and to inform them about his life, teachings, death, resurrection, and exaltation (ascension/return), with the obvious implications of these traditions for his followers. The authors of the Gospels would likely be offended if they were accused of writing unbiased historical reports."[3] That encounter with Jesus through the Gospels is meant to be transformative; the life of the Christian is to reflect the patterns of Jesus's own life. The Gospels spell out those values and ways of life that reflect this encounter with Jesus and define what authentic holiness means, both for the individual Christian and for the Christian community.

The absolute center of the Gospels' portrayal of Jesus is his death and resurrection. Late in the nineteenth century the German scholar Martin Kahler famously described the Gospels as "passion narratives with a long introduction."[4] The New Testament itself understands the meaning of the death of Jesus as an act of self-transcendence, a sacrifice driven by love, the culmination of a life poured out in service to others. The meaning of Jesus's death as an act of love coincides with Jesus's own teaching about the central command of the Mosaic Law. When asked by a lawyer what was the first commandment of the law, Jesus replies, " 'You shall love the Lord your God with all your heart, and with all your soul, and with all your mind.' This is the greatest and first commandment. And a second is like it: 'You shall love your neighbor as yourself.' On these two commandments hang all the law and the prophets" (Matt

---

[3] See John J. Collins, Craig A. Evans, and Lee Martin McDonald, *Ancient Jewish and Christian Scriptures. New Developments in Canon Controversy* (Louisville, KY: Westminster John Knox Press, 2020), p. 101.

[4] Martin Kahler, *The So-called Historical Jesus and the Historic, Biblical Christ*, p. 80, n. 11; first published in 1992, it has been reprinted by Fortress Press in 1966.

22:35–40). John's Gospel captures this core meaning in an explicit way in describing the death of Jesus as an act of love, itself expressive of God's love for the world: "No one has greater love than this, to lay down one's life for one's friends" (John 15:13). As John's passion narrative begins, the narrator notes: "Now before the festival of the Passover, Jesus knew that his hour had come to depart from this world and go to the Father. Having loved his own who were in the world, he loved them to the end" (John 13:1). Christian faith holds that Jesus's death, which to his opponents appeared as a defeat, as a "no" to his mission, is transformed into victory and affirmation through the resurrection of Jesus. God's "yes" overturns a human "no" and thereby confirms the validity of Jesus's cause.

The descriptions of Jesus's mission that lead into the gospel passion narratives illustrate the modalities of love and service that find their final expression in Jesus's death. His healings, his confrontations with the power of evil, his outreach to those pushed to the margins, his prophetic courage in the face of opposition and rejection, his words of truth—all of these are portrayed as expressions of love from the vantage point of the Gospels. All of these fulfill the primary command of the law as taught by Jesus. And all of this provides the rationale for the commitments and virtues that are to characterize the follower of Jesus, and the qualities of the community formed of such followers.

This equation between the example of Jesus and the character of Christian discipleship is found throughout the Gospels. The words of Jesus in Mark's Gospel are explicit: "If any want to become my followers, let them deny themselves and take up their cross and follow me. For those who want to save their life will lose it, and those who lose their life for my sake, and for the sake of the gospel, will save it" (Mark 8:34–35). The same fundamental commitment to "giving one's life" in service that motivated Jesus's own mission is to become a fundamental stance of the disciple as well. In Jesus's parable of the sheep and the goats found in Matthew's Gospel, the exalted "Son of Man" who comes at the end of time to judge the world bases his verdict precisely on these characteristic actions of Jesus: feeding the hungry, giving drink to the thirsty, welcoming the stranger, clothing the naked, caring for the sick, and visiting the prisoners (see Matt 25:31–46). At his final Passover with his disciples in John's account, Jesus washes their feet as an act of humble service and underscores that this is to be an example for his disciples:

> After he had washed their feet, had put on his robe, and had returned to the table, he said to them, "Do you know what I have done to you? You call me Teacher and Lord—and you are right, for that is what I am. So if I, your Lord and Teacher, have washed your feet, you also ought to wash one another's feet. For I have set you an example, that you also should do as I have done to you. Very truly, I tell you, servants are not greater than their master, nor are messengers greater than the one who sent them. If you know these things, you are blessed if you do them." (John 13:12–17)

The biblical scholar Michael Gorman has labeled these gospel virtues as "cruciform."[5] Most thoughtful moral philosophers of the ancient and modern world could name a number of qualities that characterize the moral person: honesty, a sense of fairness, fidelity, truthfulness, and so on. The virtues proclaimed in Jesus's teaching and reflected in the expectation of authentic discipleship would include similar lists. However, among this array of virtues there are some that rise to the surface because they more closely reflect the characteristic values and virtues of Jesus's own life: care for the poor and oppressed, a strong sense of justice, inclusion of those pushed to the margins, compassion and mercy, an inclination

---

[5] See Michel J. Gorman, *Cruciformity: Paul's Narrative Spirituality of the Cross* (Grand Rapids, MI: Eerdmans, 2001). This notion of "cruciformity" especially applies to Paul's ethical perspective, as we will note later.

to forgiveness and reconciliation, a commitment to service, and love for others. These reflect the deep character of Jesus's mission, grounded in his commitment to give his own life out of love for others—hence the term "cruciformity"—a way of living reflective of the spirit of Jesus crucified and risen.

The Destiny of the Disciples

The gospel portrayal of discipleship also affirms that the destiny of the disciple will share in the destiny of Jesus himself. "Eschatology" is a theological term for describing this New Testament and Christian perspective. The word *eschaton* in Greek means "final" or the "last"; "eschatology" refers to perspectives about the ultimate destiny of humanity and the world itself. Here, again, the death and resurrection of Jesus provide the foundation of Christian hopes about the "end time." Just as Jesus endured rejection, suffering, and death itself as the price of his mission, so, too, the followers of Jesus are to expect the same. But, just as God would vindicate Jesus's sacrifice with new and eternal life, the fate of the disciples of Jesus would also ultimately be victorious.

This type of scenario is described in the so-called apocalyptic discourses found in the Synoptic Gospels. In Mark 13, for example, seated on the Mount of Olives overlooking Jerusalem and its temple, Jesus warns his disciples:

> As for yourselves, beware; for they will hand you over to councils; and you will be beaten in synagogues; and you will stand before governors and kings because of me, as a testimony to them. And the good news must first be proclaimed to all nations. When they bring you to trial and hand you over, do not worry beforehand about what you are to say; but say whatever is given you at that time, for it is not you who speak, but the Holy Spirit. Brother will betray brother to death, and a father his child, and children will

rise against parents and have them put to death; and you will be hated by all because of my name. But the one who endures to the end will be saved. (Mark 13:9–13; see also Matt 10:16–22)

In the same setting in Matthew's Gospel, Jesus connects future sufferings with the future mission of the disciples:

Then they will hand you over to be tortured and will put you to death, and you will be hated by all nations because of my name. Then many will fall away, and they will betray one another and hate one another. And many false prophets will arise and lead many astray. And because of the increase of lawlessness, the love of many will grow cold. But the one who endures to the end will be saved. And this good news of the kingdom will be proclaimed throughout the world, as a testimony to all the nations; and then the end will come. (Matt 24:9–14)

Here again, John's Gospel has its own unique expression of a similar conviction about the ultimate destiny of the disciples. John's most vivid description of this is found in the final discourse of Jesus to his disciples on the eve of his death (John 13–17). Here Jesus reassures his disciples as he is about to leave them, promising that they will share his destiny with his Father. Here, too, as in the Synoptic Gospels, the Johannine Jesus warns his disciples of future suffering but also promises ultimate life with God:

I have made your name known to those whom you gave me from the world. They were yours, and you gave them to me, and they have kept your word. Now they know that everything you have given me is from you; for the words that you gave to me I have given to them, and they have received them and know in truth that I came from you; and they have believed that you sent me. I am asking on their behalf; I am not asking on behalf of the world, but on behalf of those whom you gave me, because they are yours.

All mine are yours, and yours are mine; and I have been glorified in them. And now I am no longer in the world, but they are in the world, and I am coming to you. Holy Father, protect them in your name that you have given me, so that they may be one, as we are one. While I was with them, I protected them in your name that you have given me. I guarded them, and not one of them was lost except the one destined to be lost, so that the scripture might be fulfilled. But now I am coming to you, and I speak these things in the world so that they may have my joy made complete in themselves. I have given them your word, and the world has hated them because they do not belong to the world, just as I do not belong to the world. I am not asking you to take them out of the world, but I ask you to protect them from the evil one. They do not belong to the world, just as I do not belong to the world. Sanctify them in the truth; your word is truth. You have sent me into the world, so I have sent them into the world. (John 17:6–18)

Beyond the warnings of the world's "hatred" of the disciples comes the promise of the disciples sharing in the destiny of Jesus with his Father:

I ask not only on behalf of these, but also on behalf of those who will believe in me through their word, that they may all be one. As you, Father, are in me and I am in you, may they also be in us, so that the world may believe that you have sent me. The glory that you have given me I have given them, so that they may be one, as we are one, I in them and you in me, that they may become completely one, so that the world may know that you have sent me and have loved them even as you have loved me. Father, I desire that those also, whom you have given me, may be with me where I am, to see my glory, which you have given me because you loved me before the foundation of the world. "Righteous Father, the world does not know you, but I know you; and these know that you have sent me. I made your name known to them, and I will make it known, so that the love with which you have loved me may be in them, and I in them. (John 17:20–26)

The Role of the Spirit

The Gospel of Luke, along with its second volume, the Acts of the Apostles, and the Gospel of John add another dimension of the experience of discipleship, namely the role of the Spirit. For both evangelists, the Spirit becomes the dynamic force that enables the followers of Jesus to live in the pattern of his holiness. In Luke's account, the power of God's Spirit is present from the beginning of Jesus's life. The Spirit overshadows Mary, the mother of Jesus (Luke 1:35), and animates other characters in the infancy narrative (Elizabeth in 1:41; Zachary 1:67; Simeon 2:25). The Spirit that descends on Jesus at the moment of his baptism (Luke 3:22) is also invoked by Jesus himself at the outset of his public ministry (Luke 4:18). Luke describes Jesus as "filled with the power of the Spirit" (4:14). It is this same spirit that the Risen Jesus promises to send to his disciples when he returns to his Father (24:49; see also Acts 1:5). And in the Acts of the Apostles, it is this Spirit that descends on the disciples at Pentecost and will drive the mission of the followers of Jesus "from Jerusalem to the ends of the earth" (Acts 1:8; 2:1–42). Luke mentions the decisive role of the Spirit some fifty-six times in the Acts of the Apostles (plus seventeen times in his Gospel). In effect, Luke spells out the premise we are describing in this chapter— encountering the Spirit of Jesus translates into the disciples' own experience of holiness and drives their sense of mission.

John's Gospel, too, gives an explicit role to the Spirit in Christian experience. In the first discourse of John's Gospel, Jesus testifies to Nicodemus about rebirth in the Spirit (John 3:5–8), but the Gospel's most emphatic description of the Spirit's role is in Jesus's final discourse. There Jesus, on the eve of his death, speaks of the Spirit as the "Paraclete"—a designation unique to John's Gospel. The Greek verb *parakaleo* has several layers of meaning: to "comfort," to "exhort," to "beseech" or "plead," a spread of meaning that expresses the varied dimensions of the Spirit's role. The Johannine Jesus promises to ask his Father to send the disciples "another Advocate" (John 14:16), one who protects and intercedes for them as Jesus himself had done. The Paraclete will also serve as the "collective memory" for the Christian community, helping the disciples receive and understand the teaching of Jesus (John 14:26), and this same Paraclete is the "Spirit of truth" testifying to the community about Jesus (John 15:26–27). And the Spirit Paraclete will also bolster the mission of the community in its confrontation with the world (John 16:7–11). In the resurrection appearance of Risen Jesus to his disciples in Jerusalem, he "breathes on them and says to them, 'Receive the Holy Spirit,'" empowering them for their mission ("As the Father has sent me, so I send you") and endowing them with the power to forgive sins (John 20:21–23).

Failing Disciples and Hostile Opponents

The gospel portrayal of authentic discipleship as a life of holiness drawn from the encounter with Jesus is communicated not simply by the example and teaching of Jesus and the ideals of discipleship. Also important are the negative examples of direct opposition to Jesus and the flaws and failures of his chosen disciples.

One of the remarkable features of the Gospels as "founding literature" is the refusal of the gospel writers to portray the first followers of Jesus in ideal terms. Alongside the privilege of their being called by Jesus to follow him and share in his mission, and of being witness to so much of his ministry of teaching and healing, are the multiple examples in all Four Gospels of the disciples' lack of understanding, their occasional resistance to Jesus and his teaching, and, especially in the drama of the Passion, their abandonment, betrayal, and public denial of him. Mark's Gospel seems to emphasize the flawed nature of the disciples more intensely than the other three: the disciples fail to understand the parables of Jesus; they are opposed to trying to feed the multitudes; they are confused (and termed "hard of heart") by the theophanies of Jesus's calming the storm and walking on the water; they resist his predictions of his impending passion; sleep during his prayer of anguish in the garden of Gethsemane; and, at the moment of Jesus's arrest, all of them abandon him. Peter, the apparent leader and spokesperson for the disciples, lingers behind, only to three times deny his discipleship when accosted by a servant.

Many of these incidents are repeated in Matthew and Luke, if with less intensity. When Peter resists Jesus's teaching about the necessity of the cross, Jesus calls him not only as a "Satan" but as a "stumbling block" (Matt 16:23). In Luke, at the sacred moment of the Last Passover Jesus celebrates with his disciples, an argument breaks out among the disciples over "who is the greatest" (Luke 22:24–27). And, of course, in all Four Gospels the figure of Judas, chosen as one of the Twelve, proves to be an utterly unfaithful disciple in betraying Jesus to his enemies.

In John's account, the disciples are less prominent than in the Synoptic narratives, yet here, too, there are examples of failing to understand Jesus, abandoning him (John 6:66), Peter's public denial (John 18:25–27), and Thomas's resistance to believing in Jesus's resurrection (John 20:24–25). In a beautiful scene in John 21, Jesus extracts from Peter a threefold confession of his love for Jesus to reconcile his threefold denial (John 21:15–19).

Along with the portrait of the disciples as frail and failing, the Gospels anticipate more resistance and rejection of Jesus on the part of his opponents, primarily the religious leaders of his own people. Many of the wrong attitudes of both opponents and flawed disciples are anticipated in Jesus's parables and teaching: the religious hypocrisy and false piety of the leaders (e.g. Jesus's critique of ostentatious piety in Matt 6:1–18), the arrogance of the self-satisfied virtuous ones coupled with their contempt for sinners (the parable of the Pharisee and the Tax Collector in Luke 18:9–14), the insensitivity of the rich for the plight of the poor (the story of the Rich Man and Lazarus in Luke 16:19–31), the resistance to mercy and compassion (the condemning reaction of the host to the woman who wipes Jesus feet with her hair in Luke 7:36–50) and so on. There are abundant examples of all these traits in the Gospels. The woes listed in Luke's Sermon on the Plain (Luke 6:24–26) and the severity of Jesus's denunciation of the religious leaders in chapter 23 of Matthew's Gospel are prime examples of what, ultimately, are meant to be warnings to the followers of Jesus about what not to do rather than attacks on opponents.[6] For the Gospels, the culmination of such opposition to Jesus leads finally to his condemnation and death at the hands of the Romans.

We should note that alongside this array of negative examples on the part of the disciples of Jesus and his opponents are cameo appearances of characters in the Gospel who respond wholeheartedly to Jesus and reveal the true character of what it means to be a disciple. Some examples of this include the Centurion in Capernaum who asks Jesus to heal his servant, winning from Jesus the exclamation that he had not found faith like this in Israel (Matt 8:5–13); the Syrophoenician woman who, on behalf of her sick daughter, overcomes Jesus's own resistance (Mark 7:24–30); the earnest scribe who appreciates Jesus's answer about the greatest commandment and is declared by Jesus as "not far from the kingdom of God" (Mark 12:28–34); the poor widow who gives all she has to the Temple (Mark 12:41–44); the woman of Bethany who anoints Jesus with precious oil in preparation for his burial (Matt 26:6–13); the women who, unlike the male disciples, stand by Jesus at his cross (Mark 15:40–41); and Mary Magdalene, the first in John's Gospel

[6] Christians must recognize, however, that, taken out of the context of the Gospels, these negative characterizations of the religious leaders have been be used through the ages to foment anti-Semitism. Particularly since the tragedy of the Shoah or Holocaust, most Christian denominations have strongly condemned prejudice of any kind directed at Jews.

to recognize the Risen Christ and to bring the message of the resurrection to his disciples (John 20:1–18).

Conclusion

We discover the core purpose of the Gospels in their proclamation of Jesus Christ as the embodiment of the divine presence and as the encounter point for authentic Christian discipleship. From the moment of their initial call to follow Jesus and share in his mission, through their experience of Jesus's mission of healing and exorcism and teaching, to their commission from Jesus to extend his mission to the world, and on to their promised final destiny of life with God—the Gospels' portrayal of Jesus is the source and inspiration for authentic Christian life and for the character of the Christian community formed in Jesus's name.

The Mind of Christ: Christian Holiness and Christian Community According to Paul

In chapter five we described the theology of Paul which centers on the figure of Jesus crucified and risen.[7] Although in a very different literary mode, Paul's letters share the same central focus as the Gospels: proclaiming Christ as the embodiment of God's presence and both the source of human liberation from the power of death and the basis of human hope for enduring life with God. For Paul this encounter with Christ was expressed in some of his characteristic phrases, such as "being in Christ" (see, e.g., Rom 8:1–2; Paul uses the phrase numerous times in his writings) or "Christ lives in me" (see, e.g., Gal 2:20). Although remaining deeply rooted in his Jewish heritage and identity, Paul viewed the crucified and risen

[7] See Chapter 5.

Christ as the fulfillment of God's promises to Israel and the goal and endpoint of the Law (Rom 10:4).

Thus, for Paul, as for the Gospels and their notion of "discipleship" or "following Jesus," the encounter with Christ is transformative, compelling the Christian to live in accord with the example and teaching of Jesus. For Paul, the initiation of that transformation takes place at Baptism, where the new Christian sacramentally participates in the dying and rising of Jesus, plunging into the waters of baptism and rising to a newness of life. And empowered by that participation, the Christian becomes a "new creation" (Gal 6:15), having the capacity to lead a life of holiness reflective of Christ's own life. The Christian is no longer trapped in the life of the "flesh"—Paul's favored term for a life overshadowed by the power of sin and death—but now can live in the "Spirit"—a life of virtue and hope reflective of God's own Spirit.

The Christian Community

Our goal here is not to repeat what has already been said earlier about Paul's theology and spirituality, but to consider one emphatic dimension of his view of Christian life, namely Christian life lived in community. For Paul, as for the Gospels, Christian life at its heart is not solitary but communal. Jesus's mission portrayed in the Gospels is to inaugurate the "reign" or "kingdom" of God, that is, to heal, restore, and reconstitute the people of God.[8] The core of Jesus's teaching and his interpretation of the Jewish law is expressed in the love command, love of God and love of neighbor (Matt 22:34–40). His example, his teachings, and his parables emphasize the obligations of limitless forgiveness, compassion, and care for the vulnerable. His mission has an inclusive character, reaching across boundaries to the outsider: the Gentile centurion

[8] See Chapter 4.

of Capernaum, the Syrophoenician woman of Tyre, the Gadarene demoniac of the Decapolis, the Samaritans. In what is recognized as a unique saying of Jesus, love is to be extended even to the enemy and the persecutor, an ultimate boundary in human relationships (Matt 5:44; Luke 6:27). In the Acts of the Apostles, the impact of the Spirit sent by the Risen and Ascended Jesus that floods his first followers at Pentecost creates communities of intense friendship, who "share all things in common" (Acts 2:43–47; 4:32–35). Later, Paul and Barnabas—leading figures of the Gentile mission—will join hands with Peter and James and the Jerusalem community to validate the inclusive mission of the early church, one that includes both Jews and Gentiles (Acts 15:1–29).

We also saw that this vision of an inclusive Christian community is affirmed by the post-Pauline writings such as Colossians and Ephesians, even extending the reach of Christ's redemptive power to the universe itself.[9]

This same communal vision of Christian life is strongly emphasized in Paul's undisputed writings. One of the apostle's nagging problems was the existence of factionalism and conflict in the communities under his care. The opening section of his First Letter to the Corinthians laments the divisions within and among the house churches of this community:

> Now I appeal to you, brothers and sisters, by the name of our Lord Jesus Christ, that all of you be in agreement and that there be no divisions among you, but that you be united in the same mind and the same purpose. For it has been reported to me by Chloe's people that there are quarrels among you, my brothers and sisters. What I mean is that each of you says, "I belong to Paul," or "I belong to Apollos," or "I belong to Cephas," or "I belong to Christ. (1 Cor 1:10–12)

---

[9] See earlier discussion.

Conflict within Paul's beloved community of Philippi reveals the apostle's antidote for such factionalism. He begins with an earnest plea for unity:

> If then there is any encouragement in Christ, any consolation from love, any sharing in the Spirit, any compassion and sympathy, make my joy complete: be of the same mind, having the same love, being in full accord and of one mind. Do nothing from selfish ambition or conceit, but in humility regard others as better than yourselves. Let each of you look not to your own interests, but to the interests of others. (Phil 2:1–4)

Toward the end of the letter, he addresses an apparent conflict between what are probably prominent women members of the community whom Paul also calls his "co-workers," Euodia and Syntyche, and asks other community members to assist in their reconciliation (see Phil 4:2–3). Paul's solution is to appeal to the "mind of Christ." The motivation for building a cohesive community is Jesus's own example of self-transcending love through which he "empties" himself of his own interests for the sake of others. To make his point, Paul cites what apparently was an early Christian hymn:

> Let the same mind be in you that was in Christ Jesus, who, though he was in the form of God, did not regard equality with God as something to be exploited, but emptied himself, taking the form of a slave, being born in human likeness. And being found in human form, he humbled himself and became obedient to the point of death—even death on a cross. Therefore God also highly exalted him and gave him the name that is above every name, so that at the name of Jesus every knee should bend, in heaven and on earth and under the earth, and every tongue should confess that Jesus Christ is Lord, to the glory of God the Father. (Phil 2:5–11)

Paul's Portrait of the Church

Paul's equation for finding the heart of Christian life is the same as that of the Gospels, even as they use a different form of discourse: following the example and teaching of Jesus reveals the path to authentic holiness and genuine Christian life. Although this equation is found throughout Paul's letters, one segment of his First Letter to the Corinthians is a compelling example. Among the several problems that seem to embroil the Christians at Corinth and provoke Paul's response is one that involves conflict during the Lord's Supper, one of the most important moments in the life of the several house churches that existed in Corinth. In chapter 10 Paul speaks eloquently of the origin and meaning of the Eucharist as a sign of Christian unity: "The cup of blessing that we bless, is it not a sharing in the blood of Christ? The bread that we break, is it not a sharing in the body of Christ? Because there is one bread, we who are many are one body, for we all partake of the one bread" (1 Cor 10:16–17). Despite the profound meaning of the Lord's Supper, Paul is dismayed to learn that divisions among the Christians are on display at this sacred moment:

Now in the following instructions I do not commend you, because when you come together it is not for the better but for the worse. For, to begin with, when you come together as a church, I hear that there are divisions among you; and to some extent I believe it. Indeed, there have to be factions among you, for only so will it become clear who among you are genuine. When you come together, it is not really to eat the Lord's supper. For when the time comes to eat, each of you goes ahead with your own supper, and one goes hungry and another becomes drunk. What! Do you not have homes to eat and drink in? Or do you show contempt for the church of God and humiliate those who have nothing? What should I say to you? Should I commend you? In this matter I do not commend you! (1 Cor 11:17–22)

Although the precise cause of the "divisions" is not entirely clear, it seems that the poorer members of the assembly are being embarrassed by the wealthier members, apparently because the wealthy bring elaborate food to enjoy during the celebration while the poor have nothing.

Paul's response is again to turn to the example of Jesus. This time citing the tradition he had received about the origin of the Lord's Supper as the final Passover meal of Jesus with his disciples:

> For I received from the Lord what I also handed on to you, that the Lord Jesus on the night when he was betrayed took a loaf of bread, and when he had given thanks, he broke it and said, "This is my body that is for you. Do this in remembrance of me." In the same way he took the cup also, after supper, saying, "This cup is the new covenant in my blood. Do this, as often as you drink it, in remembrance of me." For as often as you eat this bread and drink the cup, you proclaim the Lord's death until he comes. Whoever, therefore, eats the bread or drinks the cup of the Lord in an unworthy manner will be answerable for the body and blood of the Lord. Examine yourselves, and only then eat of the bread and drink of the cup. For all who eat and drink without discerning the body, eat and drink judgment against themselves. (1 Cor 11:223–226)

Paul's logic is clear: through the elements of bread and wine, the ritual of the Lord's Supper commemorates the meaning of Jesus's own death as the breaking of his body and the pouring out of his blood "for you." Christ's death as an act of self-transcending love—the love enacted in the ritual of the Lord's Supper—makes intolerable behavior that breaks the bond of unity.

Paul's wrestling with the problem of divisions in the community even at the Eucharist, and the remembrance of Jesus's own love for his disciples even to the point of death, become the key to the following sections of 1 Corinthians, a segment of the letter that contains his most ardent teaching about Christian community. Paul turns immediately to a series of fundamental images and exhortations that illustrate the meaning of the "*ekklesia*'—the "assembly" or "church." The first is to conceive of the church as a profusion of different gifts or "charisms" but all united in the one Spirit for the sake of the community: "Now there are varieties of gifts, but the same Spirit; and there are varieties of services, but the same Lord; and there are varieties of activities, but it is the same God who activates all of them in everyone. To each is given the manifestation of the Spirit for the common good" (1 Cor 12:1-11).

Paul turns next to another image for the church—the church as the "Body of Christ" (1 Cor 12:12-31). Greco-Roman literature used the metaphor of the body and its many parts to describe the ideal unity of the civic body. But Paul intensifies the significance of this metaphor. Because the Christian is "in Christ" and participates in Christ's death and resurrection, being part of the Body of Christ has a metaphysical reality that goes beyond the merely metaphorical or symbolic meaning. As Paul notes, "For just as the body is one and has many members, and all the members of the body, though many, are one body, so it is with Christ. For in the one Spirit we were all baptized into one body—Jews or Greeks, slaves or free—and we were all made to drink of one Spirit" (1 Cor 12:12-13). In describing the interrelationship of the members of the Body of Christ, Paul also reflects the "cruciform" ethics mentioned earlier—particular attention and care is to be afforded to the "weaker" and those judged "less honorable" (1 Cor 12:22-23).[10] In fact, "God has so arranged the body, giving the greater honor to the inferior member, that there may be no dissension within the body, but the members may have the same care for one another. If one member suffers, all suffer together with it; if one member is honored, all rejoice together with it" (1 Cor 12:25-26).

---

[10] See earlier discussion.

The climactic point in Paul's reflections and the foundation upon which all of his prior exhortations about the Christian community are based appears in chapter 13, in his "hymn to charity," one of the most well-known and eloquent passages in all of Paul's writings, a passage worth quoting in its entirety:

> If I speak in the tongues of mortals and of angels, but do not have love, I am a noisy gong or a clanging cymbal. And if I have prophetic powers, and understand all mysteries and all knowledge, and if I have all faith, so as to remove mountains, but do not have love, I am nothing. If I give away all my possessions, and if I hand over my body so that I may boast, but do not have love, I gain nothing. Love is patient; love is kind; love is not envious or boastful or arrogant or rude. It does not insist on its own way; it is not irritable or resentful; it does not rejoice in wrongdoing, but rejoices in the truth. It bears all things, believes all things, hopes all things, endures all things. Love never ends. But as for prophecies, they will come to an end; as for tongues, they will cease; as for knowledge, it will come to an end. For we know only in part, and we prophesy only in part; but when the complete comes, the partial will come to an end. When I was a child, I spoke like a child, I thought like a child, I reasoned like a child; when I became an adult, I put an end to childish ways. For now we see in a mirror, dimly, but then we will see face to face. Now I know only in part; then I will know fully, even as I have been fully known. And now faith, hope, and love abide, these three; and the greatest of these is love. (1 Cor 13:1–13)

Paul's word portrait of charity has been cited by some interpreters as equivalent to a portrait of Jesus's own qualities as the embodiment of divine love. In any case, the sequence found in 1 Corinthians 11–13 reveals the inner logic of Paul's ethical thinking. Divisions and conflicts in the community run counter to the deepest values of Christian discipleship. The Lord's Supper that celebrates the self-transcending love of Christ, the diverse gifts of members of the community working together for the common good through the One Spirit, the members of the community bound together as Christ's Body, with special care for the vulnerable and least honorable, and, finally, the quality of love that is not self-seeking but seeks the good of the other—these signs of authentic Christian discipleship underwrite the common life of the Christian community and derive from its encounter with Christ.

Thus, for Paul as for the Gospels, the encounter with the holiness of Jesus as the embodiment of the sacred leads to the holiness of the Christian community. In the perspective of Christian faith, the capacity of the Gospels and the Letters of Paul to mediate that encounter is the basis for them been viewed as "sacred."

Conclusion

Although we will not attempt to do so here, the case we have made for the Gospels and Paul as sources of Christian holiness can also be made about virtually all of the New Testament books.[11] The portrait of Jesus as the High Priest who enters the heavenly sanctuary to offer life-giving sacrifice for God's people leads to the letter's exhortations to persevere in faith and charity. The tradition of Jesus's care for the poor informs James's exhortations to justice and inclusion. The hope derived from the resurrection informs 1 Peter's theology of witness, even in the face of derision and possible persecution. 1 John affirms the humanity of Jesus and the centrality of his love command. The apocalyptic visions of the book of Revelation portray the victory of Christ, the Lamb that was slain, over the power of evil and death as the source of courage for Christians to resist the demonic oppression of the Roman Empire and all demonic systems.

[11] See Chapter 6.

The ensemble of virtues culminating in self-transcending love described in the various books of the New Testament is the foundation for all authentic Christian practices and spirituality. A direct line can be drawn from the New Testament portrayal of Christian holiness to the best practices of Christian faith throughout history: authentic worship; courageous witness; sacraments of healing and communion and comfort; the effort to build community; institutions of healing and care for the poor; and many more. Obviously, too, the warnings about the lingering power of sin and the multiple examples of flawed and failed discipleship in the New Testament writings also prefigure the long list of Christian infidelities through the centuries.

Other Christian writings through the centuries may also inspire holiness and provide wisdom to the Christian community. But the writings of the New Testament are rooted in the apostolic period of Christian history and hold a unique and normative place unmatched by any subsequent expression of Christian teaching. The interpretation of the New Testament writings, that is, the manner in which Christians try to appropriate the message of these texts, is not fixed or uniform but is enveloped in the ongoing history and development of the church and society. Our final consideration of the New Testament as a sacred text considers this history of interpretation.

8

Interpreting the New Testament as a Sacred Text

With this chapter we come to the conclusion of our quest for what makes the New Testament a "sacred" text—the question that guides this entire series about the sacred texts of various religious traditions. At the outset we noted that the term "sacred" can hold different meanings.[1] From a "civic" or "secular" point of view, the term "sacred" is applied to people, events, or objects that are profoundly meaningful, even venerable, because of their significance for society. However, from a religious point of view—the perspective taken here—"sacred" refers to a person or event or object that evokes the transcendent. Hagia Sophia, the remarkable sixth-century building in Istanbul, is an example of the varied meanings of "sacred." First built as a Christian church honoring "Holy Wisdom," that is, the second person in the Christian doctrine of the Trinity, it was sacred in the truly religious sense. Later in 1431, with the Ottoman conquest, its sacred character remained, but now as a Muslim mosque. In 1934, as part of the secularization process inaugurated by the Turkish leader Ataturk, it was turned into a museum—still a "sacred" building but now "sacred" in a secular sense as an example of a remarkable human architectural feat. Most recently, the current government in Turkey has rededicated it as a mosque, so the same building has regained, for Muslims at least, its religious sacred character.

[1] See Introduction.

The New Testament. Donald Senior, Oxford University Press. © Oxford University Press 2022.
DOI: 10.1093/oso/9780197530832.003.0009

The New Testament has retained its "sacred" religious character since its formation in the earliest centuries of Christianity. The foundation for its sacred character, as we have tried to demonstrate, is that it proclaims Jesus Christ, who from the point of view of Christian faith represents the embodiment of the divine, and, at the same time, offers Christians who encounter Christ through the New Testament the path to holiness.

To make this case, we first considered the make-up of the New Testament as a collection of varied "books" or texts, composed by different authors, with diverse literary forms (e.g., narratives, letters, exhortations, etc.), directed to different audiences and appearing over a span of time in the latter part of the first century.[2] This literary diversity of the New Testament finds its unity in its focus on the person of Jesus Christ and his meaning for Christian life. From the lifetime of Jesus in his historical setting through the composition of the various New Testament books, the transmission of traditions about Jesus was mediated through the life of the early Christian community itself—sustained and interpreted through its communal worship, its preaching and teaching, and even through some of the conflicts and interactions that took place both within the community and with the wider non-Christian world of which it was a part.[3]

While encompassing great diversity, the texts that form the New Testament are not independent books in a series or individual books lined up on a library shelf. In a complex process that took decades to conclude, the early church discerned in various ways which sacred and "inspired" books, in fact, would become normative for the church through inclusion in the "canon" of the New Testament.[4] We traced this complex process and its instinctive criteria for the inclusion of the twenty-seven books that became

[2] See Chapter 1.
[3] Chapter 2.
[4] Chapter 3.

the New Testament. While the major components such as the Four Gospels and the letters attributed to Paul were included fairly early on as "normative" books for Christians, some outlying books of the New Testament, such as Jude, James, and Revelation, were "disputed" by some local churches and their leaders before being finally accepted as part of the canon. Taken as a whole and incorporated into the entirety of the Old Testament and the Bible itself, the canon of the New Testament provides a new layer of context and meaning to the individual books of the New Testament.

The heart of the matter is to demonstrate that, in fact, the various New Testament books do focus on proclaiming Jesus.[5] Their goal ultimately is not simply to provide "information" about the Jesus who lived and died in Palestine in the first third of the first century, but, from the vantage point of belief in the resurrection of Jesus, to proclaim the person and message of the Risen and Exalted Jesus to those who would encounter these various writings. While drawing on history, the purpose of the New Testament books is profoundly religious in character. We reviewed the various major segments of the New Testament to make that case. Key elements of the gospel narratives carry this faith perspective in their portrayal of the Crucified and now Risen Jesus: the marvelous portents of his origin; the theophanies that mark his earthly lifetime; the nature of his mission of healing, exorcism, and teaching; the titles applied to him; and the interpretation in narrative of his climactic death and resurrection.

Different in literary form and theological style, the Pauline Letters also are intended to extend Paul's own mission of proclaiming the gospel to the Gentile world.[6] Paul gives only passing attention to the "facts" of Jesus's life and, instead, focuses on probing the meaning of the central act of Jesus's existence, namely his death and resurrection. As pastoral letters intended to give guidance to their

---

[5] Chapter 4.
[6] Chapter 5.

recipients, Paul's letters also concentrate on the meaning of Jesus for Christian life and for the nature of the Christian church. The same is true, in varied ways, for the diverse remaining books of the New Testament.[7]

While proclamation of the unique identity and mission of Jesus Christ is the primary purpose of the New Testament books, they are also intent on shaping the *response* of Christians to this proclamation, both as individuals and as a community or "church."[8] Here, too, is the rationale for considering the New Testament as "sacred." In the case of the Gospels, their portrayal of the disciples of Jesus illustrates what it means to "follow" Jesus and to shape one's life and purpose in the light of Christian faith. The Gospels describe not only the blessings of being called to Christian faith and participating in the Christian mission to the world but also offer an unvarnished look at the human frailties and failures of the first disciples—which, in turn, mirror the mixed reality of Christian life throughout history. As is true of the Bible in general and of the New Testament itself, the Gospels portray Christian life as first and foremost a life in community, held together by the love command that is at the heart of Jesus's teaching and the example of his life. And the character of the Christian mission to the world also is to reflect the commitments of Jesus's own mission: a mission of self-transcending service, of justice, of inclusion, of care, and of healing for the vulnerable,

For Paul's theology, too, Christian life is to mirror the life of Christ.[9] Through faith and baptism, the Christian is transformed and participates in the very death and resurrection of Christ. As Paul declares regarding his own experience, the Christian is to be "in Christ" and "with Christ." The Christian community is to "put on the mind of Christ" and act accordingly with the same

---

[7] Chapter 6.
[8] Chapter 7.
[9] See Chapter 5.

self-transcending love that marked the entire mission of Jesus. Through the power of the Spirit that animates the Christian, the community itself is to be united in love, with many gifts in the One Spirit, with many members in the One Body. Each in its own way, the other books of the New Testament also attend to how the encounter with Christ must lead to a transformed life within community, marked by sacrificial love, persevering hope, and courageous witness to the world.[10]

Biblical Interpretation

While a convincing case can be made about the sacredness of the New Testament through its proclamation of Jesus Christ and its guidance on the nature of Christian life, this does not mean that over time, or at any particular time, all Christians understand the message of the Scriptures in the same way. This brings us to the question of "interpretation" of the New Testament, a subset of biblical interpretation in general.

Earlier we had noted two fundamental paths or vantage points one can take in approaching the significance of the New Testament. One can choose to analyze the New Testament from a purely historical or literary point of view, without necessarily viewing these texts as having any personal religious authority or normative role. The dominant interest in this perspective is to study the New Testament writings as a prime example of ancient literature that, in fact, has had a substantial impact on human history and thereby is worthy of academic and scientific inquiry. In such a case, the New Testament writings are interesting historical artifacts but, by their nature, remain texts from the past, similar to studying Ulysses or Beowulf or Shakespeare's plays. These texts, too, could be considered "sacred" but from a non-Christian perspective, only in the secular sense

---

[10] See Chapter 6.

of the term described earlier. Such classic writings are of interest but hold no particular religious or normative authority for their interpreters A minority taking this approach might also believe that the influence of the New Testament writings has even had a negative impact on human history, fostering attitudes of anti-Semitism, for example, or denigrating the role of women in society. Obviously, those holding such a view would not ascribe any religious value to the New Testament writings or consider them "sacred" from a religious or even a civic point of view.

However, from the point of view of Christian faith, the New Testament writings do have a normative and still valid and positive religious significance for contemporary life. The notion of "sacred" here is sacred in a fully religious sense. The rationale for this religious viewpoint is what we have been tracing in this study—necessarily giving major attention to why these texts are considered sacred by Christians rather than what the New Testament might mean from a secular or nonreligious point of view.

It is important to point out, however, that these two fundamental perspectives are not necessarily mutually exclusive in all respects. A believing Christian can also approach the New Testament from a strictly historical and literary point of view, seeking the literal meaning of the biblical texts and making use of the same historical-critical methods as their nonreligious counterparts. The difference is that for the believing Christian, analyzing the New Testament from a purely historical and scientific point of view cannot be the final word. Still remaining is the question of the meaning of these sacred texts for Christian life.

Interpretation of the New Testament: A Very Short History

Here is where the question of interpretation of the New Testament enters. How do I accurately understand the message of a particular

New Testament book? How would we describe the meaning of the New Testament for Christian life today? How do we understand from a doctrinal point of view the identity of Jesus portrayed in the ensemble of the New Testament writings? What do I understand to be the defining characteristics and structures of the Christian community derived from the diverse books of the New Testament? Additionally, who has the authority to determine what is an authentic or valid answer to such questions? And what are the proper methods of extracting contemporary meaning from these ancient texts?

Such questions have been in play from the very beginning of Christianity, as they were for the Jewish community regarding the interpretation of their Scriptures. A fully adequate history of biblical interpretation and New Testament interpretation in particular is quite complex and far beyond the scope of our work here.[11] But we can trace some broad strokes of that history to give an idea of what is entailed.

Premodern, Modern, and Postmodern Biblical Interpretation

For the Christian community to accept the New Testament as sacred does not mean uniformity in how Christians interpret this sacred text. Circumstances of evolving time and culture, differing perspectives of religious authority and church structures, accumulated knowledge about the historical circumstances of early Christianity, surer knowledge of ancient languages, along with the different social contexts and religious perspectives of

---

[11] See Keith D. Stanglin, *The Letter and Spirit of Biblical Interpretation: From the Early Church to Modern Practice* (Grand Rapids, MI: Baker Academic, 2018); Henry Wansbrough, *The Use and Abuse of the Bible: A Brief History of Biblical Interpretation* (New York: T & T Clark, 2010).

the interpreters themselves are among several factors that come into play.

What could be called the evolving "technology" of texts and reading also plays a role.[12] In early centuries up to the late Medieval period, literacy was not widespread, so most Christians would not come in contact with the New Testament by reading it themselves. This would only begin to happen with the advent of the printing press in 1450 AD and the increasing availability of printed texts that would later result. Thus, for most of the centuries before the modern period, Christians became acquainted with the Scriptures through other means, most of them in a communal setting: hearing the biblical texts read in their assemblies and worship; as time went on, also viewing scenes from the Bible in the visual arts, in architecture (e.g., the decorations in churches and later Gothic cathedrals), in music, and in drama where biblical scenes were enacted. In such a traditional context, comment on the meaning of biblical passages by preachers and homilists played an especially important role. In fact, most of the theology of this period on up to and including the early Medieval period was in the form of commentary on Scripture.

In the period leading up to the Middle Ages, monasteries became important for the preservation and transmission of biblical texts as well as their interpretation. In the Middle Ages, the rise of universities also played an important role in biblical interpretation, with clergy and other students taught by master interpreters such as Thomas Aquinas, Bonaventure, Roger Bacon, and Erasmus. After the Reformation, Protestant scholars would also play a key role in the trends of biblical interpretation beginning with Martin Luther himself. As we will note, in the modern period, widespread literacy, the availability of printed copies of the Bible, and the advent of

---

[12] See Brent Nongbri, *God's Library. The Archaeology of the Earliest Christian Manuscripts* (New Haven, CT: Yale University Press, 2018); Brian J. Wright, *Communal Reading in the Time of Jesus: A Window into Early Christian Reading Practices* (Minneapolis, MN: Fortress, 2017).

historical-critical approaches would represent a sea change in the modalities of biblical interpretation.

We might trace the broad history of New Testament interpretation through three major segments or periods, realizing that the boundaries between them are porous.

Premodern: From the First Century up to and Including the Early Medieval Period

As we noted earlier, the New Testament writings themselves emerged from the traditions and experience of the apostolic church. In some ways, "interpretation" was already at work even in the New Testament texts themselves. An evangelist such as Matthew portrayed Jesus as the "fulfillment" of God's promises in the Old Testament. Jesus himself interprets the demands of the Torah or Jewish Scriptures. Likewise, Matthew and Luke can be seen as a new expression or "interpretation" of the Gospel according to Mark; their changes introduced new perspectives for the sake of the circumstances of their own time and place. Paul's writings are full of examples where the apostle interprets the Jewish Scriptures—his own Bible—in the light of his faith in Christ. And so on through the various books of the New Testament. This early tradition of rereading and reinterpreting earlier sacred texts would continue into the early centuries of the church and beyond.

One of the factors that fueled early Christian interpretation of the New Testament writings was their shared conviction that these sacred writings found their ultimate origin in God's inspiration.[13] As such, Christian interpreters believed that the biblical writings had a surplus of meaning beyond the plain literal meaning of the text. The early preachers, teachers, and church leaders were intelligent and aware of the need to attend to the "literal" meaning of the

[13] See the discussion of revelation and inspiration Chapter 3.

text. One had to understand the language used by the author, the literary form of the text, and its meaning within the overall context of the writing. Jerome, who translated the Bible into Latin and offered commentary on major parts of it, made it a point to learn Hebrew, even consulting with Jewish scholars to ensure accuracy. In fact, Christian interpreters of the New Testament through the modern period accepted the historical truth of the biblical text at face value. Historians point to the so-called Antioch school of interpretation that stressed the importance of this literal meaning supplied by the biblical author. But these early interpreters also fervently believed that there was meaning in the text beyond its historical surface and that the intent of the human author did not exhaust the meaning that God intended the text to proclaim. There was a "spiritual" meaning or meanings in the sacred texts that went beyond the original intent of the author or the literal meaning of the text. Famous bishop and teacher John Chrysostom (c. 347–407) makes a comparison that would be repeated many times in later Christian writings, namely that the biblical text was like the Incarnation itself; that is, Jesus was both human and divine. Similarly, the biblical text had a "human" dimension but also a divine or spiritual meaning beyond the literal sense.

A favorite way for many interpreters to express this latent spiritual meaning was through allegory; that is, the conviction that beyond the literal meaning there was this deeper and alternate meaning to be found in the text, particularly in narratives. There are obvious allegories throughout the Bible, as there are in other literature. A famous allegory is that of Israel portrayed as the vine planted and tended by God in Isaiah 5, an allegory repeated in Jesus's parable of the vineyard in Matthew 21:13–46 and the image of the vine and branches in John 15:1–11. Old Testament texts such as Isaiah 7:14, where the prophet challenges King Hezekiah to recognize the sign of a young woman bearing a child as a portent of the protection of Jerusalem from siege, is read by later Christian interpreters as a prediction of the virginal conception of Jesus and a portent of the salvation of the world. Other allegories were much more elaborate, such as St. Augustine's famous allegorical interpretation of the story of the Good Samaritan in Luke's Gospel. In Augustine's interpretation, the man who fell among thieves is really Adam, who is accosted by the power of evil. The priest and the Levite who pass by the wounded man represents the Old Testament, and the Good Samaritan is Jesus who saves the man.[14]

An important feature of this early period of interpretation is the conviction that the biblical text had a capacity not just for one literal meaning but additional "spiritual" meanings. This conviction became codified in the widespread notion of the four senses or levels of meaning in the Scriptures: (1) the literal sense derived from a study of the language and context of the biblical text; (2) the allegorical sense which reveals the hidden meaning behind the literal; (3) the moral sense in which the biblical text instructs how one should live; and (4) the anagogical sense whereby the Scriptures "lead" (the root meaning of *anagogical*) to the revelation of heavenly mysteries. The three levels beyond the literal represent "spiritual" meanings of Scripture.[15] Paradoxically, the recognition that the biblical text has more levels of meaning than the literal sense intended by the original author coincides with a conviction of the postmodern period that texts have levels of meaning beyond the so-called intention of their authors.[16]

[14] See Augustine, *Quaestiones Evangeliorum*, II, 19.

[15] In the twentieth century, some Catholic biblical scholars spoke of a "fuller sense" of Scripture, again pointing to levels of meaning embedded in the text beyond the literal level. This terminology is seldom used today. See Raymond E. Brown, "The History and Development of the Theory of a *Sensus Plenior*," *Catholic Biblical Quarterly* 15 (1953): 141–162.

[16] See later discussion.

Modern Period: from Reformation and Enlightenment to the Twentieth Century

As in so many aspects of life, particularly in Western cultures, the so-called Enlightenment marks a sea change in biblical interpretation. The Enlightenment was a period in the seventeenth and eighteenth centuries that emerged from the Renaissance, itself a high point in the development of Western culture and art stemming from the high Middle Ages in the fifteenth and sixteenth centuries, and anticipating the subsequent onrush of the scientific advances of the nineteenth and twentieth centuries. Important to the Enlightenment was the primacy of reason or rational perspectives and the emphasis on empirical inquiry. The realm of the transcendent and the miraculous was often considered illusory or the result of "magical" thinking. The French Revolution, one of the defining events of the eighteenth century, saw itself as the triumph of reason and rationality, and viewed traditional religious thinking and structures as contemptuous and an obstacle to human progress.

Coupled to these powerful movements in Western culture was the Reformation itself, which in many ways broke the grip of the Catholic Church on Western society and had a profound impact on biblical interpretation. Luther (1483–1546) reacted against what he saw as the corruption of the Catholic Church, expressive of authoritarian structures and religious formalities. His response was to contrast the state of late medieval Catholicism with the charismatic spirit and fluid structures of the church of the New Testament. Luther compared the formalities and legalism of the Church to what he considered the legalism and religious hypocrisy of the first-century Judaism condemned by Jesus.[17] The Scriptures should be the sole norm of Christian faith and practice,

---

[17] It should be noted that in this Luther continued a stereotype of first-century Judaism that plagued Western Christianity until the latter part of the twentieth century.

leading to the formula: *sola scriptura*, "only scripture"—a norm that countered the traditional church's claim to magisterial authority in matters of faith and morals. The Catholic Church itself would react to the currents of the Reformation, beginning with the Council of Trent (1545–1563), which inaugurated a "counterreformation" that called for church reform but also reasserted what it considered the legitimate teaching authority of the church's magisterium.

Emerging from these powerful movements and counter movements were two important consequences for modern biblical interpretation. First of all, the triumph of reason and empirical science was also applied to biblical scholarship and interpretation. Biblical scholars, whether working from a secular viewpoint or from the vantage point of faith, began to apply critical historical methods to an analysis of the biblical text: concentrating on its sources, its original social and religious contexts, its various literary forms, its manner of composition, and its actual historical accuracy weighted against its theological interests. More and more, the task of biblical interpretation was dominated by the academy rather than by the context of worship and preaching that had been the crucible of traditional biblical interpretation. Likewise, especially in Protestant traditions, the availability of the printed biblical text and the emphasis on individual devotional reading and interpretation of Scripture in some ways moved further away from the authority of the church in biblical matters. Paradoxically, some denominations with a tradition of strong biblical piety would, perhaps unconsciously, adapt a strong empirical approach to biblical interpretation. "Fundamentalism" adheres to the strictly literal meaning of the biblical text, rejecting in principle any symbolic or metaphorical interpretation of the biblical text but considering it objectively historical and without any error.[18]

---

[18] The connection between empiricism and fundamentalism is emphasized by James Barr, *Fundamentalism* (originally published in 1977, it is now reissued by Eugene, OR: Wipf & Stock, 2018).

Until the middle of the twentieth century, the Roman Catholic Church and Orthodox Christian communities were wary of modern biblical scholarship. Church leaders feared that much of historical-critical biblical scholarship was reductionist in spirit, considering the spiritual character of the Bible as superstition, and thus a viewpoint posing a danger to traditional Christian faith. But gradually, assured by trustworthy Catholic biblical scholars in the field who demonstrated that historical critical scholarship was not inherently opposed to faith, Catholic church leaders eased their fears.[19] Catholic biblical scholarship began to flourish under the leadership of Pope Pius XII's groundbreaking encyclical *Divino Afflante Spiritu* in 1943, which firmly endorsed modern biblical scholarship, and especially with the impetus of the Second Vatican Council (1962–1965), resulting in the flourishing of biblical scholarship and biblical piety in modern Catholicism. Most liberal Protestant denominations readily accept modern methods of biblical analysis, while Evangelical and fundamentalist groups continue to resist such approaches.

Postmodern Period

Over the past few years there have been some trends worth noting in biblical interpretation. While the historical-critical approach remains valid and widely used, more scholars have emphasized the limits of such an approach. As the interpreters of the first centuries of the church realized, there are additional levels of meaning in a text beyond the literal sense. For modern scholarship, that realization has dawned from thoughtful analysis of how any text operates. First of all, retrieval of the intention of the original author or authors of a text is not assured. One can make educated guesses

---

[19] On the history of modern Catholic biblical scholarship, see Donald Senior, *Raymond E. Brown and The Catholic Biblical Renewal* (New York: Paulist Press, 2018).

from the language used, from the known patterns of language that the original audience may have anticipated, and so on. But texts, many modern linguistic philosophers note, have a life of their own and their meaning can often exceed that intended by their composer. In the case of some New Testament texts such as the Gospels, more than one "author" may have been involved, as various traditions about Jesus were handed down in the community before being incorporated in the finished product. And the gospel narratives themselves may have gone through several editions before their final form.

Particularly important in the interpretation of a biblical text is the relationship between the text and the reader—what is sometimes referred to as the "world in front of the text."[20] Readers of a text bring their own experience and perspectives to bear as they encounter a New Testament text. Not only are their own personal and individual experiences in play, but they are probably part of an ecclesial tradition that influences what they expect of a passage from the Gospels or a segment of Paul's letters. A Roman Catholic may approach the biblical text with a different set of assumptions from that of a Lutheran or a Pentecostal Christian. As we mentioned earlier, one's "social location" also plays an important part. Reading Jesus's words about "Blessed are the poor" will resonate differently with a Bolivian peasant than with the CEO of an international corporation—even if both share the same Christian faith and belong to the same ecclesial community.

A diversity of biblical methodologies has developed, particularly in the academic community. Feminist interpretation is aware that the cultural backdrop of the biblical world was patriarchal and there is a poverty of women's voices in the Scriptures. Reading the text from a feminist perspective is alert for the place of women's perspectives within the biblical text and helps bring a balance.[21]

[20] See Schneider, *The Revelatory Text*, pp. 157–179.
[21] See Barbara E. Reid., *Wisdom's Feast: An Introduction to Feminist Interpretation of the Scriptures* (Grand Rapids, MI: Eerdmans, 2016).

Other approaches also work from what might be called an ideological or experiential perspective such as postcolonial, or liberationist perspectives. Some modern approaches apply sociological models that have been fruitful in analyzing contemporary social groups and structures and adapt these models to understand more deeply the circumstances and perspectives of ancient texts such as the New Testament.

The diversity of experience and expectation that readers bring to the interpretation of a biblical text—whether listening to it read in worship or studying with a group—is also a great asset for biblical interpretation and makes a case for it being read not just in individual devotion but as a community of faith. The basis of such communion is Scripture, which we cannot read merely on our own. As noted by Jerome, the great biblical scholar of the early church, "The Bible was written by the People of God for the People of God, under the inspiration of the Holy Spirit. Only in this communion with the People of God can we truly enter as a 'we' into the heart of the truth that God himself wishes to convey to us."[22] The insights of each person in a community help draw out the meaning of a text with so many layers of meaning as the New Testament holds. The great twentieth-century Roman Catholic exegete Raymond E. Brown made this point about interpreting the New Testament with an ecumenical consciousness. Various Christian denominations may find authentication for their particular ecclesial traditions in this or that New Testament text. Catholics, for example, may gravitate toward the Gospel of Matthew with its emphasis on the role of Peter as "rock on which I build my church" (Matt 16:18) and see here an affirmation of the Petrine ministry of the Pope. Protestant denominations, however, may find confirmation of their own less hierarchical structures in the Letters of Paul and his insistence on a community made up of many gifts and one spirit (1 Cor 12:4–11). Brown affirmed his appreciation of this process but suggested

[22] Jerome Cf. Ep. 125, 12: CSEL 56, 131.

that each community of faith could also be enriched by listening to the voices of other interpreters and ask if their own conception of church could be challenged and enriched by those aspects of the New Testament that may not play a major role in one's own ecclesial tradition.[23]

Conclusion

Our quest has been to determine why the New Testament is considered a "sacred" text by Christians. While modern biblical scholarship has developed a variety of ways of reading the biblical text, one fundamental requirement remains. For the New Testament to retain its quality as a sacred text today, biblical interpretation cannot remain solely focused on a past historical level. The New Testament is not sacred simply because it is old and still "in print." For all of its fascinating historical and literary features which draw the attention of scholars, the key is that interpretation must move beyond the past historical significance of the New Testament writings to the spiritual meaning they might have for the community of Christian faith today. For Christians, the sacred writings of the New Testament remain both the source and norm of authentic Christian faith.

[23] Raymond E. Brown, *The Churches the Apostles Left Behind* (New York: Paulist Press, 1984), pp. 146–150.

Bibliography

Augustine. *Quaestiones Evangeliorum*. Vol. II, 19.

Barr, James. *Fundamentalism*. Eugene, OR: Wipf & Stock, 2018. (Originally published in 1977)

Bauckham, Richard. *The Gospels for All Christians: Rethinking the Gospel Audiences*. Grand Rapids, MI: Eerdmans, 1997.

Bond, Helen K. *The First Biography of Jesus. Genre and Meaning in Mark's Gospel*. Grand Rapids, MI: Eerdmans, 2020.

Boring, M. Eugene. *An Introduction to the New Testament. History, Literature, Theology*. Louisville, KY: Westminster John Knox Press, 2012.

Brown, Raymond E. *The Churches the Apostles Left Behind*. New York: Paulist Press, 1984.

Brown, Raymond E. *The Community of the Beloved Disciple: The Life, Loves, and Hates of an Individual Church in New Testament Times*. New York: Paulist, 1979.

Brown, Raymond E. *The Death of the Messiah from Gethsemane to the Grave: A Commentary on the Passion Narratives in the Four Gospels*. Vol. 2. New York: Doubleday, 1994.

Brown, Raymond E. *The Epistles of John*. The Anchor Bible. New York: Doubleday, 1982.

Brown, Raymond E. "The History and Development of the Theory of a *Sensus Plenior*." *Catholic Biblical Quarterly* 15 (1953): 141–162.

Brown, Raymond E. *An Introduction to the New Testament*. Anchor Bible Reference Library; New York: Doubleday, 1997.

Burridge, Richard. *What Are the Gospels? A Comparison with Graeco-Roman Biography*. 3rd ed. Waco, TX: Baylor University Press, 2018.

Collins, John J. *The Apocalyptic Imagination: An Introduction to Jewish Apocalyptic Literature*. 2nd ed. Grand Rapids, MI: Eerdmans, 1998.

Collins, John J., Craig A. Evans, and Lee Martin McDonald. *Ancient Jewish and Christian Scriptures: New Developments in Canon Controversy*. Louisville, KY: Westminster John Knox Press, 2020.

Cook, John Granger. *Crucifixion in the Mediterranean World*. WUZNT 327; Tübingen: Mohr Siebeck, 2014.

Crossan, John Dominic. *The Cross That Spoke: The Origins of the Passion Narrative*. San Francisco: HarperCollins, 1988.

Dunn, James D. G. "Has the Canon a Continuing Function?" In *The Canon Debate*, edited by Lee Martin McDonald and James A. Sanders. Grand Rapids, MI: Baker Academic, 2019, pp. 558–579.

Dunn, James D. G. *Jesus According to the New Testament*. Grand Rapids, MI: Eerdmans, 2019.

Dunn, James D. G. *The Theology of Paul the Apostle*. Grand Rapids, MI: Eerdmans, 1998.

Elliott, John H. *A Home for the Homeless: A Sociological Exegesis of I Peter, Its Situation and Strategy*. Philadelphia: Fortress, 1981.

Elliott, John H., and I. Peter. *A New Translation with Introduction and Commentary*. The Anchor Bible; New York: Doubleday, 2000.

Eusebius of Caesarea. *Vita Constantini*. IV, *36*.

Fiorenza, Elisabeth Schüssler. *Revelation. Vision of a Just World*. Proclamation Commentaries; Minneapolis, MN: Fortress Press, 1991.

Gorman, Michael J. *Apostle of the Crucified Lord: A Theological Introduction to Paul & His Letters*. 2nd ed. Grand Rapids, MI: Eerdmans, 2017.

Gorman, Michael J. *Cruciformity: Paul's Narrative Spirituality of the Cross*. Grand Rapids, MI: Eerdmans, 2001.

Hansen, Ryan Leif. *Silence and Praise. Rhetorical Cosmology and Political Theology in the Book of Revelation*. Minneapolis, MN: Fortress, Press, 2014.

Hays, Richard B. *The Moral Vision of the New Testament: Community, Cross, New Creation. A Contemporary Introduction to New Testament Ethics*. San Francisco: Harper, 1996.

Hengel, Martin. *Crucifixion in the Ancient World and the Folly of the Message of the Cross*. Philadelphia: Fortress, 1977.

Jerome. *The Letters of Saint Jerome by Saint Jerome and Aeterna Press*. Letter 125, 12: CSEL 56, 13; London: Aeterna Press, 2016.

Johnson, Luke Timothy *The Writings of the New Testament: An Interpretation*. Minneapolis, MN: Fortress, rev. ed., 1999.

Johnson, Luke Timothy. *The Real Jesus: The Misguided Quest for the Historical Jesus and the Truth of the Traditional Gospels*. San Francisco: Harper, 1996.

Johnson, Luke Timothy. *Constructing Paul*. Vol. 1. *The Canonical Paul*. Grand Rapids, MI: Eerdmans, 2020; Vol. 2. *Interpreting Paul: The Canonical Paul* (Grand Rapids, MI: Eerdmans, 2021).

Kahler, Martin. *The So-called Historical Jesus and the Historic, Biblical Christ*. Minneapolis, MN: Augsburg Fortress, 1988. (Original German edition published in 1892)

Keener, Craig S. *Christobiography. Memory, History, and the Reliability of the Gospels*. Grand Rapids, MI: Eerdmans, 2019.

Kempis, Thomas à. *The Imitation of Christ*. Mineola NY: Dover Publications, 2003.

Kysar, Robert. *John the Maverick Gospel*. Revised ed. Louisville, KY: Westminster John Knox Press, 1993.

Litwa, M. David. *How the Gospels Became History: Jesus and Mediterranean Myths*. New Haven, CT: Yale University Press, 2019.

Matera, Frank. *New Testament Ethics. The Legacies of Jesus and Paul*. Louisville, KY: Westminster John Knox Press, 1996.

McDonald, Lee Martin. "Identifying Scripture and Canon in the Early Church: The Criteria Question." In *The Canon Debate*, edited by Lee Martin McDonald and James A. Sanders, pp. 416–439.

McDonald, Lee Martin, and James A. Sanders, eds. *The Canon Debate*. Grand Rapids, MI: Baker Academic, 2019.

Meier, John P. *A Marginal Jew: Rethinking the Historical Jesus. Volume One: The Roots of the Problem and the Person*. Anchor Bible Reference Library; New Haven, CT: Yale University Press, 1991.

Moloney, Francis J., SBD. *The Apocalypse of John: A Commentary*. Grand Rapids, MI: Baker Academic, 2020.

Nongbri, Brent. *God's Library. The Archaeology of the Earliest Christian Manuscripts*. New Haven, CT: Yale University Press, 2018.

O'Collins, Gerard. *Inspiration: Towards a Christian Interpretation of Biblical Inspiration*. New York: Oxford University Press, 2018.

Pagels, Elaine. *The Gnostic Gospels*. Vasalia, CA: Vintage Press, 1989.

Rahner, Karl. *Inspiration in the Bible*. 2nd ed. Quaestiones Disputatae 1; New York: Herder and Herder, 1966.

Reid, Barbara E. *Wisdom's Feast: An Introduction to Feminist Interpretation of the Scriptures*. Grand Rapids, MI: Eerdmans, 2016.

Rowe, C. Kavin. *World Upside Down: Reading Acts in the Graeco-Roman Age*. New York: Oxford University Press, 2009.

Schenck, Ken. *The Letter to the Hebrews*. Franklin, TN: Seedbed Publishing, 2018.

Schneider, Sandra M. *The Revelatory Text: Interpreting the New Testament as Sacred Scripture*. New York: HarperCollins, 1991.

Schnelle, Udo. *Apostle Paul: His Life and Theology*. Grand Rapids, MI: Baker Academic, 2005.

Seitz, Christopher R. *Convergences. Canon and Catholicity*. Waco, TX: Baylor University Press, 2020.

Senior, Donald C. P. *Raymond E. Brown and The Catholic Biblical Renewal*. New York: Paulist Press, 2018.

Senior, Donald C. P. *The Landscape of the Gospels: A Deeper Meaning*. New York: Paulist Press, 2020.

Senior, Donald C. P. *1 Peter*. Sacra Pagina. Collegeville, MD: Liturgical Press, 2003.

Stanglin, Keith D. *The Letter and Spirit of Biblical Interpretation: From the Early Church to Modern Practice*. Grand Rapids, MI: Baker Academic, 2018.

Vawter, Bruce. *Biblical Inspiration*. Theological Resources; Philadelphia: Westminster, 1972.

Wall, Robert. "The Significance of a Canonical Perspective of the Church's Scripture." In *The Canon Debate*, edited by Lee Martin McDonald and James A. Sanders, pp. 528–540.

Wansbrough, Henry. *The Use and Abuse of the Bible: A Brief History of Biblical Interpretation.* New York: T & T Clark, 2010.

Wolter, Michael. *Paul: An Outline of His Theology.* Waco, TX: Baylor University Press, 2015.

Wright, Brian J. *Communal Reading in the Time of Jesus: A Window into Early Christian Reading Practices.* Minneapolis, MN: Fortress, 2017.

Index

For the benefit of digital users, indexed terms that span two pages (e.g., 52–53) may, on occasion, appear on only one of those pages.